THE MESSIAH IN THE OLD TESTAMENT

D1111037

Other Books by Walter C. Kaiser, Jr.

Classical Evangelical Essays in Old Testament Interpretation (editor)
The Old Testament in Contemporary Preaching
Toward an Old Testament Theology
Ecclesiastes: Total Life
Toward an Exegetical Theology: Biblical Exegesis for Preaching and Teaching
A Biblical Approach to Personal Suffering: Lamentations
Toward Old Testament Ethics
Malachi: God's Unchanging Love
The Uses of the Old Testament in the New
Quest for Renewal: Personal Revival in the Old Testament
Quality Living: Bible Studies in Ecclesiastes
A Tribute to Gleason Archer: Essays in Old Testament Studies (coeditor)
Have You Seen the Power of God Lately? Studies in the Life of Elijah
Toward Rediscovering the Old Testament
Hard Sayings of the Old Testament
"Exodus," in *The Expositor's Bible Commentary* (vol. 2)
Back Toward the Future: Hints for Biblical Preaching
More Hard Sayings of the Old Testament
The Communicator's Commentary: Micah to Malachi
The Journey Isn't Over: Pilgrim Psalms [120–134] for Life's Challenges and Joys
"Leviticus," in *The New Interpreter's Bible*
An Introduction to Biblical Hermeneutics: The Search for Meaning (coauthor)
Proverbs: Wisdom for Everyday Life
Psalms: Heart to Heart With God

STUDIES IN
OLD TESTAMENT BIBLICAL THEOLOGY

THE MESSIAH IN THE OLD TESTAMENT

WALTER C. KAISER, Jr.

ZondervanPublishingHouse
Grand Rapids, Michigan

A Division of HarperCollinsPublishers

The Messiah in the Old Testament
Copyright © 1995 by Walter C. Kaiser, Jr.

Requests for information should be addressed to:

ZondervanPublishingHouse
Grand Rapids, Michigan 49530

Library of Congress Cataloging-in-Publication Data

Kaiser, Walter C.
    The Messiah in the Old Testament / Walter C. Kaiser, Jr.
      p.   cm.
    Includes bibliographical references and indexes.
    ISBN: 0-310-20030-X (pbk.)
    1. Messiah—Biblical teaching. 2. Bible. O.T.—Criticism, interpretation, etc.
    3. Messiah—Prophecies. I. Title.
    BS1199.M44K35 1995
    232'.12-dc 20   95-8263
                                                          CIP

All Scripture quotations, unless otherwise indicated, are taken from the *Holy Bible: New International Version®*. NIV®. Copyright © 1973, 1978, 1984 by International Bible Society. Used by permission of Zondervan Publishing House. All rights reserved.

All rights reserved. No part of this publication may be reproduced, stored in a retrieval system, or transmitted in any form or by any means—electronic, mechanical, photocopy, recording, or any other—except for brief quotations in printed reviews, without the prior permission of the publisher.

Edited by Verlyn D. Verbrugge

Printed in the United States of America

02 03 04 /DC/ 18 17 16 15 14 13 12 11 10

◆ Contents ◆

Dedicated to
two wonderful granddaughters
Christine Margaret Coley
and
Sarah Elise Coley
Psalm 128:5–6

————————

◆ Preface to the Series ◆

The editors are pleased to announce the "Studies in Old Testament Biblical Theology" series, with the hope that it contributes to the field of Old Testament theology and stimulates further discussion. If Old Testament theology is the queen of Old Testament studies, she is a rather neglected queen. To write in the area of Old Testament theology is a daunting proposition, one that leads many to hesitate taking on the task. After all, Old Testament theology presupposes an understanding of all the books of the Old Testament and, at least as conceived in the present project, an insight into its connection with the New Testament.

Another reason why theology has been neglected in recent years is simply a lack of confidence that the Old Testament can be summarized in one or even a number of volumes. Is there a center, a central concept, under which the entire Old Testament may be subsumed? Many doubt it. Thus, while a number of articles, monographs, and commentaries address the theology of a source, a chapter, or even a book, few studies address the Old Testament as a whole.

The editors of this series also believe it is impossible to present the entirety of the Old Testament message under a single rubric. Even as important a concept as the covenant fails to incorporate all aspects of the Old Testament (note especially wisdom literature). Thus, this series will present separate volumes, each devoted to a different theme, issue, or perspective of biblical theology, and will show its importance for the Old Testament and for the entire Christian canon.

One last word needs to be said about theological approach. Gone are the days when scholars, especially those who work in a field as ideologically sensitive as theology, can claim neutrality by hiding behind some kind of scientific methodology. It is, therefore, important to announce the approach taken in this series. Those who know the editors, authors, and publisher will not be surprised to learn that an evangelical approach is taken throughout this series. At the same time, however, we believe that those who do not share this starting point may still benefit and learn from these studies.

The general editors of this series, Willem A. VanGemeren and Tremper Longman III, wish to thank the academic publishing department of Zondervan, particularly Stan Gundry and Verlyn Verbrugge, who will be working most closely with the series.

Willem A. VanGemeren
Professor of Old Testament and Semitic Languages
Trinity Evangelical Divinity School

◆ Abbreviations ◆

ASV	American Standard Version
BDB	Brown, Driver, Briggs, *Hebrew and English Lexicon of the Old Testament*
Bib	*Biblica*
BSac	*Bibliotheca Sacra*
CBQ	*Catholic Biblical Quarterly*
GTJ	*Grace Theological Journal*
HBT	*Horizons in Biblical Theology*
ICC	International Critical Commentary
IEJ	*Israel Exploration Journal*
JBL	*Journal of Biblical Literature*
JETS	*Journal of the Evangelical Theological Society*
JSOT	*Journal for the Study of the Old Testament*
JSS	*Journal of Semitic Studies*
KJV	King James Version
MT	Masoretic Text
NASB	New American Standard Bible
NEB	New English Bible
NIV	New International Version
NKJV	New King James Version
NovT	*Novum Testamentum*
NT	New Testament
OT	Old Testament
OTS	*Oudtestamentische Stüdien*
PTR	*Princeton Theological Review*
TToday	*Theology Today*
VT	*Vetus Testamentum*

◆ 1 ◆

Introduction:
The Study of Messianism

"What is a 'Christian'?" asked James H. Charlesworth. He responded: "Most people would answer: one who believes that Jesus of Nazareth was 'the Christ' Jews were expecting. Many Christians, Jews, and most citizens of the modern world would tend to agree on this definition. It is however, misleading and, indeed, inaccurate," continued Charlesworth, "[because] it assumes three things: (1) that the title 'Christ' fully categorizes Jesus, (2) that Christians are clear and in agreement on what this title, 'Christ,' denotes, and (3) that all, or virtually all, Jews during the time of Jesus were looking for the coming of the Messiah or Christ."[1]

This study of the concept of the Messiah in the OT will attempt to show that "most people," according to Charlesworth's estimate, are not that far off the mark, if they are off at all. It will also attempt to recover what Anthony Collins lost

---

[1]James H. Charlesworth, "From Messianology to Christology: Problems and Prospects," in *The Messiah: Developments in Earliest Judaism and Christianity*, ed. James H. Charlesworth (Minneapolis: Fortress, 1992), 3. Also see Charlesworth, "From Jewish Messianology to Christian Christology: Some Caveats and Perspectives," in *Judaisms and Their Messiahs*, ed. J. Neusner, W. S. Green, and E. Frerichs (Cambridge: Cambridge Univ. Press, 1988), 225–64.

when he published in 1724 a volume entitled *Discourse of the Grounds and Reasons for the Christian Religion*, and its sequel in 1727 entitled *The Scheme of Literal Prophecy Considered*.[2] In both of these works Collins attempted to show that the use of the literal meaning of certain messianic proof-texts from the OT could not support the messianic interpretation placed on them by the NT. According to him, only the original (i.e., the literal) sense could be declared as the valid and true meaning of the text. The so-called "complete" or "spiritual" fulfillment of these OT texts that many were applying to Jesus, Collins concluded, could be no more than an illustration; in any case, they did not amount to a specific "proof" that Jesus had been anticipated as the "messiah" with certain characteristics and works in the prophets' own times.

Thus the eighteenth century began the long debate, which has continued to this very hour, about the apologetic "argument from prophecy" for the Messiah. It is interesting to note that in 1742, less than twenty years after the first volume authored by Collins appeared, George F. Handel's oratorio *The Messiah* had its first performance. That work, which continues to be a favorite across many cultures to this day, uses the basic compilation of Scriptural passages and reflects the type of conclusions that "most people" have about the significance and meaning of the OT passages cited.

A. DEFINITIONS

It is helpful to define several of the terms we use in this study of Messianism in the OT, using the methodology of Bib-

---

[2]These references were supplied to me from the article by Ronald E. Clements, "Messianic Prophecy or Messianic History?" *HBT* 1 (1979): 87. Clements refers to J. O'Higgins, *Anthony Collins: The Man and His Works*, International Archives of History of Ideas 35 (The Hague: Nijhoff, 1970), 155ff., for Collins' works on biblical prophecy. Also H. W. Frei, *The Eclipse of Biblical Narrative. A Study in Eighteenth and Nineteenth Century Hermeneutics* (New Haven: Yale Univ. Press, 1974), 66 ff.

lical Theology. This is particularly helpful since the debate has attracted so much attention and the stakes in the argument are, from many points of view, as fundamental as the very definition for "Christianity" itself.

1. *Messianic*. One source of confusion is that the term "messianic" has a much wider range of meaning than "Messiah." "Messianic" usually is applied to everything in the OT when it refers the hope of a glorious future. This suggests that the central feature of the coming golden age is the expectation of the Savior and King Messiah. But that fact is hotly debated, for in the minds of most scholars today, the oldest and most general expectation was for a coming era of happiness. Only in much later times, according to this academic consensus, was the hope of the Messiah connected with this expectation.

The chronological question of what was early and what was late in Scripture will always be a source of vigorous debate, especially when the arguments are based almost exclusively on internal evidence. This opens the door for a large measure of speculation and subjectivity. But the majority of passages that speak about the glorious future do not refer to a future king at all; instead, they are usually about Yahweh, who acts either in judgment or deliverance. Accordingly, many of the passages scholars believe are mistakenly called messianic are better placed simply under the category of eschatology. The problem we will have to face is the one where the identity and work of Yahweh *coincides* or *overlaps* with that of Messiah. If the text develops a link between the person and work of Yahweh and that of Messiah, most of the objections to including messianic materials under the rubric of "Messiah" will disappear.

2. *Messiah*. What about the term *messiah*? The Hebrew term *māšîaḥ* appears thirty-nine times in the OT and is rendered in the Septuagint by the Greek *christos*, which became the official designation for Jesus in the NT and, at first, a pejorative way of referring to his followers: "Christians."

The Hebrew form is a verbal noun derived from *māšaḥ*, which is similar in meaning to what the participle *māšûaḥ* means (e.g., 2Sa 3:39), translated "anointed." In the prevailing sense of this root (except for the two uses in Isa 21:5; Jer 22:14), the idea is one of consecrating objects or persons for sacred purposes—the altar, the basin, etc. The noun, however, is only applied to animate objects: those who were consecrated in this category were priests, prophets, and kings.

While many scholars claim that the term *messiah* was used in a more general sense as an epithet of kings, priests, and prophets (indeed, even of the foreign King Cyrus; cf. Isa 45:1), and never in its later technical sense, the text seems to argue the reverse in at least nine of its thirty-nine occurrences. These nine passages did picture some "anointed one" who would be coming in the future, usually in the line of David, and who would be Yahweh's king: 1 Samuel 2:10, 35; Psalms 2:2; 20:6; 28:8; 84:9; Habakkuk 3:13; Daniel 9:25, 26. But this term was neither the most frequent nor the clearest in the OT to depict the expected King who would reign on David's throne. If a more promising title were to be chosen, based on frequency alone, it would be "Servant of the Lord."

The way that the title *messiah* gained its technical status happened as Saul was being rejected as king. In his place, the Lord looked for a "man after his own heart" (1Sa 13:14). That man turned out to be David, the son of Jesse. David was first anointed by the prophet Samuel (1Sa 16:13), then anointed as king of Judah (2Sa 2:4), and eventually anointed as king over all Israel (2Sa 5:3). Prior to this, Saul had been called the "anointed of the LORD" (*māšîaḥ YHWH*; 1Sa 24:6[7], 10[11]; 26:9, 11, 16, 23; 2Sa 1:14, 16), but now David was God's "anointed," and "from that day on the Spirit of the LORD came upon David in power" (1Sa 16:13). David was called the Lord's "anointed" ten times.

The fact that the same title, "anointed," was also used of priests and prophets should not surprise us. The great antitype, the Christ of the NT, embraced all three offices and functions of prophet, priest, and king. In that sense, the Messiah would be "set ... above [his] companions" (Ps 45:7 [8]), that is, above the "christs" or "anointed ones" of old. Some preparation for this triple assimilation of titles and functions can be seen in the fact that some of Messiah's "companions" or forerunners in the OT exercised two offices or functions: Melchizedek was both a priest and a king, Moses was a priest and a prophet, and David was a king and prophet.

The primary meaning of the term *messiah* as anointing and the limitation of its use as a verbal noun to persons who were either prophets, priests, or kings is what began to shape its technical status. In that sense, the concept had a much earlier emergence as a significant term and concept than many in the scholarly tradition set by Collins in 1724 and 1727 would allow.

The relationship of Yahweh with "his anointed," the king, was cemented in the Nathan prophecy of 2 Samuel 7. Here David and his line of kings assumed a unique position that guaranteed to him and to his reigning sons a kingdom that would be "established" by Yahweh "forever" (vv. 12–16). Without using the word *māšîaḥ*, Nathan represented a significant advance in the progressive revelation of what the concept of Messiah entailed. And Psalm 89, in commenting on the 2 Samuel 7 event, referred to the promise delivered by Nathan as one that the Lord had sworn (Ps 89:3–4[4–5]; 132:11–12), since God had made a "covenant" with David to be his "chosen one," his "servant" (89:3–4[4–5], 35; 132:10), his "firstborn," and "the most exalted of the kings of the earth" (89:27[28]), for whom God would be his "father" (89:26[27]). Here, then, was the messianic prototype. Therefore, the psalmist could pray in 132:10, "For the sake of David your servant, do not reject *your anointed one*" (*mᵉ šîḥekā*, italics ours).

3. *Futurism and eschatology.* Some prefer to place all expectations and hopes for the future that have a historically ori-

ented and completely Davidic stamp on them as a royal messianism that is limited to the future of the Jewish people of that time and to the state of Israel. Such a concept of futurism is often used in order to separate it from the future of the "last things" connected with the glorious reign of Yahweh. Eschatology, according to this same set of distinctions, is reserved for the new promises of God that the prophets saw beyond the break with the people, the state, and the reign of David.

But these distinctions introduce a division of thought where the OT did not call for one. In fact, the historically oriented problems, successes, and failures of David and his times were directly linked with what God was going to do in that final day of judgment and deliverance. Only those who insist that the promise of the land, the centrality of Zion, and restoration of the people is either a historical *fait accompli* or an offer now defunct must make this type of division. In our view, God has not withdrawn his promise to give the land to Israel, to restore them back to that territory, or to place one of David's descendants on his throne in Zion.

B. STARTING POINTS

How can the study of the messianic features in the OT be approached? Where does one begin? How is the progress of the doctrine to be charted? Is the original meaning of the OT context durable enough to suggest anything like what "most people" think the OT says, let alone what the NT claims for this doctrine of the Messiah?

Probably the best way to initiate study in this area is to trace briefly what approaches have been tried and found to be lacking before we set forth our own proposal. We can list seven different methods that have been used to surmount Anthony Collins' challenge to what he wrote about as the traditional way of understanding the messianic texts of the OT.

1. *Dual meaning.* The first rebuttal that came to the criticisms raised by Collins was exemplified by Thomas Sherlock's

The Use and Intent of Prophecy (London, 1732).[3] He argued for some type of dual meaning in prophecy. What Collins had maintained about the literal meaning, Sherlock conceded, might indeed be true of the original meaning in the OT text, but there had to be a later, fuller meaning, to which the messianic interpretation and application could be attached. This tactic was to become a popular one, right up to the present, but it would be at the price of forfeiting most of the predictive value of the anticipations of the Messiah in their OT context.

2. *Single meaning.* Just as the dual meaning interpretation was being used to solve the new challenges to OT prophecy and messianic forecasting, J. G. Herder (1744–1803) and J. G Eichhorn (1752–1827) emerged at the end of the eighteenth century to propose a new approach to the study of prophecy and messianic interpretation. For Herder, and especially Eichhorn, the whole idea that the OT contained a prediction of a coming Savior was merely a dogmatic imposition on the text of Scripture. Prophecy could only have one meaning—the meaning that was understood in the prophet's own time and milieu. So sure was Eichhorn that he had eradicated the whole idea of messianic proof-texts and predictive prophecy from the OT that he was able to claim in 1793, "The last three decades have erased the Messiah from the OT."[4] In order to compensate for this loss, Eichhorn replaced the older messianic predictions of the OT with a broader-based understanding of what hope for the future was in the OT. Instead of depending on "foretelling" (*Weissagung*), he suggested that "discernment" (*Ahndung*) replace it as the category of thought to be applied to prophecy. What this did was to turn the interpreter's attention away from the text of the OT and direct it instead to the prophet himself.

---

[3]I am indebted to Clements, "Messianic Prophecy or Messianic History?" for the general outline of the positions noted here.

[4]The work of Herder and Eichhorn on prophecy is recorded in E. Sehmsdorf, *Die Prophetenauslegung bei J. G. Eichhorn* (Göttingen: Vandenhoef, 1971), 153–54, as cited in Clements, 89.

With the prophet discernment first came into being and was first expressed.

As a result, by the end of the eighteenth century the very notion of messianic prophecies, especially as understood in the past, all but disappeared from discussions of prophecy. What little discussion of the messianic hope remained was so broadened that one could hardly recognize it any longer.

3. *New Testament meaning.* Another massive attempt to arrest this newer approach to messianic prophecy appeared in a three-volume set from 1829 to 1835, written by E. W. von Hengstenberg. Between 1854 and 1858, a second edition (in four volumes) by this same author appeared with the title, *Christology of the Old Testament and a Commentary on the Messianic Predictions* (Edinburgh).[5] While treating the isolated passages on the messianic idea in their chronological order, Hengstenberg allowed the NT to be his final arbiter in difficult places.

Scholars tended to fault this successor to W. M. L. DeWette's chair at University of Berlin for not paying as much attention as he could to the historical circumstances of the passages. While Hengstenberg inveighed against the "rationalistic" interpretations of others, they accused him of imposing dogmatic schemes over the text, devoid of the wider historical aspects. In that sense, the debate had not moved much in one hundred years. It is worth noting, however, that Hengstenberg's volumes are still being reprinted over 150 years later while all his nemeses's books have long since been out of print.

4. *Developmental meaning.* Another conservative writer, Franz Delitzsch, broke with Hengstenberg's NT principle of control, since he also realized that, like the dual meaning, it

---

[5]The first edition of von Hengstenberg's work was published in Berlin by Oehmigke. This edition was translated into English by Reuel Keith and published in Alexandria by Morrison (1836–39). It was abridged by Thomas Kerchever Arnold (London: Francis and John Rivington, 1847) and reprinted by Kregel in Grand Rapids, Michigan, as *Christology of the Old Testament and a Commentary on the Messianic Predictions* (1970), with a "Foreword" by Walter C. Kaiser, Jr.

had failed to win any confidence in the scholarly community.[6] This scholar agreed with many of the traditional arguments from prophecy, but he also insisted that every interpretation of OT prophecy had to meet two criteria: (1) that of placing the prophecy in the times and circumstances of the original prophet, and (2) that of allowing only a single meaning for every prophecy, without resorting to a typological or spiritual meaning in order to rescue a passage for a messianic interpretation. Delitzsch conceded that some of the passages previously used as proof-texts for the traditional argument for the Messiah could no longer bear that weight. In these procedures and concessions, Delitzsch seemed to be giving ground to the nonconservatives.

In order to get back to the traditional interpretation of the messianic texts, Delitzsch proposed the idea of development. This allowed Delitzsch to have the OT say *less* than its fulfillment in Jesus required, but to provide for the OT to say *more* when the original OT prophecy was filled out by later doctrine and Christian experience. This method also had little or no impact on the nonconservative world of scholars.

5. *Goal meaning.* While Hengstenberg and Delitzsch were working out two different kinds of conservative attempts to rehabilitate traditional understandings of the messianic doctrine, other more radical and critical arguments were being prepared. The best known representative of this group was a book by A. F. Kirkpatrick.[7] In his chapter "Christ the Goal of History,"[8] Kirkpatrick depicted Christ as the goal of prophecy, but the goal was an ethical and moral goal. Christ was not the goal in the sense that he fulfilled specific and detailed promises of his coming; instead, he was the goal in that he united all the lines

---

[6]Delitzsch's contribution was entitled *Messianic Prophecies in Historical Succession* (Edinburgh: T. & T. Clark, 1891).

[7]A. F. Kirkpatrick, *The Doctrine of the Prophets* (New York: Macmillan, 1897).

[8]Ibid., 517 ff.

of prophecy by filling them with new meaning. Once again, the prophetic hope was so broadened that any particular prophetic utterances became vague, to the point of being archaic, incidental, and practically useless.

6. *Relecture meaning*. A more recent attempt to connect the OT prophecy with the NT fulfillment is by a process known as a *relecture*: that is, the process of reading earlier prophecies in a new way, so that they are filled with new meaning.[9] In many ways, this is a return to the "dual meaning" with which this whole cycle began. Since the OT prophecies were not the work of single authors and came by a long process of interpretation and reinterpretation, or so it was argued, there was no one final way to understand their meanings. The subjectivity of this process of interpreting the text could not hold a serious constituency for long. It was slippery and had no validating potentiality in anything that could be seen as objective.

7. *Theological meaning*. The twentieth-century solution to this tug of war that had been going on between the historical and theological claims of the text swung toward the theological side. One must acknowledge, this view pleaded, that the NT saw Christ as being the end of Israel's history, even if it were only a theological and not a historical judgment. The *hidden* messianic theme had had its part to play in the NT representation of the OT. Therefore, the history of Israel would find its consummation and final stage of growth, argued H. G. A. Ewald, in the appearance of the Christian church.[10]

The price paid here, of course, is the transfiguration of Israel into the church, which becomes the last stage of that na-

---

[9]R. E. Clements points to the following representatives of this method: J. Vereylen, *Du prophète Isaïe à l'apocalyptique. Isaïe I-XXXV miroir d'un demi-millenaire d'expérience religieuse en Israel* (2 vols.; Paris: J. Gabalda, 1977–78), 2:655ff. Cf. also B. S. Childs, *Biblical Theology in Crisis* (Philadelphia: Westminster, 1970), 155ff.

[10]H. G. A. Ewald, *The History of Israel* (4th ed.; 8 vols., London: 1883–86), 6:7, 9.

tion. But this runs counter to the clearly expressed hopes of the OT prophets themselves that God will conclude in space and time what he has promised to do long ago, namely, to give Israel the land and to grant the world a new Davidic king.[11]

So what will it be? Does the OT contain specific and particular prophecies about the person and work of a coming Messiah? Or were these prophecies more general in their expectations, while their particulars dealt only with the historical realities of what was happening right then and there in the prophet's own day? How can we break this Gordian knot?

C. A PROPOSAL

Let us begin by admitting that the nontraditionalists have been justified in their insistence on the two criteria that must be used for interpreting prophecies: (1) the meaning of the OT references to the Messiah must reflect the author's own times and historical circumstances, and (2) the meaning must be a meaning that is reflected in the grammar and syntax of the OT text. To deny these two working hypotheses introduces pandemonium into the interpretive process.

Conservatives have not been successful in their attempts to cut this Gordian knot by appealing to a dual sense, a NT messianic sense, or to some secondary development behind, under, or around the text in a spiritual or typological meaning that could be validated only from later theology or experience. Everyone of these procedures has proved to be self-defeating, for they only led to parochial, private, or preferential points of view. The advantage of the commonality of language was forfeited in favor of an in-house key that could be supplied only to those who first participated in the esoteric mysteries of the conservative group. All the alleged apologetic advantages of appealing to the OT texts by the apostles and the four Evange-

---

[11]For a full presentation of this point, see Walter C. Kaiser, Jr., "An Assessment of 'Replacement Theology,'" *Mishkan* 21 (1994): 9–20.

lists of the NT became nonexistent in one stroke by these two-track hermeneutical systems of interpreting messianic passages.

1. *Epigenetical meaning*. What was left, then, that had not already been tried? One method that had not received a fair airing in scholarly and popular descriptions of messianic interpretation is one we will designate as the *epigenetical meaning* of the text. This one takes both the historical conditions in which the original word was given and its predictive particulars in equal seriousness, for it links both to the text's implantation of seminal ideas organically imbedded within the one, single truth as understood by the author in his own times and circumstances.

The seven meanings discussed above tended to focus as the only point worthy of theological reflection either on the side of a historical word, appropriate for a special time or particular setting, or on the side of the consummated event(s), which took the ultimate fulfillment. What was neglected by both sides of this debate was the actual progress of the word between the prediction and the fulfillment as it worked out its fulfillment in the subsequent history of Israel. This aspect was seen more or less as an unnecessary nuisance between the word and its fulfillment. *But that was the whole point of the messianic doctrine*. God was not only predicting what would happen; he was just as mightily working his promise-plan out in the everyday course of events in the arena of history in accordance with the same announced word given in advance. And what the working in history and the working in the distant future shared in common was that the same word spoke both to the *immediate* future and to the *distant* future.

Some will object to our making any provision for the reality of prediction or foretelling in the biblical text. That debate, however, is a philosophical one—one that David Hume introduced and has been answered many times since then. That cannot be our stopping point here. We must assume the possibility that God does know the future and that he was able to communicate that future to mortals by means of revelation. That, in fact, is the consistent claim of the writers of the OT. To pause to make a full explication of that point would deter us from the more important point that is usually neglected in these discussions.

But certain caveats and definitions must be stated before we can proceed.

2. *Single meaning.* The first is the meaning of "single *or* literal meaning." This term means no more than this: the words of the authors of Scripture must mean what they ordinarily meant when they were accorded their *usus loquendi*, that is, their spoken sense in similar contexts of that day.

3. *Corporate solidarity.* What is often neglected by those who affirm the single meaning, however, is that the single meaning may entail the use of the concept of "corporate solidarity." "Corporate solidarity" is that the *one* who represents the group and the *many* who are represented are equally a part of the same single meaning intended by the author. Usually these two aspects are incorporated into a collective singular noun, just as in the English phrases "one deer" or "ten deer;" the noun remains the same! But when the single meaning is frozen into a monolithic, time-bound entity that has neither ties with an informing past nor connections with a continuing future, as specifically provided for by the original context, single meaning has become a reductionist interpretive tool that insulates and isolates the past into its own time-capsule.

One need only consider what the exegete does with concepts such as the "seed," the "servant of the LORD," the "branch," the "firstborn," and the like in order to see evidence of the reductionist type of single meaning systems about which I am complaining here. The prophets' consciousness of such corporate solidarities of the one and the many are all too common to be missed. It may have been this aspect of the messianic hermeneutic that Franz Delitzsch, and to a lesser extent, E. W. von Hengstenberg, were attempting to get at.

4. *Unity of the plan of God.* There is another matter that is equally as serious. The Bible is to be read with an appreciation of its wholeness, its unity, and its concept of a divine plan that is being enacted both in immediate historical fulfillments and in a final, climatic fulfillment in the last days. Modernity has placed far too much weight on the particularity and the details of the text and has devoted hardly any time to the unity of the Bible. James Orr put the matter exactly where it needs to be. He argued:

> The Koran, for instance, is a miscellany of disjointed pieces, out of which it is impossible to extract any order, progress, or arrangement. The 114 Suras or chapters of which it is composed are arranged chiefly according to length—the longer in general preceding the shorter. It is not otherwise with the Zoroastrian and Buddhist Scriptures. These are equally destitute of beginning, middle or end. They are, for the most part, collections of heterogeneous materials, loosely placed together. How different everyone must acknowledge it to be with the Bible! From Genesis to Revelation we feel that this book is in a real sense a unity. It is not a collection of fragments, but has, as we say, an organic character. It has one connected story to tell from beginning to end; we see something growing before our eyes: there is plan, purpose, progress; the end folds back on the beginning, and, when the whole is finished, we feel that here again, as in primal creation, God has finished all his works, and behold, they are very good.[12]

We have argued in *Toward an Old Testament Theology*[13] that one way of conceiving the Bible's own unity (indeed, a case that grows out of the OT text itself rather than one that is imposed over it as a grid) is to watch how the *promise-plan* of God unfolds diachronically throughout the biblical text of the

---

[12]James Orr, *The Problem of the Old Testament* (New York: Charles Scribner's Sons, 1907), 31–32.

[13]Walter C. Kaiser, Jr., *Toward an Old Testament Theology* (Grand Rapids: Zondervan, 1978), especially 1–69.

OT. The fact that God has a fixed plan for history can be seen from the programmatic text of Genesis 12:3b, "In your seed [Abraham], all the families of the earth shall be blessed" (pers. tr.). This became the most succinct statement of God's plan for all who believe and his plan for the work of the one who would represent the whole group. But this was by no means the only statement of purpose found in the biblical text.

The unity that Scripture exhibited was not static—a flat-Bible type of uniformity; it had an organic or epigenetical aspect to it that defied an easy categorization or simplification. Even in its earliest OT statements, that divine word (which had no single designation, such as the NT's "promise" [*epangelia*], but a constellation of terms such as the "covenant," the "oath," the "word," etc.) had within it seminal ideas that only later amplifications would unfold from the germs of thought that were just barely visible when first announced. That is why the metaphor from biology is an apt one: prophetic truth had an organic, epigenetical nature. The fixed core of ideas connected with the promise-plan of God and the representative of that promise remained constant. But as time went on, the content of that given word of blessing, promise, or judgment grew in accordance with seed thoughts that were contained within its earliest statements, much as a seed is uniquely related to the plant that it will become if it has life at all.

That is the aspect of the messianic doctrine that has been missed in the debate over whether to emphasize the original context of the OT writer or its NT fulfillment. That tension calls for us to jump the chasm and declare ourselves to be on either one side or the other. We sympathize with most of the traditional understandings of messianic prophecy in the OT as they were used to point to Jesus of Nazareth as the Coming One, but we cannot reach these conclusions by adopting some form of a dual meaning, an eisegesis that reads the NT automatically into the OT, or by a type of reader-response hermeneutic that assigns new meanings by some process such as *relecturing* or *sensus plenior*. Of what value would the claims of the NT Evangelists and apostles be if the original OT meanings did not anticipate in some adequate way what eventually took place during the days of Jesus of Nazareth?

D. THE PROMISE-PLAN OF GOD

Rather than contending for a messianic doctrine that results from a number of scattered predictions throughout the OT, the OT presents the concept of the Messiah and his work in the context of an eternal plan, which was unfolded before the eyes of Israel and the watching world. Predictions tend to focus the listener's or reader's attention only on two things: the word spoken before the event and the fulfilling event itself. While there is a limited amount of legitimacy about that narrower view of the future, it fails to capture the essence of the messianic story in all its fullness. Willis J. Beecher described what such a truncated analysis missed:

> [It left out] the *means* employed for that purpose. The promise and the means and the result are all in mind at once. ... If the promise involved a series of results, we might connect any one of the results with the foretelling clause as a fulfilled prediction. ... But if we permanently confined our thought to these items in the fulfilled promise, we should be led to an inadequate and very likely a false idea of the promise and its fulfillment. To understand the predictive element aright we must see it in the light of the other elements. Every fulfilled promise is a fulfilled prediction; but it is exceedingly important to look at it as a promise and not as a mere prediction.[14]

1. *Prediction or promise?* The promises of God were interrelated and usually connected in a series. They were not disconnected and heterogeneous prognostications randomly announced in the OT or arbitrarily chosen for use by the NT.

---

[14]This is taken from Beecher's famous Stone Lectures, presented at Princeton Seminary in 1905: Willis J. Beecher, *The Prophets and the Promise* (Grand Rapids: Baker, 1963 [reprint of 1905]), 376 (emphasis added).

Instead, it is amazing how the depictions concerning the coming Messiah and his work comprised one continuous plan of God. Each aspect was linked into an ongoing stream of announcements beginning in the prepatriarchal period, supplemented by the patriarchal, Mosaic, premonarchial, monarchial, and prophetic periods, down to the postexilic times of Israel's last leaders and prophets. The promise was a single one; yet it was cumulative in its net results. Indeed, its constituent parts were not a collection of assorted promises about a Messiah who was to come: instead, they formed one continuous pattern and purpose placed in the stream of history.

2. *Separate or cumulative?* In the past, the great traditional apologetic works correctly pointed to literally hundreds of predictions about the Messiah. In fact, in some 558 rabbinic writings there are 456 separate OT passages used to refer to the Messiah and the messianic times[15]—a number that is probably exaggerated because of the spiritualizing tendencies for interpreting Scripture that had entered into Judaism in the first century A.D. J. Barton Payne listed 127 personal messianic predictions involving 3,348 verses; this list included any and all references to typological predictions of the Messiah and his times. Payne's list of *direct personal* messianic foretellings came to a remarkable 574 verses.[16] But what was lacking was the Bible's own case for the unity and cumulative force of all these prophecies. The brute fact that many of these earlier prophecies were repeated in later predictions should have pointed us to the fact that God's revelations were building on what had previously been announced.

---

[15]This statistic comes from Alfred Edersheim, *The Life and Times of Jesus the Messiah*, 2 vols. (Grand Rapids: Eerdmans, 1953), 2:710–41 (Appendix 9). The distribution of the 456 OT passages is as follows: Pentateuch, 75; Earlier and Later Prophets, 243; Writings, 138.

[16]J. Barton Payne, *Encyclopedia of Biblical Prophecy* (New York: Harper and Row, 1973), 667–68. Payne found 103 *direct* messianic predictions in eighteen books of the OT, including 25 in Isaiah, 24 in the Psalms, and 20 in Zechariah.

3. Temporal or eternal? By now it should be clear that the messianic prophecies came in a series of predictions that belonged together as a single plan of God that was constantly being updated and renewed. The time-sweep was indeed staggering in that it moved from the Garden of Eden with its promise of a "seed" to the everlasting kingdom of God in the new heavens and new earth. Little wonder, then, that the plan was called in a number of places, the "eternal covenant" (e.g., Heb 13:20) of God. The promise had temporal enactments and constant fulfillments that were part of the single ongoing purpose that God had built into the fabric of history; but that fact in no way detracts from the climactic fulfillment his plan would have in the eternal state.

4. Cosmopolitan or nationalistic? Since the promises made with David and the patriarchs were so obviously nationalistic in that they pointed to the nation Israel and her land, did this not therefore limit their usefulness for those outside the boundaries of that nation and her times? Too frequently in post-Reformation thought the tendency has been to capture the essence of the OT for the church by using a replacement theology—one that replaces "Israel" with the "church."[17]

But what God was going to do for Israel was just as eternal as the promise of the coming of that messianic "seed" and the "gospel" (see Gal 3:8). In Abraham's seed "all nations will be blessed." In Beecher's Princeton lecture mentioned above, he sternly warned against any bifurcation or division of the promise whereby Israel was dissolved or collapsed into the new reality of the Church:

> ... if the Christian interpreter persists in excluding the ethnical [*sic*] Israel from his conception of the fulfillment, or in regarding Israel's part in the matter as merely preparatory and not eternal, then he comes into conflict with the plain witness of both testaments [and since May 1948, we might interject, with history itself].... Rightly interpreted,

---

[17]See Kaiser, "An Assessment of 'Replacement Theology.'"

the biblical statements include in the fulfillment both Israel the race, with whom the covenant is eternal, and also the personal Christ and his mission, with the whole spiritual Israel of the redeemed in all ages. The New Testament teaches this as Christian doctrine, for leading men to repentance and for edification, and the Old Testament teaches it as messianic doctrine, for leading men to repentance and for edification. ... The exclusive Jewish interpretation and the exclusive Christian interpretation are equally wrong. Each is correct in what it affirms, and incorrect in what it denies.[18]

We conclude, therefore, that the messianic doctrine is located in God's single, unified plan, called in the NT his "promise," which is eternal in its fulfillment but climactic in its final accomplishment, while being built up by historical fulfillments that are part and parcel of that single ongoing plan as it moved toward its final plateau. Thus, what began simply as a "word" about who God was and what he was going to do for a select group of people became a word that was intended from the start to be cosmopolitan in its effects, for it announced simultaneously who God was and what he would do for all the other nations on earth through this one group.

E. PROBLEMS IN MESSIANIC INTERPRETATION

Before we conclude this introductory section on messianic prophecy, something must be said about some of the problems posed by interpreting passages connected with this theme.

1. *Double meaning*.[19] It should be clear from what we have already argued that this writer cannot agree with those who force a distinction between the sense the prophets attach to their own utterances and what God intended in these utterances.

---

[18]Willis J. Beecher, *The Prophets and the Promise*, 383.

[19]For a survey of a number of authors advocating this view, see David Jeremiah, "The Principle of Double Fulfillment in Interpreting Prophecy," *Grace Journal* 13 (1972): 13–29.

According to Bernard Ramm, "One of the most persistent hermeneutical sins is to put two interpretations on one passage of Scripture."[20] Likewise, Milton Terry warned, "If the Scripture has more than one meaning, it has no meaning at all."[21] Even E. W. von Hengstenberg joined this chorus of declamations by advising:

> Several interpreters, endeavouring to find a middle course, adopt the notion of a double sense of prophecy; the one, that which the Prophets conceived, the other, that which God designed. This assumption, which is entirely untenable, arises from neglecting to discriminate between the *objective* meaning of a prophecy and its *subjective* meaning or meanings. In every composition, the former can be but *one*, the latter may be *as various as its readers are numerous*. It is only with the former that we are concerned [as interpreters]. . . .[22]

2. *Prophetic ignorance.* In order to enhance the divine source of these messianic prophecies and to further back up the doubtful case for double or dual meaning, some scholars have attempted to appeal to 2 Peter 1:19–21 to show that the prophets did not always understand what they wrote. But the apostle Peter makes the opposite point, for he declares in verse 16 that he and his companions had "not followed cleverly devised fables," for they were eyewitnesses of Jesus' glory on the Mount of Transfiguration (vv. 16–18). Instead, they had found in the OT prophecies a "stronger and more secure prophetic word" (v. 19a, pers. tr.).

These OT Scriptures were not a matter of one's own "loosing" (*epiluseōs*, v. 20), "because prophecy came not in old time by the will of man, but holy men of God spoke as they were moved by the Holy Spirit" (v. 21, pers. tr.). To make the

---

[20]Bernard Ramm, *Protestant Biblical Interpretation* (Boston: Wilde, 1950), 87.

[21]Milton Terry, *Biblical Hermeneutics* (New York: Eaton and Mains, 1890), 384.

[22]E. W. Hengstenberg, *Christology of the Old Testament*, 114. Italics are his.

word *epiluseōs* mean in this context an "explanation" or "interpretation," as some do, would be to argue that no prophet can interpret his own message. But that claim is too bold, for that would mean that *all* prophetic writings were closed to their human authors. Furthermore, the substantive *epilusis* in classical usage means a "freeing," "losing," or "destroying"—in other words, an unleashing from life. This is the only instance of this form in the NT. Even the Septuagint gives us no examples. The verbal form, however, appears to mean "to set at liberty," "to let go," "to loose," while it came to mean secondarily, "to explain, unfold, or interpret" (see Mk 4:34).

Peter urges his readers to give heed to these OT prophecies, "as to a light shining in a dark place," because the Spirit of God has revealed through these prophets what is certain, plain, and intelligible through the Father of lights. Had Peter's advice been, "Give heed to the light shining in a dark place since no prophet understood or could explain what he said, but he wrote as he was carried along by the Holy Spirit," then the light would have been darkness, and how could any audience, then or now, including the prophets themselves, have given heed to that enigmatic word? This would call for a second miracle—the inspiration of the interpreter.[23]

3. *Three types of prophecies.* This is not to say that all prophecies are equally easy to interpret. In the nineteenth century August Tholuck distinguished between three types of quotations of OT prophecies: direct prophecies, typical prophecies, and applications of OT statements.

Direct prophecies are those in which the OT author looked directly at the messianic age, and his readers understood it as a prophecy about the Messiah. For example, almost all Jews and Christians recognize that Micah 5:2 declared that the

---

[23]See Walter C. Kaiser, Jr., "The Single Intent of Scripture," in *Evangelical Roots: A Tribute to Wilbur Smith*, ed. Kenneth S. Kantzer (Nashville: Nelson, 1978), 123–41; *Back Toward the Future: Hints for Interpreting Biblical Prophecy* (Grand Rapids: Baker, 1989), 127–45.

birthplace of Messiah would be Bethlehem. It is true that Micah claimed Bethlehem was "small" in comparison to the other "clans of Judah," while Matthew 2:6 claimed that Bethlehem was "by no means least." But this was not a contradiction between the OT and NT authors, only a difference in emphasis, for both agreed that Bethlehem was the city to watch.

Likewise, Malachi 3:1 predicted that a messenger would announce the coming of Messiah while Zechariah 9:9 declared that Zion's king would enter the city riding on a donkey. The point with all these prophecies is that their fulfillment was readily apparent and fairly uncomplicated.

Typical prophecies are different from direct prophecies in that their immediate referent in their own day was separate from that to which their ultimate referent pointed, though they were joined as one single meaning in that they shared at least one thing in common, which was at the heart of the prediction. In this category we have persons, institutions, or events that were *divinely designated* in the OT text to be models, previews, or pictures of something that was to come in the days of Messiah.

Especially noteworthy are the parts, services, and attendants of the tabernacle, for Exodus 25:8–9, 40 informs us that Moses was instructed to make that structure according to a "pattern" of what the real was. Thus, God suggests that the *copy* will be replaced as soon as the *actual* shows up in space and time. In other words, the sacrifices, the furniture, and the high priest of the tabernacle were all on notice that they were working with what would be obsolete when the real, of which they were only shadows and patterns, came on the scene. Because of the brevity of our treatment and the fact that this type of prophecy raises separate hermeneutical considerations, this book will not treat many of the numerous types that pointed to the Messiah.[24]

---

[24]See our commentary on "Leviticus," in *The New Interpreter's Bible* (Nashville: Abingdon, 1994), for further details on how these types functioned.

The third type of prophecies quoted in the NT are *applications*. Here the language of the OT text is used or appropriated, but no specific prediction was intended by the OT or claimed by the NT writer.

Some suggest that Hosea 11:1, as cited by Matthew in 2:15, "Out of Egypt I called my son," is the prime example of this category. However, they are wrong to do so, for most miss the point that the words emphasized in the text are not "*out of* Egypt"; rather, the emphasis falls on "my son." The point of the citation is the corporate solidarity between all Israel being rescued and delivered by God and the One who was God's "Son" *par excellence*, not the Exodus from Egypt. Had the departure from Egypt been the point of commonality between the two, the citation from Hosea 11:1 should have appeared not in Matthew 2:15, when Jesus went *into* Egypt, but at verse 21!

The best illustration of an application of the words of the OT, borrowed for a new situation is Matthew 2:23: "and he went and lived in a town called Nazareth. So was fulfilled what was said through the prophets: 'He will be called a Nazarene.'" Apparently, Matthew is referring to Isaiah 11:1, where the word for "Branch" is *nezer*. By assonance, *nezer* became "Nazarene." Matthew must have had a twinkle in his eye as he set forth that pun, a literary device that the prophets loved to employ.

One final question remains: How do we know whether we are dealing with a direct, typological, or application type of prophecy? Typical prophecies require that the immediate context supply an explicit notification that they are divinely designated to be only patterns of what the real will be like when it/he comes. Applications are the most suspect and should be used rarely, if at all, and with great caution. Certainly, no one should build any part of the main messianic doctrine on them. The most straightforward procedure will be to deal with the direct prophecies; those are the ones we will focus on in this study of OT biblical theology.

◆ 2 ◆

The Messiah
in the Pentateuch

There are six direct messianic predictions in the Pentateuch: two in the pre-patriarchal times (Ge 1–11), two major ones in the patriarchal era (Ge 12–50), and two dominating ones in the Mosaic epoch (Ex–Dt). All six are interconnected and relate to the promise-plan of God that is the main backbone of the narrative and theology of the OT.

The first two prophecies in these five books of the law declared that the coming man of promise would be from the "offspring" of a woman (Ge 3:15), but he would also later on be none less than God come to dwell among the families of Shem (9:27).

The second set of promises announced that there would be two marvelous results that would accompany the coming of this man of promise. By means of Abraham's offspring, blessing would be mediated to all the families of the earth (Ge 12:3). However, as the plan gathered more specificity and was attached particularly to one of Jacob's sons, namely Judah, it became clear that this coming one would be given not only the rule and authority over all the nation of Israel, but also authority over the nations (49:10).

During the Mosaic era of revelation, two events stood out with regard to this emerging and accumulating doctrine of the coming man of promise. In the prophecies of a Gentile named

Balaam, this same coming man (in the seed or offspring of Eve, Shem, Abraham, Isaac, Jacob, and Judah) would act as a victorious king as he crushed his enemies (Nu 24:17). In addition to his function of ruling as a king, Moses declared he would be a prophet as well (Dt 18:18).

Thus, even when sketched in its boldest and simplest strokes, the Pentateuch set forth in rudimentary forms lines of thought that were anchored seminally in truth that would be enlarged in later revelation. Already, this person would be known by his titles of "Seed," "Shiloh," "Scepter," "Star," "King," and "Prophet."

However, we must be careful not to take any one of these prophecies or titles in abstraction by itself, for they can only be appreciated in their biblical context as they belong to the ongoing announcements and fulfillments of the promise theme. This coming person cannot be separated from the contents of the covenant God repeatedly affirmed with the patriarchs and Moses. Intertwined in this one plan of God were provisions for a name, a blessing, a land, a gospel, a people, a divine dwelling in the midst of the people, and an affirmation that God would be their personal deity. It is best that we follow the story of this promise-plan through these six high watermarks for the Messiah in the Torah.

A. THE EDENIC PREDICTION (GENESIS 3:15)

Genesis 3:15 has commonly been called the *protoevangelium* (the "first gospel") because it was the original proclamation of the promise of God's plan for the whole world. While it is true that it is found in a sentence that denounced the tempter of Eve in the Garden of Eden, yet it gave our first parents a glimpse, even if only an obscure one, of the person and mission of the one who was going to be the central figure in the unfolding drama of the redemption of the world. The "seed/offspring" mentioned in this verse became the root from which the tree of the OT promise of a Messiah grew. This, then, was the "mother prophecy"[1] that gave birth to all the rest of the promises. Charles Briggs agreed: Genesis 3:15 was "the germ of promise which unfolds in the history of redemption."[2]

Strange as it may seem, the history of the human race begins with the sin of our first parents and their expulsion from the Garden of Eden. But that is not where it ended, for in the middle of the bleakness and the dark tragedy of God's curse on the tempter, the woman, and the man came the first rays of light and hope embodied as the gospel of the grace of our God.

"The serpent" is named as the tempter of the woman. Little progress will be made on this text until we can identify this tempter. It is evident for a number of reasons that something more than a mere reptile is intended here. Note the intelligence, conception, speech, and knowledge the serpent possesses—indeed, a knowledge that surpasses either what the man or woman have. The tempter speaks as if he has access to the mind of God—or at least to the supernatural world.

"The serpent" is clearly being individualized, for the pronoun used of him in Hebrew is the second person masculine singular pronoun. Furthermore, the serpent of the temptation is the serpent of the final conflict; he is someone whom a future male descendant of the woman will strike with a crushing blow to his skull. Thus, the designation "the serpent" (*hannāḥāš*) is probably a title, not the particular shape he assumed or the instrument he borrowed to manifest himself to the original pair. Even the alleged demotion of the means of locomotion for reptiles from a upright walking position to that of crawling on one's belly and eating dust (Ge 3:14) is insufficient to demonstrate that this being had a reptilian form when he appeared to the first couple. Had not God already made creeping things

---

[1]This expression comes from James E. Smith, *What the Bible Teaches About the Promised Messiah* (Nashville: Nelson, 1993), 38.

[2]Charles A. Briggs, *Messianic Prophecy* (New York: Charles Scribner's Sons, 1886), 73.

that crawled on their bellies in the first chapter of Genesis and called them "good" (1:24–25)? The words of the curse on the serpent, therefore, must be figures of speech, vividly picturing those who had been vanquished and who must now lie face down in the dirt while the conquering king literally makes these enemies his footstool.[3] When all these details are taken into account, the identity of the tempter can be none other than Satan, that old dragon, the serpent.[4]

Who then is the "seed" or "offspring" mentioned in this text? Clearly the term "seed" is a generic term for the entire race that came from the woman on the one hand, while the "seed" of the serpent embraces all the evil race derived from him. However, the very fact that the noun "seed" is a collective singular deliberately provides for the fact that it may include the one who represents the whole group as well as the group itself. The fact that there is such a one specified in this text as a male descendant of the woman opens up this text to its messianic possibilities.

That is the most striking thing that happens in verse 15—the suffix on the Hebrew word "heel" is singular ("*his*"). This suffix cannot refer to the woman, since any reference to her must be feminine; nor can it refer to the serpent, since he will be the object of this male's attack. Moreover, the reference to "his heel" bears out the correctness of understanding Hebrew *hû'* as a singular masculine pronoun in the phrase "*he* will crush your head."

---

[3]For a more complete discussion, see my *Toward an Old Testament Theology* (Grand Rapids: Zondervan, 1978), 77–79. The same concept of going on one's belly as a symbolic expression for total defeat occurs in Ge 49:17; Job 20:14, 16; Ps 140:3; Isa 59:5; Mic 7:17.

[4]Later, the NT identified the serpent of Genesis 3:15 as Satan, as when in Romans 16:20 Paul prayed, with obvious reference to this OT text, "The God of peace will soon crush Satan under your [i.e., the church's] feet"; in 2 Corinthians 11:3, 14 he warns, "Eve was deceived by the serpent's cunning. . . . for Satan himself masquerades as an angel of light." Revelation 12:9 is even plainer: "The great dragon was hurled down—that ancient serpent called the devil, or Satan, who leads the whole world astray."

Further evidence for the correctness of this conclusion is supplied by the Septuagint, the Greek translation of the OT, made about three centuries before Jesus Christ was born. The Hebrew masculine personal pronoun, as R. A. Martin has pointed out,[5] occurs 103 times in Genesis, but only in 3:15 did the translators of the Greek text break their own grammatical rules, which require that the pronoun agree with its antecedent in gender and number. Martin concludes,

> It seems unlikely that this is mere coincidence or oversight. First of all, the quality of the Greek translation of the Pentateuch is, generally speaking, higher than other parts of the OT. Second, in all other instances where such literalness would have resulted in violence to agreement in Greek between the pronoun and the antecedent the translator avoided such literalness and used the required feminine or neuter pronoun. The most likely explanation for the use of [masculine pronoun] *autos*[6] [rather than the neuter pronoun *auto*] in Gen 3:15 to refer back to [the neuter noun] *sperma* is that the translator has in this way indicated his messianic understanding of this verse.[7]

Herein lies, even if only in germ form and somewhat enigmatically stated, the roots of the messianic doctrine. It is also noteworthy that this text was understood by the Jewish community to point to the Messiah almost three hundred years before Jesus was born. That male will turn out to be the Messiah himself. However, at this stage of history, it is enough to know that God will provide an antidote for the terrible state that sin introduced into the world.

---

[5]R. A. Martin, "The Earliest Messianic Interpretation of Genesis 3:15," *JBL* 84 (1965): 425–27.

[6]Martin (ibid., 427, n. 6) also considered the unlikely possibility that the final *sigma* (*s*) on *autos* might be a case of dittography for the initial *sigma* from the following word in Greek, *sou*. However, he discounted this possibility because the textual tradition was unanimous on reading the masculine form.

[7]Ibid., 427.

This is how it will happen. God deliberately places an "enmity" (a word that, in its five uses in the OT, indicates person-to-person hostility, never hostile actions exchanged by animals) between (1) "the serpent," i.e., Satan, and (2) the woman, Eve. God also plans that that "enmity" will continue between (3) Satan's "seed/offspring" and (4) the woman's "seed/offspring." The most surprising thing is that there suddenly emerges a male descendant of the woman (4a, to continue the numbering above) who will "crush"[8] the head of Satan while the latter merely "crushes" or "bruises the heel" of this unnamed and unidentified male "seed." The victory is to be complete and decisive.

Three battles are depicted here: a personal one between the woman and Satan in that day (1 and 2 above); another between the posterity of both the woman and Satan in the future (3 and 4 above); and the final battle, presumably in the end times, that leads to a mortal blow to the skull of the Evil One by an as yet unnamed or unidentified male descendant of the woman (4a).

The *protoevangelium* is a presentation of the entire history of humanity in a miniature declaration. Relief will come from the same God who created all things. But exactly how? And when? Such questions as these went unanswered as the centuries rolled on.

Some hint of what these early mortals may have understood from this announcement is evident in Eve's response after she had given birth to her first son (Ge 4:1). She named

---

[8]The Hebrew word for "crush" or "bruise" is the same word, *šûf*. The word only appears three times in the OT. One of its three instances is probably not supported by the best texts (Ps 139:11), which leaves only Job 9:17 as a comparison for our text in Genesis 3:15. The parallelism with Job 9:17 favors the meaning of "crush *or* bruise," as does the Syriac, Vulgate, Arabic, Targum of Jonathan, and Samaritan Targum. The Septuagint and the Targum of Onkelos favor the unlikely meaning of "watch *or* guard." The contrast between crushing the head and crushing or bruising the heel is the difference between a mortal blow to the skull and a slight injury to the victor.

him "Cain" and explained, "I have gotten [the verb sounds like the noun "Cain"] a man," adding "even the LORD." That is the way Luther rendered the appositional clause that came at the end of this verse. Such a translation is possible, for there is no word for "help," as most modern versions generally render it: "*with the help of* the LORD" (italicized words are not in the Hebrew text). If this suggestion is correct, then Eve understood that the promised male descendant of human descent would be, in some way, divine, "the LORD." If so, then Eve's instincts about the coming Messiah were correct, but her timing was way off!

B. THE NOAHIC PREDICTION (GENESIS 9:25–27)

It is impossible to say how much time elapsed from the promise given in Eden to this post-flood event, but it was on the order of several thousand years. Once again, a crisis had arisen in the family of humanity; sin had brought the judgment of a worldwide flood. Then Genesis 9:18–24 relates how Noah became drunk and the sin of Ham ensued in the course of those events. What Ham did in connection with viewing the nakedness of his drunken father we are not told. It was enough, however, to call forth a curse from Noah after he woke up from his drunken stupor and was told what his youngest son had done.

The son of Ham, Canaan (Ge 10:6), who either already evidenced the same sinful perversions as were evident in his father or as Noah prophetically envisioned would eventually be true, was given a triple curse by Noah (vv. 25, 26, 27). Contrariwise, Noah pronounced a dual blessing on Ham's brother, Shem: "Blessed be the LORD, the God of Shem! May he [i.e., God] dwell in the tents of Shem" (v. 27, pers. tr.). Clearly, as Briggs observes, "Shem is the central figure of the prophecy."[9]

---

[9]Charles A. Briggs, *Messianic Prophecy* (New York: Charles Scribners' Sons, 1889), 81.

The patriarch turned from Ham to his brothers, especially to Shem, his firstborn, and blessed the God of Shem.

What Noah said next has been hotly debated, for verse 27 simply says, "May God provide ample space for Japheth, may he dwell in the tents of Shem, and may Canaan be his slave" (pers. tr.). The controversial point was this: Who is the referent of the pronoun "he" in "may *he* dwell"? Was Japheth to dwell in the tents of Shem? What would that mean? Or was God to dwell there? Either translation was possible grammatically if the contextual questions are left aside.

Those who argue that the subject to be supplied is Japheth (cf. NIV) usually raise three arguments to support their case. (1) Since the refrain in verses 26 and 27 is, "May Canaan be his servant/slave," one would expect verse 27 to apply throughout to Japheth, since verse 26 was given over to Shem. (2) The plural "tents" is not applicable to the abode of Yahweh, for in parallel passages we always read of his dwelling in "his tent" on his holy hill of Zion. (3) Inasmuch as both brothers acted in concert to resist Ham's apparently lewd suggestion, one would expect a corresponding blessing to be shared by the two of them.[10]

But the question remains: What would Japheth's dwelling in the tents of Shem mean? Some crassly suggest that it meant that Japheth's Indo-European descendants would one day take over the land of the Shemites and subjugate them. This view has been rejected by most in favor of a spiritual interpretation, that the Japhethites would participate in the saving blessings of the Shemites, for there is no indication here of a forcible conquest of Shem by Japheth. But if a non-military conquest is intended, then, as Franz Delitzsch argued, "The fulfillment is plain enough, for we are all Japhethites dwelling in the tents of Shem; and the language of the New Testament is

---

[10]These three reasons are given in C. F. Keil and F. Delitzsch, *Biblical Commentary on the Old Testament: The Pentateuch* (Grand Rapids: Eerdmans, 1956), 1:159.

the language of Javan [Greece] entered into the tents of Shem."[11] In other words, the gospel was preached in Greek in Israel, even though Israel was subdued by the imperial power of Rome. Thus, Greek entered into the tents of Shem and became their spiritual conqueror.

But all of this sounds too much like special pleading. It is better to take *Elohim*, "God," as the subject and proper antecedent of "he will dwell" in Genesis 9:27 for five reasons.[12] (1) The Hebrew language presumes that the subject of a previous clause will carry over to the next one when no other subject is interjected, especially when, as here, it is in a parallel line of Hebrew poetry.

(2) Structurally, the heptastich (seven poetic lines) in verses 25–27 is subdivided into three parts with the curse on Canaan as a refrain. In the first part, a distich (two lines), only Canaan appears. In the second part, also a distich, Canaan and Shem appear. In the third part, a tristich, all three sons appear. This justifies making God the subject of the verb to dwell in the second of the three lines, since then Shem is being talked about and not a second statement being made about Japheth.

(3) In the narrative, beginning in Genesis 9:18, the place of honor and prominence goes to Shem, in that his name comes first. Thus he seems to be the leader; a fact that does not comport well with Shem's being placed in some sort of subordination to Japheth in verse 27.

(4) Since God blesses Shem in the previous distich of verse 26 and thereby identifies himself in a distinctive sense as being related to Shem, it is most natural to expect that this distinctiveness will manifest itself in some way, such as God's decision to take up his abode somewhere within the Semitic world.

---

[11]Ibid., 160.

[12]These five reasons follow closely those given by Charles A. Briggs, *Messianic Prophecy*, 82–83, n. 1.

(5) The most natural interpretation of the blessing of expansion for Japheth and Japheth's alleged dwelling in the tents of Shem, despite modern protests to the contrary, would be that Japheth would conquer Shem, or at least occupy his territory. But this would humiliate Shem, making him little better off than the curse set upon Canaan. Therefore, the meaning of Genesis 9:27 is God's announcement that his advent will take place among the Shemites, later known through the Greek form of their name as the Semites.

The concept of God's "dwelling" among humankind was startling, to say the least. But how? How could the immortal God, so to speak, contaminate himself with the stuff of our humanity? Here again, the germ of the messianic idea presses itself upon humanity with tantalizing brevity. But the promise doctrine never shrinks back from this basic, but seminal concept. One day the living Word of God will become flesh and will dwell (or "tabernacle") among us (Jn 1:14). Revelation subsequent to Noah's era, largely confined to the Mosaic and premonarchial periods, will enlarge on what is meant by the "rest" or "dwelling" of God among humankind. For instance, the story of the *shekinah* (i.e., the "dwelling") glory of God hovering over the tabernacle and in the pillar of cloud by day and fire by night reveals what else God intended by this theme of his dwelling among mortals. In addition, the whole concept of the "glory of God" is a rich source for detailing what it means to have the presence of God in the midst of his people.

For now, clearly God promises to come in his advent in the line of a woman (Ge 3:15), the human side of the messianic redemption, and as God on high to dwell among the people of Shem (Ge 9:27), the divine side of the coming Messiah. "These two lines of Messianic prophecy, the human and the divine, henceforth develop side by side in Messianic prophecy; they approximate at times, but never converge till they unite in the person of Jesus Christ, the God-man, at His first advent, and still more at His second advent."[13]

C. THE ABRAHAMIC PREDICTION
(GENESIS 12:1–3, ETC.)

From among the Shemitic/Semitic tribes to whom God had given his promise to dwell among them, he called one Semitic couple, Abram and his wife Sarai, to leave the plush surroundings of Ur in southern Mesopotamia and go about 1100 miles away to an unnamed land he would show them. This "call of Abram," as the episode will later be called, begins a new era in history and a new epoch in the disclosures about the promise-plan of God with its central character, the Messiah.

On at least six occasions the divine promise was announced to Abraham (Ge 12:1–3, 7; 13:14–18; 15:4–5, 13–18; 17:1–8; 18:17–19; 22:15–18). On two other occasions the same prophetic words were given to Isaac (26:4, 23–24), and twice more this same covenant, with its same promises, was repeated to his son Jacob (28:14–15; 35:9–12).

God made eight promises to Abraham: (1) He would make him into a great nation; (2) he would bless him; (3) he would make his name great; (4) Abraham and his seed would be a blessing to others; (5) God would bless those who blessed him; (6) he would curse those who cursed him; (7) through Abraham and his "seed" (or "offspring") God would be the channel of blessing to all the peoples on earth; and (8) God would give to Abraham's "seed" the land he had entered after leaving Ur of the Chaldeans. The first seven promises appeared in his "call" in Genesis 12:2–3, while the eighth was added when he arrived at Shechem in Palestine (v. 7).

The seventh of these eight promises became the one that was emphasized, for it always appears in the climactic posi-

---

[13]Ibid., 82–83.

tion, even though it was repeated to Abraham three times and once each to Isaac and Jacob (Ge 12:3; 18:18; 22:18; 26:4; 28:14). This is where the messianic aspect of the promise to the patriarchs resided: it was this as yet unspecified "seed" that embraced the potentiality for including at one and the same time the One who represented the group as well as all who participated by faith in that group.

The fivefold emphasis on the statement "through you/your offspring all nations on earth will be blessed" pointed to the heart of the gospel as well as to missions. Rather than the blessing being a work of the patriarchs, it would come from God as a gift. That is why the apostle Paul wrote that this promise was "the gospel"—the heart of the "good news" itself (Gal 3:8). Elsewhere Paul argued that it came to Abraham while he still was uncircumcised (Ro 4:10–12). Both arguments were correct and fair to the OT text. Human works were definitely excluded as the means for obtaining God's blessing or favor.

Thus, what had seemed as an unfair narrowing of the privileges given to the Shemites, in that God would live only in their tents, was to be the very means for extending those benefits to all the nations and to all the Gentiles. The blessing of God was imparted, then, on the condition that the people who first benefited from this gift were to be the source for introducing these privileges to the heathen. This was missions of the highest order!

A problem, however, is raised with regard to this seventh promise. Two different forms of the verb "to bless" were used. The *Niphal*, or the passive voice in English, was used in three cases: Genesis 12:3; 18:18; 28:14. But in the other two, 22:18 and 26:4, the *Hithpael* or reflexive form of the verb was used. The tendency of scholars in the twentieth century has been to level all five instances out to the reflexive form, arguing that the later passages are clearer and should therefore be regarded as an interpretation on the former.

In response, we should note that all five passages are rendered as passives in the Samaritan version and in the Babylonian (Onkelos) and Jerusalem (Pseudo-Jonathan) Targums.[14] But even if the *Hithpael* has a separate meaning, as it well might here, the distinction is that in the reflexive idea, the nations reflect on how fortunate they are to have been blessed through the seed of Abraham (rather than the nations deciding to "bless themselves" by doing what was done to Abraham), while the passive form stresses that the nations are blessed by an outsider (i.e., by God) as Abraham was blessed—not by any work of their own, but by means of God's provision of this "seed."

This idea, of course, is already brought out in Genesis 12:2, where the divine blessing is attached to Abraham's person: "And you [or "it"; referring to Abraham's name or nation] will be a blessing." Thus, Abraham did not bless himself, nor was he merely a formula of blessing; he was the medium and agency through which the divine blessing would come. The two result or purpose clauses in verse 3 (generally translated as "and," but surely the Hebrew *waw* functions more precisely here as a purpose or result clause) state that what God gave to Abraham was in order that he (or his "seed") might be a blessing to all the nations of the earth (see the fourth and seventh promises). One should also notice that the references found in the Apocrypha and in the NT consistently render the idea of the blessing through Abraham in the passive voice: Abraham was only to be a channel.

How were Abraham, Isaac, and Jacob to be a channel of God's blessing to the entire world? And who is this "seed"? Already in Genesis 3:15 we have come to understand that this

---

[14]The most definitive discussion on this problem, which has never received an answer in this century, is by O. T. Allis, "The Blessing of Abraham," *PTR* 25 (1927): 263–98. See especially p. 281, where Allis lists the following as probable examples of a passive meaning for the *Hithpael*: Ge 37:35; Nu 31:23; Dt 4:21; 23:9; 1Sa 3:14; 30:6; 1Ki 2:26; Job 15:28; 30:16, 17; Pss 107:17, 27; 119:52; Isa 30:29; La 4:1; Eze 19:12; Da 12:10; Mic 6:16. Gesenius's *Grammar* makes a similar point.

"seed" can be a collective noun and embrace one's whole biological progeny. At the same time, however, there is something distinctively singular and individualistic about this seed, for a certain "he" will have it out with the Evil One in some future day (3:15), even though "he" acts only as one of the woman's many descendants. Paul picked up the same theme in Galatians 3:16, insisting that the text of the OT said "seed" (a collective singular noun), not "seeds" (a plural noun). He was not appealing to some midrashic or rabbinic principle of interpretation, as many have recently argued, echoing the latest eddies of thought stimulated by recent discoveries from Qumran and by rabbinical studies; he was carefully observing that the divine revelation had distinctly chosen the collective singular word over the plural in order to provide for the single but inclusive concept of corporate solidarity[15] between the one and the many.

The word "seed" must be understood in some exclusive way, for not all of Abraham's biological progeny are intended (e.g., none of Keturah's children or the child Hagar bore Abraham). That is, only a portion of Abraham's seed is marked as being the objects of this designation. This narrowing of the promise is likewise seen in the posterity of Isaac (Esau is excluded) and of Jacob (where the blessing bypassed the eldest son, Reuben, and the next oldest brothers, Simeon and Levi, but came to the fourth son, Judah).

Before we leave this section, it will be of some interest to inquire what Jesus referred to when he claimed in John 8:56, "Your father Abraham rejoiced at the thought of seeing my day; he saw it and was glad." The natural reply of the Jewish

---

[15]"Corporate solidarity" is not to be confused or equated with "corporate personality" as defined by H. Wheeler Robinson, *Corporate Personality in Ancient Israel*, 2d ed. (Philadelphia: Westminster, 1980), but instead with D. Joyce, "The Individual and the Community," in *Beginning Old Testament Study*, ed. J. W. Rogerson (Philadelphia: Westminster, 1982). See also J. W. Rogerson, *Anthropology and the Old Testament* (Atlanta: John Knox, 1979). See below, chap. 6, pp. 138–39.

audience was, "You are not yet fifty years old . . . and you have seen Abraham!" (v. 57). When could Abraham have seen the "day" of Christ? And what did Jesus mean by "day"? If "day" functions the same way as "time" and "hour" do in "his time had not yet come" (7:30), or he "prayed that if possible the hour might pass from him" (Mk 14:35), or "the hour has come for the Son of Man to be glorified" (Jn 12:23), then Christ's "day" refers to the events that surrounded his passion and work of redemption on the cross.

But when could Abraham have seen anything on that order of sophistication? Probably when he took his son Isaac up on Mount Moriah to be offered, even though he had waited so long for him and would probably never get another to replace him. Abraham presumably believed God would raise the slain Isaac up from the dead, for he distinctly told the men accompanying him to wait at the foot of the hill, for he and the boy would go and worship and both would return (Ge 22:5)![16] God instead provided a substitute—a ram caught in the thicket, which appeared as God called a halt to the test (v. 13). That is why Abraham named the place "Yahweh Jirah," "The LORD Will Provide" (v. 14).[17] In other words, Abraham saw that God himself would provide a substitute, someone in that coming "seed" who would somehow be connected with the sacrifice and deliverance of Isaac, the son of promise.

D. THE JUDAIC PREDICTION (GENESIS 49:8–12)

Jacob's family increased to twelve sons, reaching seventy individuals (including grandchildren and dependents) by the time the family left for Egypt (Ex 1:5). But it was his fourth son,

---

[16]Cf. also Heb 11:19.

[17]For more details on this narrative and its function in this messianic context, see Walter C. Kaiser, Jr., "Sacrifice Your Son as a Burnt Offering," in *Hard Sayings of the Old Testament* (Downers Grove, Ill.: InterVarsity, 1988), 52–56.

Judah, whom God singled out to be the channel through which the messianic line would continue.

This prophecy (Ge 49:8–12) comes in the context of the patriarch Jacob's final blessing on each of his sons. He passed over his first three sons as the channels of this designated man of promise in favor of Judah, the fourth oldest of the twelve. Judah was promised: (1) the praise of his brothers, (2) the pre-eminence in Israel, (3) victories over his enemies, (4) the obedience of the nations, and (5) unusual prosperity in his fields and herds.

The interpretation of this prophecy, however, depends in a large measure on what meaning is assigned to the Hebrew word *šylh* (v. 10). In most English translations this word is translated as a proper name ("Shiloh") and acts as the subject of the verb "comes." We may rightly reject the city of Shiloh (which is never spelled *šylh*), the alleged Akkadian reading of *šîlu(m)* meaning "Prince, ruler, king" (which does not occur in Akkadian), and the reading "tribute is brought to him" (because the unexpressed subject cannot be the "staff" or "scepter").[18]

The meaning of "until Shiloh comes" can be best explained if the pointing of the vowels is changed from *šîloh* to *šelloh* or *šeloh*, a form supported by thirty-eight Hebrew manuscripts. In that case *šeloh* is a compounded word from *še*, the shortened form of the so-called relative particle *'ašer* ("which, whose"), *le* ("belonging to"), and the suffix *ôh* for *ô*, ("him"). This accords perfectly with the longer form that is spelled out more distinctly in Ezekiel 21:27 [32], "until he comes to whom it rightfully belongs." The Septuagint and Theodotion understood something close to this when they read: "until that comes which belongs to him [Judah]"—that is, dominion over the world. Aquila, Symmachus, and the Targum Onkelos read this

---

[18]See W. L. Moran, "Genesis 49:10 and Its Use in Ezekiel 21:32," *Bib* 39 (1958): 402–25, for a full discussion of these options; also David Baron, *Rays of Messiah's Glory: Christ in the Old Testament* (Grand Rapids: Zondervan, n.d. [reprint of 1886]), 258–62.

way: "until he comes to whom it [i.e., the scepter, or the rule] belongs." The personal reference (i.e., "to him") is the preferred way of taking it, for that reading is based on the number of manuscripts that support it and it accounts for a wide spectrum of earlier authorities that treat it that way. The fact that Ezekiel seems to allude to this verse in his book tends to clinch the argument from a revelational standpoint.

Two things are foretold in this verse: the tribe of Judah will not cease to exist as a people, and Judah will have a government of its own until the Messiah appears on the scene. The word "until," however, needs further investigation. Hebrew ʿad often takes an inclusive sense, suggesting that Judah's rule and reign will reach up to the coming of Shiloh and beyond. That surely indicates that Shiloh will be part of Judah. What clinches this understanding of "until" is the fact that the extent of Judah's domain will be worldwide, for "the obedience of the nations [will be] his." That is, the peoples of the world will one day come in homage and submission to Shiloh, that is, to the One to "whom [dominion rightfully] belonged."

Under "Shiloh's" rule, Israel's land will enjoy unusual prosperity (vv. 11–12). One will be able to "tether his donkey to a vine" (v. 11a), because there would be such an abundance of vines that the possible damage to one vine will not be missed. Another indication of the abundant harvest is that one's garments will be washed in wine (v. 11c). That is, the winepress will be so full after squeezing out the juice from the grapes in the large vats by stamping on them with one's feet that one's clothes will be saturated with grape juice. Moreover, the eyes will be dark from drinking so much wine and teeth will be white as milk from drinking from the overflow of the milking herd (v. 12).

The only other option is to understand "Shiloh" as meaning "peacemaker, pacifier," even though nouns of this form do not denote, as it must here, a doer of an action. But if the word originally had an abstract meaning such as "rest," then the move from the abstract to the concrete can explain the anomalous form. This is our second option if the preferred reading adopted above should prove to be incorrect. The theme of "rest" and the concept of "peace" are a major part of the ongoing promise-plan of God, as can be seen from its appearance during the days of the judges (cf. also Heb 3:7–4:11) and from Solomon's own name being closely tied in with *šalôm*, "peace."

But on the preferred reading of *šylh*, Genesis 49:10 means the following: "The scepter [an insignia of dominion] shall not depart from Judah, nor the ruler's staff from between his feet [i.e., "from him"], until he [i.e., the Messiah] comes to whom it [i.e., the rule, reign, and/or dominion] belongs." Thus Judah will continue to govern until Messiah comes. Shiloh is best understood, therefore, as a cryptic but shorthand form of a personal name for the Messiah. While some may object that this personal messianic meaning was not known until the sixteenth, or, as others protest, as late as the nineteenth century A.D., it can be shown that there is an old Jewish tradition going back to the Targum of Onkelos that reads, "until Messiah come" (the Jerusalem Targum reads, "until the time that King Messiah shall come"). Thus, we are more than justified in concluding that this verse is a messianic text that adds to the Messiah's credentials the fact that he will govern, not only the nation Israel, but all the nations of the world. The reason he can claim such a high prerogative is because it is his right to do so, for all rule and authority are derived from him.

E. THE BALAAMIC PREDICTION
(NUMBERS 24:15–19)

Jacob and his family spent 430 years in Egypt, after which they were miraculously delivered by God under Moses (Ex 12:40). After they escaped the clutches of Pharaoh, they wandered for forty years in the desert, for what could have been not more than an eleven-day journey, once they had arrived at Sinai (Dt 1:2).

In the fortieth year of wandering, the king of Moab, Balak, sought to hire Balaam, the son of Beor, who lived at Pethor (also known as Pitru), near the Euphrates River in northern Mesopotamia. He wanted Balaam to come and place a curse on the hordes of Israelites that appeared to be on the verge of crossing over into his territorial boundaries. After Balaam refused to accept because Yahweh had forbidden him to go, stating that a blessed people could not be cursed, the prophet eventually capitulated when a second request came, even though it displeased the Lord.

Three times the Moabite king, Balak, situated the prophet Balaam so that he would throw a spell or a curse on Israel and thereby, apparently, make it easier for him to conquer them in battle; alas, Balaam ended up blessing Israel each time. In the fourth oracle, one that Balak no longer wanted, Balaam again described the future of Israel under the inspiration of God. This time it was a spectacular prediction of a coming powerful ruler who would arise from Israel to gain an unprecedented victory over that nation's enemies. This time the prophecy included the theme of royal messianism as one of its key predictions.[19]

Balaam stated high claims for the source of his disclosure about this coming "ruler" and "star" who would arise from Israel, which would happen "in days to come" (Nu 24:14). The divine revelation came to him personally, opening his eyes and hearing so that he could see and hear the words of God (v. 15). It imparted nothing less than "knowledge from the Most High" (v. 16). In the most succinct terms possible, what he received was a propositional revelation that gave a whole new perception of God.

---

[19]For a detailed study on Balaam, see Walter C. Kaiser, Jr., "Balaam, Son of Beor, in Light of *Deir 'Allā* and Scripture: Saint or Soothsayer?" in *Festschrift for Dwight Young*, ed. Joseph Coleson and Victor Matthews (Winona Lake, Ind.: Eisenbrauns, forthcoming).

What was the content of this oracle of God? What Balaam saw was a man, though not one who was already present (v. 17a). He would come sometime in the future; he would be an Israelite and a king who would triumph (v. 17b). The symbols of his reign would be a "star" and a "scepter." Jewish interpreters early on decided that this ruler announced here was the Messiah. One clear piece of evidence for that point of view can be seen in the adoption of the name "star" by the pseudomessiah Simeon Bar Kochba, "Simeon son of the Star." Bar Kochba led a revolt against the Roman emperor Hadrian in A.D. 132, in order to oppose Hadrian's founding the non-Jewish city of Aelia Capitolina on the ancient site of Jerusalem. His "messiahship" came to such a bitter end that this virtually ended all future discussions about a Messiah for the Jews.[20]

Others claim that the Magi in Matthew 2 followed the star to Jerusalem because they believed, on the basis of Numbers 24:17, that the birth of Messiah would be marked with the appearance of a "star." While this may be the reason for their connecting the two, it is puzzling why Matthew did not appeal to this text in Numbers, as he did so for so many of the other prophecies surrounding the Messiah.

Balaam foresaw that Israel, and the ruler that emerged from the midst of her, would subdue the nations and destroy all her enemies. First Moab would be conquered, then Edom. David did, indeed, subjugate Moab and Edom (1Sa 14:47; 2Sa 8:1, 14), but much later Jeremiah repeated Balaam's prophecy and still placed it in the future (Jer 48–49). Even later, a Jewish leader named John Hyrcanus conquered Edom (129 B.C.) and forced circumcision on all, thereby assimilating them, for all intents and purposes, into Israel. The Edomites are not heard from after A.D. 70. Is that the end of the matter, or will these same territories, if not the same national and ethnic group, be finally subjugated by the coming Messiah?

---

[20]Such discussions broke out again around the sixteenth century among the diaspora in Eastern Europe.

It is not clear who the "sons of Sheth" (v. 17c) are either. If the actual son of Adam named Seth is intended, then Balaam could be referring to the whole human race, since all are descended from Seth through Noah. The realm that is claimed for Messiah, in this case, is nothing less than worldwide.

Israel's archenemy, Amalek, who had harassed the elderly, sick, and young at the end of their line of march (Dt 25:17–19), would also come to ruin at the hands of this ruler and people (Nu 24:20). Thus, those who were the "first among the nations"—in that they were the first nation to attack Israel after the Exodus (Ex 17:8ff.)—would be the ones on whom God concluded his work of judgment. In that case, they may represent the kingdom of humankind opposing the kingdom of God.

All other challengers to this ruler would also be captured or rewarded, depending on their response to him. The Kenites (v. 21), of whom Moses' father-in-law Jethro was one, left the safety of their surroundings to travel with the Israelites (Nu 10:29; Jdg 1:16). But since they also maintained a distance from the people of God and were never fully part of them, the Assyrians would take them captives. Seven hundred years after Balaam, the Assyrians came to power and terrorized the whole Near East, including northern Israel; for the Kenites it meant genocide.

Finally, Balaam spoke of the death of the Mesopotamian powers (vv. 23–24). The old empires of the Near East would be invaded by the west, here called "Kittim" (i.e., Cyprus). We have not yet seen anything on the scale suggested by Balaam thus far in history, for the prophet gasps, "Ah, who can live when God does this?" (v. 23b). What precedes this event in history only signifies the usual "now" versus the "not yet" tension often present in what has come to be known as "inaugurated eschatology."

We conclude, therefore, that the nations listed here must be understood in the manner that Briggs had argued.

[They were] types and forerunners of all those nations who

war against the Israel of God, as they are presented to us in later prophecy; the enemies of this stadium of history being the advanced guard, the front line of an innumerable host, advancing in every epoch of history, until the final conflict with Gog and Magog at the end of the world (Rev xx. 8 sq.). Explicitly the prophecy is generic, and refers to the kingdom of God as thus triumphant; but implicitly it involves in the subsequent development of the idea of the royal house of David, and his subjugation of the nations, and still further, the royal sceptre of David's greater son.[21]

The picture painted by Balaam of the "star," "scepter," and "ruler," the man who would arise out of Israel and be awesome in his conquests and decisive in his actions, is a picture of the coming Messiah. Indeed, "Who can live when God does this?" This portion mainly depicts what will take place at the second advent of Messiah. He will literally clean house of all evil and all opposition to his rule and reign.

F. THE MOSAIC PREDICTION (DEUTERONOMY 18:15, 18)

The sixth and final messianic prediction in the Pentateuch is found in Deuteronomy 18:15, 18. At the end of the forty years of wandering in the desert, God spoke once again to his people, this time through Moses. Moses pointed to "a prophet" whom God would raise up from among the people and who would be like Moses.

This prediction is singular in number throughout this passage. In fact, the word "prophet" is placed in the emphatic position, in front of the Hebrew verb, in verses 15 and 18. Clearly, a single person is intended here. But it also seems that this singular noun must have a collective, or at least a distributive, sense, for it appears in a context where classes of officials

---

[21]Charles A. Briggs, *Messianic Prophecy*, 108–9.

are being mentioned, including "judge" (17:8–13), "king" (17:14–20), "priest" (18:1–8), and "false prophets" (18:9–14). How, then, shall we understand *nābî'*, "prophet," in Deuteronomy 18:15–22? Is it a collective noun with a distributive sense or a simple singular noun? Does it embrace the prophetic order and simultaneously point to one particular prophet? Or is it solely about the coming personal Messiah?

Jewish and most modern commentators have seen the "prophet" here as a generic and collective term. It is not without significance that all previous messianic prophecies in the Pentateuch have been generic in nature, for they envisaged the Messiah as coming from the seed of the woman, from the race of Shem, from the seed of Abraham, from the tribe of Judah, or from the sons of Jacob. Not one of the five previous direct messianic prophecies has pointed to a specific person, even though it was clear that the coming one would be an individual. By virtue of specifying a singular "prophet," the revelation in Deuteronomy 18:15, 18 may have taken a deliberate turn to set an individual at the heart of this prophecy.

Given the context of chapters 17–18, it is best to understand this text, in part, to refer to the succession of prophets whom God would raise up in Israel.[22] But there is some aspect in which none of the prophets who followed Moses were like him or could quite match him. Deuteronomy 34:10–12 asserts:

> Since then, no prophet has risen in Israel like Moses, whom the LORD knew face to face, who did all those

---

[22]David Baron, *Rays of Messiah's Glory*, 181–83, n. 1, strenuously objects to viewing this prophecy as including a succession of prophets, one after another. He writes: "But against this interpretation we have, first, the fact that *nābî'* (prophet) is singular—God says not prophets, but 'a prophet'—secondly, that this word *nābî'* is never taken collectively, nor are the prophets elsewhere spoken of collectively; thirdly, that sacred history points out no such succession of one prophet; and fourthly, this and the preceding interpretations are all contrary to two plain passages of Scripture: Numbers xii. 6–8 ... and Deuteronomy xxxiv. 10–12, a passage inserted probably by Ezra, asserts that 'there arose no prophet like unto Moses.'"

miraculous signs and wonders the LORD sent him to do in Egypt—to Pharaoh and to all his officials and to his whole land. For no one has ever shown the mighty power or performed the awesome deeds that Moses did in the sight of all Israel.

Likewise, Numbers 12:6–8 also speaks of the uniqueness of Moses apart from all his prophetic colleagues that followed him:

> When a prophet of the LORD is among you,
>   I reveal myself to him in visions,
>   I speak to him in dreams.
> But this is not true of my servant Moses;
>   he is faithful in all my house.
> With him I speak face to face,
>   clearly and not in riddles;
>   he sees the form of the LORD.
> Why then were you not afraid
>   to speak against my servant Moses?

In some vital aspect, all the other prophets missed something that Moses had because of his unique relationship with God. In this regard, then, this promise to Moses served to unite him with the coming one, the Messiah.

But the meaning of these two passages does not force us to assume that no prophet in the OT ever had the mind of God revealed to him as Moses had, or that no prophet enjoyed the same communion with God that Moses enjoyed. Moses is special precisely because of the directness and the clarity with which his messages came, as he was unique in the public nature of the miracles that attended his declarations to the pagan nation of Egypt. Thus he founded a class of prophets, just as he exemplified the uniqueness of only one of that class who was to come.[23]

---

[23]Some Jewish commentators (e.g., Rashi, Iben Ezra) thought that this prophet referred to Joshua. But Joshua had already been raised up in Numbers 27:18–23, so the exclusionary clause of Deuteronomy 34:10–12 would also apply to him.

The coming prophet would be (1) an Israelite ("of your brothers"; Dt 18:15, 18); (2) "like" Moses (vv. 15, 18); and (3) authorized to declare God's word with authority (vv. 18–19). He would enjoy unusually intimate fellowship with the Father, just as Moses talked with God on the mountain "face to face" (34:10). He would perform miracles in public before the nations, as Moses had done (34:11–12), not in private, as Elijah and Elisha for the most part did. He would be a lawgiver, exactly as Moses had given the Ten Commandments, and a mediator who would pray as earnestly for his people as Moses did for Israel's preservation (Ex 32:11ff., 31–35). He would also be a deliverer, just as Moses had been used by God to deliver his people from slavery in Egypt.

It is no wonder, then, that so many Jews in the first century expected the Messiah to be that great "prophet" who would come. When they saw the miracle of the feeding of the five thousand they exclaimed, "Surely this is the Prophet who is to come into the world" (Jn 6:14). They said the same thing when they heard him teach at the Feast of Tabernacles (7:40)—though there was some confusion among them, for they had asked John the Baptist if he were that "Prophet" (1:21). When John declared that he was not, they turned on him, saying, "Why then do you baptize if you are not the Christ [Messiah], nor Elijah [the messenger who was to prepare the way], nor the Prophet?" (1:25). Philip found Nathaniel and announced to him, "We have found the one Moses wrote about in the Law, and about whom the prophets also wrote" (1:45). Even the Samaritan woman concluded that Jesus must be that "prophet" (4:19, 29) who was to come.

Peter was clear on this matter by the time he was used by God in the book of Acts. In his second temple message he quoted Deuteronomy 18:15, 18–19 as properly pointing to Jesus as the Prophet that was to come and who had now come (Ac 3:11–26). Stephen made the same connection between this prophet and Jesus (7:37).

The debate may still be pressed whether the passage also instituted a succession of prophets along with a personal Messiah. Willis J. Beecher offered a variation on the collective idea when he explained that the word "prophet" may be used distributively rather than collectively. In this case, each prophet became a type of the final prophet who was to appear.[24] This is an appropriate compromise between the Messianic-only and the collective-institution-of-the-prophets-only interpretations.

As in the previous five prophecies of the Messiah in the Pentateuch, here too the coming final prophet comprehended in his person all that prophets oftentimes only weakly demonstrated. Yet Moses, the prophet, was unique in his miracles, his direct access to God's revelation, his giving of the law, his actions as deliverer, and his office as judge over the people. In everyone of these functions, and more, he distinctly anticipated the Messiah who was to come.

APPENDIX: THE MESSIAH IN JOB

It is difficult to know where to place the messianic allusions that come from the book of Job. In many ways, they are best classified as wisdom literature, for the genre it uses is more easily recognized as belonging to that literary form. However, since we are attempting to carry out a diachronic study of the messianic materials as part of a biblical theology, it seems best that we attach this brief discussion of Job to the Pentateuchal materials. Many of the cultural allusions place the events of the book during the time of the patriarchs,[25] antedating Solomon and the sages. In some older arrangements of the Hebrew Bible, Job was also placed among the prophetic books,

---

[24]Willis J. Beecher, *The Prophets and the Promise* (Grand Rapids: Baker, 1970 [reprint of 1905]), 351.

[25]For a statement of some of the reasons why many place the writing of this book in the patriarchal period, see E. Dhorme, *A Commentary on the Book of Job*, tr. Harold Knight (Nashville: Nelson, 1984), xx–xxviii.

perhaps a sign of its intense concern with the aspects of human redemption, resurrection, and the judgment in the final day.

There is little doubt that the book of Job touches on the messianic theme. The key texts are Job 9:33; 16:19–21; 19:23–27; 33:23–28. Four times in this book a cry surfaces for someone to act as a go-between, a mediator, between God and mortals. This arbitrator is variously named: (1) a mediator, (2) a witness in heaven, (3) a kinsman-redeemer, and (4) an interpreter.

Job 9:33. Job is here responding to Bildad's first speech. He desperately longs for someone to "arbitrate" (*mokîah*)—or, as older translations call him, "a daysman"[26]—between himself and God. This is a call for someone who has the authority and ability to represent his client; in this case, hopefully, in a divine court of law. Such a person brings two parties at odds with each other together and acts as a friend to both as he straighten things out to their mutual satisfaction. Job wants this arbitrator to lay his hand on both so that what he perceives as being unfair may be removed. Otherwise, he feels as if he is in an unequal contest with God. How can he, a mere mortal, continue to dispute with God?

Only someone who can go between both God and a human being can effect the needed reconciliation. But how can that desired individual be a mere mortal? To adjudicate this dispute, this mediator will himself need to be divine! One can see the logic building for some person who will be no less than the Son of God if he is to bridge the gulf created by this situation.

Job 16:19–21. Once again Job makes his appeal to heaven. He is confident that he has someone he can call "my witness [*'ēdî*] . . . in heaven," who will act as his "advocate . . . on high." It is unthinkable for Job to conclude that he will be abandoned by God and left without any representation on high.

---

[26]A "daysman" is an archaic expression for an umpire or a mediator.

In fact, Job refers to this person here as "my intercessor," "my friend." He is the one who "on behalf of a man ... pleads with God." This advocate must represent Job before God the Father; yet he must also reside in heaven and be on high. This amounts to an expectation that such a dispute-settler must himself be, in some way, divine! Job wants nothing less than an advocate with the Father, a longing that will find expression much later in 1 John 2:1.

Job 19:23–27. This passage has given rise to an enormous amount of literature, both pro and con. It does, as a matter of fact, have a number of textual variant readings, but this does not mean that we cannot affirm its main points with regard to its messianic argument.

Job makes a number of definite assertions about this coming Messiah. He is, first of all, one he knows as "my Redeemer" The Hebrew word, *gôʾel,* refers to the closest relative, the one on whom the duties of fulfilling the levirate marriage fell, redeeming property that was in danger of being removed from the family inheritance, or on whom avenging the blood of a murdered relative fell. Job thinks that God will provide just such a person for him, thereby redeeming him from his trouble. This "Redeemer" will be a living person whom God will raise up "in the end," i.e., who will appear on the earth at the end of all things. At that time, he will stand on the earth as the final vindicator of the beaten-down Job and vindicate him.

Job himself expects to be around to see all of this, for he declares that even after he has died, he still anticipates that in his flesh and his own eyes he will look on God himself. This is what he yearns to see, for otherwise there is little prospect of his deliverance.

Job 33:23–28. One final time in the book of Job the longing for a mediator to intervene between this afflicted man and his accusers is raised, only in this instance by Elihu;[27] this is a

---

[27]Elihu seems to represent the divine point of view, for he is not reprimanded by God as Job's other three "friends" were (Job 42:7).

call for a messenger who will act as an "interpreter" (*mēlîṣ*). Perhaps this person can reveal the meaning of the events that have taken place and thus help mediate between God and mortals. This "interpreter" cannot be fulfilled by any ordinary angel, or even by a prophet from the ranks of other mortals; he can only be "one out of a thousand, to tell a [person] what is right for him" (v. 23). The expression "one out of a thousand" may mean that God had an enormous number of angels from which he can draw for such a task, but it is better to take it as Franz Delitzsch did: "one who soars above the thousands, and has not his equal among them (as Eccl vii.28)"[28]; that is, one who is preeminent beyond the thousands of angels.

Accordingly, Job envisions the messianic person as having angelic-like qualities, but to exceed them by a thousandfold. Nevertheless, this interpreting angel will be gracious to him and provide a ransom for all his troubles. He will redeem him from the pit, so that Job may live to enjoy the light (v. 28).

Job presents us with early but poignant anticipations of several key aspects and roles found in the messianic concept. These models come to him by revelation, to be sure; but ultimately, they are borne out of the deep pathos and torment of his soul as he longs for some type of relief and vindication from God. The Messiah will be an arbitrator, a mediator, a heavenly advocate and witness, a redeemer, and an interpreter of the enigmas of his life.

---

[28]Franz Delitzsch, *Biblical Commentary on the Book of Job* (Grand Rapids: Eerdmans, 1949), 230.

◆ 3 ◆

The Messiah Before
and During the Davidic
Monarchy

After Moses left the scene, the glory days of Israel seemed past for more than three centuries. The days after Moses began well enough, for Joshua prepared the people to enter the land of Canaan by observing the rite of circumcision and the Passover. And the fact that the basic conquest of the land took place in almost *Blitzkrieg* fashion was a further evidence that the same God who was with Moses was still delivering the nation under Joshua.

But that was quickly lost as the desire for carrying through with mopping-up exercises against the remaining pockets of Canaanite infestation of the land were abandoned and the people grew lax in their service and love for God. Instead, a new syncretism engulfed the people as they adopted the gods and practices of the Canaanites they should have conquered and destroyed.

Because of these conditions, as Charles A. Briggs reminded us,

> the period of the judges was ill adapted for the development of the Messianic idea. The conquest of the Holy Land and the settlement of the tribes in the midst of the conquered Canaanites whom they had failed to drive out,

resulted in breaking up the national unity, in lowering the spiritual tone through the influence of the people of the land, and in the decay of the religious life of the nation.[1]

The light of revelation reappeared somewhat toward the end of this dark period. First was the wife of a farmer, an ordinary woman named Hannah, who was chosen to be the mother of a prophet who would, in effect, introduce the Davidic age. Then came the priest Eli, whose priesthood God had declared he would maintain, even though he would have to remove the family of Eli from that office and transfer it to another family. But few things could have prepared Israel, or the reader of the revelation of God, for the startling announcement made by the prophet Nathan to David. When we come to the Davidic promise, we have reached one of the high watermarks of the messianic concept in the OT.

In other words, there are three major prophecies given in the era leading up to David's reign over the nation Israel: one to Hannah (1Sa 2:1–10), another to an unnamed prophet who prophesies the removal of Eli's family from the office of the high priesthood (2:27–36), and the third to Nathan, who gives the famous prophecy about the house of David in 2 Samuel 7. The path to the dizzy heights of 2 Samuel 7 must be carefully laid if we are to understand the concept of royal messianism as it emerged in David.

A. HANNAH AND THE KING: GOD'S ANOINTED ONE

The story of Hannah is one of an admittedly poor, needy, and especially frustrated, barren woman, who prayed to God to remove the stigma of her inability to have children. Her prayer at the tabernacle in Shiloh was at first misinterpreted by the priest Eli, who thought she was drunk. Eventually God gave this woman the son named Samuel, who became one of

---

[1]Charles A. Briggs, *Messianic Prophecy*, 121.

the most important figures in the history of God's promise-plan of redemption, particularly since he was to play a key role in moving from the age of the judges to that of the king, who would carry in his person and office the promise of the coming Messiah.

Samuel. Samuel lived and ministered during one of Israel's most crucial transitional periods of history. He was the first in the line of prophets whom Moses had announced, but he also served as the last of the line of judges who exercised political leadership over the nation. But most important, Samuel was the one who transferred his political authority as judge over to the office of king. This act set up the most explicit foundations for the messianic theme known up to that point in time. Samuel was the one who introduced the Davidic age.

Hannah. First, however, we must examine the role that pious Hannah played, for she unexpectedly became a mother. Little did she realize that her son would be the prophet whose actions prepared the way for David, through whom the promised Messiah would come. Like Sarah of old, who also was barren, God suddenly opened her womb, and the son God gave her she named Samuel.

In accordance with the vow she had made, she took her son to the tabernacle after she had weaned him. At that time she broke out into a magnificent prayer that was filled with joy, thanksgiving, hope, and praise to God. While some scholars have complained that a plain farmer's wife could not possibly have composed such a sophisticated piece of poetry, much less such developed theology as is recorded in 1 Samuel 2:1–10, others have noted that most of the expressions used in her prayer came from biblical texts that already existed. For example, Gerard van Groningen notes some of the striking comparisons between Moses' song of victory in Exodus 15:1–18 and Hannah's prayer.[2]

---

[2]Gerard van Groningen, *Messianic Revelation in the Old Testament* (Grand Rapids: Baker, 1990), 271.

Moses	Hannah
I will sing (v. 1)	My heart rejoices (v. 1)
The LORD is my strength (v. 2)	In the LORD my horn is lifted high
He has become my salvation	I delight in your deliverance
The LORD is a warrior (v. 3)	The LORD brings death and makes alive (v. 6)

The genuineness of Hannah's prayer. The prayer-song of Hannah is genuine enough, for what this woman discerned in her own experience were the same general laws by which God had already acted so many times in the past. The case is as Maas states it:

> A number of reasons lead us to suppose that [Hannah] acted as a prophetess in pronouncing her canticle. Her personal piety and sanctity, the publicity of her divine praises, the occasion of the canticle (Samuel's presentation before the Lord), and the fact that [Hannah] dwells wholly on the public and national benefits bestowed by God on Israel, are strong motives for considering [Hannah] as favored by the prophetic light when she gave forth the canticle of divine praise.[3]

The substance of Hannah's prayer. So what did this prayer include, and where did the messianic angle come in? Hannah did not focus on herself or her needs: rather, she represented the cry of the pious, who some ten times are depicted in these ten verses as "the poor," "the needy," "those who were hungry," and "she who was barren." Meanwhile, the ungodly are represented four times as proud and arrogant. Yet neither of these groups dominate the prayer; God is the dominant person. Yahweh appears nine times by that name and fifteen times by other names or pronouns.[4] The living Lord, not this woman

---

[3]A. J. Maas, *Christ in Type and Prophecy,* 2 vols. (New York: Banziger Brothers, 1896), 2:36.

[4]This observation was suggested by Gerard van Groningen, *Messianic Revelation,* 270.

or needy ones similar to her, formed the central concern of her declarations.

The structure of Hannah's prayer. The prayer has been variously analyzed into several structures. James Smith divides it up into four sources of joy: Hannah rejoices in (1) her experience (v. 1), (2) her God (vv. 2–3), (3) her observations about life (vv. 4–8), and (4) her hope (vv. 9–10).[5] Charles Briggs divides the text up into four strophes (vv. 1–2, 3–5, 6–8, 9–10) of 8, 10, 10, 8 lines each, respectively.[6] Maas follows Bickell's analysis by placing the whole prayer into eight stanzas of four lines each.[7] Our primary focus is on the one section that all parties seem to agree belongs together, namely, the hope found in verses 9–10.

The theme of Hannah's prayer. The theme of Hannah's song appears in verse 10c, "The LORD will judge the ends of the earth." With such a fair, just, and righteous governor, the godly have nothing to fear, for the Lord himself will protect his saints and silence the mouths of the wicked, who vaunt themselves against the righteous (v. 9).

Messiah in Hannah's prayer. At this point in her prayer Hannah suddenly introduces the "king" to whom God will give strength (v. 10d); in parallelism to this king comes the promise that God will also "exalt the horn of his anointed [i.e., his Messiah]."

Similar terminology about the Lord judging the ends of the earth and about an empire being given to his Messiah-King appears in Psalms 2 and 110. In those texts the references are clearly messianic; therefore, it seems fair to propose that those texts possibly used Hannah's prayer as an informing theology for their own thoughts on the Messiah.

---

[5]James E. Smith, *What the Bible Teaches About the Promised Messiah* (Nashville: Nelson, 1993), 76.

[6]Briggs, *Messianic Prophecy,* 124–25.

[7]Maas, *Christ in Type and Prophecy,* 34, n. 1.

Some see the prediction that "[God] will thunder against them from heaven" (v. 10) as fulfilled in 1 Samuel 7:10, when God delivered Israel from the Philistines at the battle at Mizpah by bringing on a violent storm with severe thunder and lightning. However, that cannot be the ultimate meaning, for the clause about the thunder is parallel with "the LORD will judge the ends of the earth"—words much more universal in scope than one mere battle with the Philistines during a violent thunderstorm. It is true, of course, that every triumph in the series of God's deliverances that lead up to his final victory at the end of the age is embraced in the one meaning the text seeks to get across. This is part of the concept of inaugurated eschatology, in which there is both a "now" and a "not yet" aspect to predictions of God's climactic work in his kingdom.[8]

The application of Hannah's prayer. To apply Hannah's words about God's humbling the proud and destroying his enemies to her rival, Peninnah (1Sa 1:2), is without basis. Regardless of Peninnah's faults, nothing she did deserves the massive judgment mentioned in this text. Instead, the taunts of Hannah's rival induce the prophetess not only to think of the victory she has witnessed, but the victory that all of Israel will gain over their enemies, especially through the ministry of the coming Messiah.

This word from Hannah about a future judgment over all of God's enemies and about the expected Messiah is given by God shortly before the capture of the ark and the destruction of Shiloh. More than any others, these two events stimulate a demand in the people for a king that will ensure a permanent dynasty, one not dependent on waiting for God to call some individual directly. While such a demand for a king was well within the divine plan and purpose (see Dt 17:14–20), it is a premature request and one that has the wrong motives behind it.

---

[8]For further discussion of this hermeneutical phenomenon, see Walter C. Kaiser, Jr., *Back Towards the Future: Hints for Interpreting Biblical Prophecy* (Grand Rapids: Baker, 1989), 117–24.

The conclusion of C. F. Keil and Franz Delitzsch is worth noting:

> Hannah's prayer rises up to a prophetic glance at the consummation of the kingdom of God. As certainly as the Lord God keeps the righteous at all times, and casts down the wicked, so certainly will He judge the whole world, to hurl down all His foes, and perfect His kingdom which He has founded in Israel.... *The king*, or the *anointed of the Lord*, of whom Hannah prophesies in the spirit ... [is] the actual king whom Israel received in David and his race, which culminated in the Messiah. The exaltation of the horn of the anointed of Jehovah commenced with the victorious and splendid expansion of the power of David, was repeated with every victory over the enemies of God and His kingdom gained by successive kings of David's house, goes on in the advancing spread of the kingdom of Christ, and will eventually attain to its eternal consummation in the judgment of the last day, through which all the enemies of Christ will be made His footstool.[9]

It is interesting to note that later on, Peter comes to the same conclusion in Acts 3:24: "All the prophets from Samuel on ... foretold these days" (i.e., the days of the Messiah). Where does Samuel make reference to any messianic prediction except in Hannah's prophecy, which he records or leaves behind from his ministry? It is no surprise, then, to find that the Targum renders verse 10 about "exalt[ing] the horn [a symbol of strength and dignity as in Pss 89:24; 112:9; 132:17] of his anointed" by these words: "and will magnify the kingdom of his Messiah."[10] The anointed one in this text is clearly the coming Messiah.

---

[9]C. F. Keil and Franz Delitzsch, *Biblical Commentary on the Books of Samuel*, tr. James Martin (Grand Rapids: Eerdmans, 1950), 33–34 (emphasis theirs).

[10]Likewise, Augustine rendered this passage as predictive of Christ in his *City of God*, 1.17.6. Gregory the Great did the same in his commentary on 1 Samuel (=1 *Regnum*), 3:47, as quoted in A. J. Maas, *Christ in Type and Prophecy*, 2:34.

The four stages in royal messianism. Here, then, is a fourth stage in the royal theme of messianism. First, Abraham had been promised that "kings will come from you" (Ge 17:6, 16), and God reaffirmed the same promise to Jacob: "Kings will come from your body" (35:11). In the second stage, the symbols of rule and authority (the "scepter" and "ruler's staff") were given to Judah (49:10); accordingly, this royalty was promised the "obedience of [all] the nations." The third stage speaks of this coming king crushing his enemies, as Balaam predicted of the one he called the "star ... out of Jacob" and the "scepter ... out of Israel" (Nu 24:17). Now in 1 Samuel 2:10, the fourth stage is reached: the Messiah as the exalted King will be the judge of all the earth.

B. ELI AND THE FAITHFUL PRIEST: GOD'S ANOINTED ONE

Along with the theme of a royal messianism was the germ of a priestly messianism that had roots in the days when the Ten Commandments were given. While Israel was camped at Sinai, God had designated the whole nation of Israel to be a "kingdom of priests" (Ex 19:6), so that each and every Israelite might carry out the mission God had given to them. They were to do this by being a light to the nations—the instruments by which all the nations of the earth would be blessed (Ge 12:3).

But by and large, the people shrank back from such a holy calling, insisting that Moses be their representative to approach God. When the people heard God's voice speaking out of the thunder and lightning, they found the whole scene too awesome and terrifying for sinful men and women. They wanted Moses to represent them (Ex 20:18–21) while they stayed a good distance away.

The ordination of the high priestly line. As a result, God ordained Aaron, Moses' brother, and Aaron's family to officiate as priests before him (Ex 29:9). As Israel came to the end of their desert pilgrimage, God made a covenant with Aaron's grandson Phinehas for an "everlasting priesthood" (Nu 25:12–13). Briggs, commenting on these verses, concludes: "The Messianic feature is in the establishment of an *everlasting* priesthood. This is a generic prophecy which culminates in the everlasting priesthood of the Messiah."[11]

Scripture records the way this covenant with Phinehas came about. Aaron had two sons who survived him, Eleazar and Ithamar. God determined had that Eleazar was the one who would succeed his father Aaron in the high priest's role (Nu 20:25–28). Later the succession passed to Eleazer's son Phinehas, because of his zeal for the Lord in the Baal Peor incident (25:12–13). Apparently, however, during the period of the judges the high priestly line shifted to the family of Ithamar, though the reasons and circumstances of that shift are not given. Eli, the high priest in the days of Samuel, was a descendant of Ithamar.[12] Then, in the time of David, it switched back to a descendant of Eleazar, Zadok. He served for a short time along with Abiathar and Ahimelech, descendants of Eli (2Sa 8:17; 20:25), until he emerged as the sole high priest.

Clearly, neither of Eli's two sons, Hophni and [a later] Phinehas, could not succeed their father as high priest. They were arrogant and sinful in the parts of the sacrifices they demanded from the people, and they were immoral by sleeping with the women that served at the entrance of the tabernacle (1Sa 2:14, 22). Eli asked his sons why they did such things, but he did so without any decisiveness and after it was too late to make any change (vv. 22–25).

---

[11]Briggs, *Messianic Prophecy,* 110 (emphasis his).

[12]We know from 1 Chronicles 24:3 that Eli's great-grandson Ahimelech was a descendant of Ithamar. Also, Josephus (*Antiquities of the Jews,* 5.11.5) describes how Eli, of the sons of Ithamar, received the high priesthood after Ozi had had it from Eleazar, Aaron's other remaining son after Nadab and Abihu had been consumed for offering unauthorized fire to the Lord (Lev 10:1–3).

The prophecy of the unnamed prophet. For all of this, God sent an unnamed prophet to Eli, who told him the following: (1) Eli had wrongfully honored his sons more than he honored God (v. 29); (2) God would now remove the high priesthood from his father's (Ithamar's[?]) house; (3) distress would come to Eli's house; (4) both of Eli's sons, Hophni and Phinehas, would die on the same day as a sign to Eli; and (5) God would raise up "a faithful priest, who will do according to what is in [God's] heart and mind" (v. 35). This last statement raises the prospect of the Messiah, for the next declaration announces, "I will firmly establish his house, and he will minister before my anointed one always" (v. 35c-d).

The time of the prophecy. The unnamed prophet gave a word that far exceeded the days of Eli or his immediate descendants, for verse 31 places some of the events, especially those in verses 35–36, in "the time is coming." The prophets frequently used this formula to announce future, and especially distant, events (e.g., 2Ki 20:17; Isa 39:6; Jer 7:32; Am 4:2; 8:11; 9:13).

The faithful priest. Who, then, is this "faithful priest"? He cannot be Samuel, for he had no enduring house in the priesthood even though he occasionally functioned in the priestly role. Others have pointed to Zadok and Abiathar as possible candidates for this role of "faithful priest," but Abiathar is the last in the line of Eli to serve in that role. That is the point of 1 Kings 2:27: Abiathar was deposed by Solomon as priest in accordance with the Lord's word announced concerning the house of Eli in Shiloh. Neither can a case be made for Zadok as being that "faithful priest," for I Kings 2:27 gives no go-ahead sign at this time to Zadok either.

Who, then, is this "faithful priest"? The Hebrew word translated here as "faithful" is *ne'emān*—the same word (with a slight variation) used of David's dynasty in 2 Samuel 7:16, whose "house and ... kingdom *will endure* forever." In 1 Samuel 25:28, the word is used again of David's dynasty, that it will be a "*lasting* dynasty." Thus, the house of the coming priest will be secure, firmly established, and reliable.

The identity of the faithful priest. Keil and Delitzsch suggest that the expression used here is a collective, embracing all priests whom the Lord raises up as faithful servants at his altar and who collectively culminate in Christ, the only real faithful priest.[13] Thus, both Samuel and Zadok were in this line of faithful priests, but its highest fulfillment comes in Jesus Christ. This view fits in with the previous generic prophecies we have seen so far in this study.

The problem with this identification is that it leaves us puzzled over the equivalent for "firmly establish[ed] house." It cannot refer to either Samuel or Zadok, for while both men were great, they did not always do "according to what was in [God's] heart and mind" (1Sa 2:35). That latter statement can only be true of our Lord, who "always [did] what pleases" the Father (Jn 8:29).

The firmly established house. Thus, it is best to regard this passage as referring solely to the Messiah, who would one day come and be given a "house." Just as Moses was "faithful in all [God's] house" (Nu 12:7), so Messiah would also be a faithful priest over God's house.

The writer of Hebrews makes the same point. "But Christ is faithful as a son over God's house" (Heb 3:6a), just as "Moses was faithful as a servant in all God's house, testifying to what would be said in the future" (v. 5). But that author surprises us with his next statement: "And we are his house, if we hold on to our courage and the hope of which we boast" (v. 6b–c). Thus, the house of Messiah is composed of the enormous offspring and spiritual seed to which he came to minister as the high priest and as the one who would sacrifice himself for our sins.

The one ministering/walking before the Messiah. But if the Messiah is that "faithful priest," who then is this one who "will

---

[13]Keil and Delitzsch, *Commentary on the Books of Samuel*, 46–47.

minister before my anointed one [my Messiah] always?" (1Sa 2:35d). Most conclude that this eliminates the faithful priest from being identified with the Messiah, since it is usually taken that he is the one who "will minister [lit., will walk] before my anointed one always [lit., all the days]." However, James Smith points out what no one else seems to have grasped:

> The immediate antecedent of the verb *walk* is the noun *house*. It is the house of the faithful priest which is under the supervision of the anointed one, the Messiah. The idea of the walking house is already in verse 30. The faithful Priest and the Anointed One (Messiah) in verse 35 are one and the same person. The Messiah's house is the New Testament royal priesthood (I Peter 2:9).[14]

That, we believe, is the correct solution. More accurately, then, verse 35 should read:

> I will raise up for myself a faithful priest, who will do according to what is in my heart and mind. I will firmly establish his house, and *it* will minister before my anointed one always. [emphasis mine]

The future lifestyle of the priestly line. Verse 36 concludes this prophecy by describing how the members of the old priestly line of Aaron will bow down to the authority of this faithful messianic priest. Those once fattened by robbing the people of what they themselves wanted from their sacrifices are now reduced to depending on the Messiah for a piece of silver or a loaf of bread.

Perhaps, as Keil and Delitzsch suggest, there is a hint here of the vision that Ezekiel saw of the new temple, in which the sons of Zadok draw near to God in order to perform his service in the new organization of the kingdom of God (Eze 40:46; 43:19; 44:15; 48:11). This will be accomplished when Christ and his kingdom are fully established.[15]

---

[14]James E. Smith, *What the Bible Teaches About the Promised Messiah*, 80.
[15]Keil and Delitzsch, *Commentary on the Books of Samuel*, 47–48.

C. NATHAN AND THE ESTABLISHED DYNASTY AND KINGDOM OF DAVID

God had promised Abraham that kings would some day come from him (Ge 17:6, 16); he repeated the promise to Moses that some day his people would have a king (cf. Dt 17:14–20). In Samuel's day, however, the people could not wait for God's timing and insisted instead that he give them one right away, just like the other nations. In response to their demand (1Sa 8:4–6, 20), God instructed Samuel to anoint Saul (8:10–19). For twenty years of what appears to be a forty-year reign, Saul ruled Israel and conquered all his enemies (14:47; 2Sa 1:17–27). However, when young David came on the scene and gained popularity by slaying Goliath, Saul's jealousy for his own praise and for his son Jonathan's position as his successor grew to gigantic proportions.

Earlier experiences with kingship. This was not the first time a demand for a king had come up. Already in the days of the judges, the people offered Gideon an opportunity to "rule over" the Israelites after his stunning defeat of Midian (Jdg 8:22). As an added inducement, they insisted that the offer of kingship carried with it a hereditary rulership: "you, your son and your grandson." But Gideon firmly declined the offer, asserting the principle, "The LORD will rule over you" (v. 23).

Gideon's son Abimelech, however, was not as reluctant or as theologically bound to the concept of God's rule as his father. After Gideon's death, Abimelech accepted the offer of one city, Shechem, to become their king (Jdg 9:15–18). It also appears that he changed his name, for Abimelech means "My father is king." Did he thereby make the tacit claim that he was the legitimate heir to the throne since his father *could have been* a king? The irony of the episode is brought out in Judges 9:6, where the root *mālak* ("to be king, to reign") appears twice, giving this literal translation: "And they kinged 'my-father-is-king' [i.e., Abimelech] as king." The entire affair ended in tragedy both for Abimelech and his "kingdom."

The situation with King Saul did not end on a much happier note. When the Lord rejected him as king, he looked for a "man after his own heart" (1Sa 13:14). That man was David, the eighth son of Jesse, who was subsequently anointed by the prophet and judge, Samuel (16:13), later by the whole tribe of Judah (2Sa 2:4), and finally by the entire nation of Israel (5:3).

Just as King Saul had been called ten times the "anointed of the LORD" (*māšîaḥ YHWH*, the word from which we get our word "Messiah"), so David would also be called ten times "the anointed of the LORD." He became Yahweh's king, who ruled Israel and Judah for the next forty years. But more than a mere kingship was at stake here. Third in importance only to the protoevangelium of Genesis 3:15 and the Abrahamic promise of Genesis 12:2–3 is 2 Samuel 7 (see also 1Ch 17; Ps 89), God's promise to David. This chapter sets the tone for the promise-plan of God throughout the rest of the OT.

Nathan's prophecy. After King David had been given rest from all his enemies in Canaan and the surrounding countries and after he had finished building his famed cedar palace, he expressed the wish to the prophet Nathan to build a house for God. After all, he felt, it was not proper for him to be living in cedar while the Shekinah Glory of God lived in curtains that might have been as old as the tabernacle—some four hundred years!

Nathan's immediate reaction was positive: David should proceed with his plans to build a new house for God. Not everything a prophet says, however, is inspired! Only when a prophet speaks as the oracle of God and attributes what he says directly to God can it have any claim to being a revelation from God. That night God warns Nathan that what he told David was his own opinion and not a divine instruction. Nathan is then told to deliver to David one of the most sensational predictions in the Bible.

David's house/dynasty. God's point is decisive: Instead of having David build a "house" for the Almighty, God will make a "house" out of David (2Sa 7:13). He will do this by conferring on him and his "seed/offspring" (v. 12) the promises he gave to the patriarchs—and more.

Seven main provisions are included in this promised dynasty:

(1) "I will make your name great" (2Sa 7:9; cf. Ge 12:2; et al.);

(2) "I will provide a place for my people Israel and will plant them" (2Sa 7:10; cf. Ge 15:18; Dt 11:24–25; Jos 1:4–5);

(3) "I will also give you rest from all your enemies" (2Sa 7:11; cf. Dt 12:9; Jos 21:44–45; Ps 95:11);

(4) "I will raise up your offspring [seed] to succeed you" (2Sa 7:12, cf. Ge 17:7–10, 19);

(5) David's seed will "build a house for [God's] Name" (2Sa 7:13; 1Ki 8:18–20; 1Ch 28:6, 7);

(6) "I will be [your seed's] father, and he will be my son" (2Sa 7:14, cf. Ex 4:22–23; Ps 89:26–27);

(7) David's dynasty, kingdom, and authority will endure forever (2Sa 7:16).

All of this leads David to conclude that something of gigantic proportions is happening to him, and that it is directly related to the plan that God repeatedly announced to those carriers of the promise who preceded him.

The charter for humanity. When David realizes what is being offered to him, he enters before the Lord and sits down. In his confused astonishment, he begins by praying,

> Who am I, O Adonai Yahweh, and what is my family, that you have brought me this far? And as if this were not enough in your sight, O Adonai Yahweh, you have spoken about the future of the house of your servant. This is the charter for humanity, O Adonai Yahweh!" (2Sa 7:18–19, pers. tr.).[16]

---

[16]One of the most astonishing mistranslations in most versions, including the NIV, is verse 19. The NIV renders it, "Is this your usual way of dealing with man, O Sovereign LORD?" The Hebrew reads: *wezōt tôrat hāʾādām.* The

David realizes that he is getting much more than he could ever have imagined or even thought. The ancient promises that he had grown up on and had counted on as the foundation of his own hope for salvation and for the future are now being repeated to him and placed in his offspring—and there will be no termination point in its provisions! David cannot believe what is happening to him.

In his prayer, five times David uses the exceptional name of God "Adonai Yahweh" (2Sa 7:18, 19[bis], 22, 28, 29). Nowhere else does this compounded form of the name of God appear in Samuel or Chronicles. The special significance of this name, as R. A. Carlson points out, is that this is the name God used when he promised Abraham a "seed" in Genesis 15:2, 8.[17] Its repeated use here is too striking to be an accident; David wants to show that what God is telling him is indeed part of the same promise-plan that was given to Abraham, Isaac, and Jacob.

The implications of this being a charter for all humanity are clear: what David received is to be conveyed to everyone, including all the Gentiles and nations of the earth. This is a further reinforcement of the gospel motif announced in Genesis 12:3, that in Abraham's seed all the nations of the earth would be blessed. Rather than viewing the gifts that God has just conferred on him in a selfish way, David sees them missiologically. The "charter for humanity" is nothing less than God's plan for

---

word *tôrat*, "law, charter," or the like, is rendered in the NIV as "your usual way of dealing with." Like Alice said to Humpty Dumpty, "That's an awful lot to make one word mean." Indeed it is, in spite of my vigorous protests over the years. For more on this issue, see Walter C. Kaiser, Jr., "The Blessing of David: A Charter for Humanity," in *The Law and the Prophets*, ed. John Skilton (Philadelphia: Presbyterian and Reformed, 1974), 298–318.

[17]R. A. Carlson, *David the Chosen King: A Traditio-Historical Approach to the Second Book of Samuel*, tr. Eric Sharpe and Stanley Rudman (Stockholm: Almquist and Wiksell, 1964), 127. The other five instances of "Adonai Yahweh" are Dt 3:24; 9:26; Jos 7:7; Jdg 6:22; 16:28. Note the promise content in each prayer. In Kings the double name occurs only in 1Ki 2:26; 8:53, while "Adonai" by itself appears in 1Ki 3:10, 15; 22:6; 2Ki 7:6; 19:23.

the whole human race. All humanity can profit from what he has just been told about his house/dynasty, kingdom, and throne.

An everlasting reign. Jacob had seen that the leadership of the tribes would fall to his fourth son, Judah; Balaam had predicted that a star and a scepter would arise out of Jacob that would crush all his enemies. But Nathan now predicts that the one family in Judah on whom the mantle of ruling will descend is David's family. And that rule, kingdom, and authority will not be limited; three times he emphasizes that it will be "forever" (2Sa 7:16). While the word "forever" (*'ad 'ôlām*) in certain contexts may be limited to a long duration but not necessarily without end, the use of this thrice-repeated expression here reappears with the same emphasis in Psalm 89 (esp. vv. 29, 36–37), which serves as a commentary on this event: God "will establish his line *forever*, his throne as long as the heavens endure ... [so] that his line will continue *forever* and his throne endure before me like the sun; it will be established *forever* like the moon" (emphasis mine).

Surely there is little debate about the present longevity of the sun and moon. They have outlasted David or any of his children. Therefore, God means that the kingdom, rule, and reign of David will be in perpetuity from that time on. Never has the reign of any mortal endured like the sun and moon have over these millennia.

That is why the angel Gabriel announces to Mary, the mother of the Messiah, that "the Lord God will give [Jesus] the throne of his father David, and he will reign over the house of Jacob forever; his kingdom will never end" (Lk 1:32b–33). The angel is merely repeating the promise that had been made to David.

The Son of God. God declares that David's son will be God's own son. Part of this promise appeared as early as Exodus 4:22–23, where the whole nation was declared "my son." Ethan, a native Canaanite, who was converted and later wrote

Psalm 89 under the inspiration of God, expands on the meaning of 2 Samuel 7:14. He declares (Ps 89:26–27):

> He will call out to me, "You are my Father,
>   my God, the Rock my Savior."
> I will also appoint him my firstborn,
>   the most exalted of the kings of the earth.

God had promised to regard David's son as his own "firstborn." "Firstborn" is itself a messianic term, for it indicates not the child who is born first in chronological order, but the one who is first in preeminence, first in rank, and first in privilege. Note how Jacob (i.e., Israel) is called God's "firstborn" (Ex 4:22), even though Esau came out of his mother's womb as the first of the twins. Likewise, Ephraim is called the "firstborn" (Jer 31:9), even though Manasseh, his brother, was older. That is also why Christ is called the "firstborn of all creation" in Colossians 1:15, and why Hebrews 1:6 uses this same term to designate Jesus in his comment that God brought his "firstborn [= Christ] into the world." At the same time, the idea of the collective singular is not far away from this technical term, for Hebrews 12:23 addresses the whole church of believers as the "firstborn." Just as the "seed" includes all who believe as well as the one who represents them all, so the "firstborn" heads up the whole body of the "firstborn."

An eternal covenant. David later reflects on what God has done for him and summarizes his conclusion in his last words in 2 Samuel 23:1–7. Especially pertinent are his words in verse 5, which we translate this way:

> Certainly, my house stands firm with God,
>   because he has made an eternal covenant with me,
> arranged in every part and guaranteed;
>   for all my salvation and my every desire
> he will cause to branch out.

Everything that God spoke to David is guaranteed and certain: it depends only on God and not one whit on David, his family, or his nation. Every point it mentions will truly come to pass; it is a unilateral covenant in which God binds himself to perform its promises totally, without condition or bilateral obligations. It is an eternal covenant.

The messianic character of the Davidic promise. Nathan's prophecy, then, predicts several important new features about the coming Messiah: (1) The Messiah will come from David's flesh and seed; (2) he will be David's heir; (3) he will also be God's natural son, (4) he will have a kingdom, rule, and reign that will never end; and (5) he will surely come one day in the future.

Thus we move from the "seed of the woman," who will be victorious over Satan, to the "seed of Abraham," who will be a blessing to all the earth, to the "seed of David," who will have a rule that will never end. This last advance on the organic nature of the messianic promise-plan of God is so significant that it is worth our examining two commentaries on this aspect of the promise, Psalm 89 and Psalm 132.

D. DAVID'S DYNASTY AND THE PSALMS

So unique was the promise of a "house" or a dynasty to David that several psalms expound on this fact in some detail.

Psalm 89

The circumstances behind Psalm 89. Psalm 89 was composed by Ethan, who played a major role in the worship program of Solomon's temple (1Ch 15:17, 19). He must have been well aware of the prior existence of 2 Samuel 7, for he reflects much of its terminology and provisions in his psalm.[18] He was

---

[18]"It seems difficult to resist the priority of the text of II Sam 7," concluded Tomoa Ishida, *Royal Dynasties of Ancient Israel* (New York: Walter de Gruyter, 1977), 82. Scholars who assume that 2 Samuel is the original text for 1Ch 17:1–15 and Ps 89 include F. W. Grosheide, *De Psalmen* (Kampen: Kok, 1955); J. Ridderbos, *De Psalmen* (Kampen: Kok, 1958); Derek Kidner, *Psalms 73–150* (London: Inter-Varsity, 1975); and S. R. Hirsch, *The Psalms*

moved by the Holy Spirit to reflect on its provisions as an act of worship, perhaps in the light of some present defeat suffered by a Davidic king or some foreseen disaster that lay up ahead of the Davidic kingship.

The dating of Psalm 89. Some have unnecessarily dated Psalm 89 as late as the fall of the kingdom of Judah in 587 B.C., but others have more realistically placed its composition at a time when the Davidic dynasty was under some unusual strain, bordering on collapse. B. D. Eerdmans thought that might have been at the beginning of the reign of Rehoboam, when the empire was divided after Solomon's death.[19] Certainly that was an unstable time for the Davidic house and the oracle Nathan had made concerning it. Others have pointed to several occasions in the reigns of David and Solomon when the hope of an eternal dynasty was threatened. Regardless of what event was the triggering device, several are clear possibilities. The point of the psalm is that Nathan's grand prediction of an eternal kingdom was threatened with collapse.

The structure and argument of Psalm 89. The development of the psalm proceeds in this manner: (1) The psalm's theme: God's mercies, faithfulness, and reliability in granting the promise to David (vv. 1–4 [MT, 1–5]); (2) a hymn of praise (vv. 5–18[6–19]); (3) Yahweh's promises to David (vv. 19–37[20–38]); (4) a lament over a reversal in the expected success of the Davidic kingdom (vv. 38–45[39–46]); and (5) an appeal from the psalmist (vv. 46–51[47–52]).

The messianic section of Psalm 89. The messianic part of this psalm is the third section. This section begins (vv. 19–20) by setting forth five statements that form the background for

---

(New York: Feldham, 1966). Other views project the existence of an original prophecy from which 2Sa 7, 1Ch 17, and Ps 89 borrowed; or that 2Sa 7 and 1Ch 17 are dependent on this original source with Ps 89 being a recension of it (see Gerard van Groningen, *Messianic Revelation*, 310, n. 1).

[19]B. D. Eerdmans, *OTS* 4(1947): 428, as quoted by John L. McKenzie, "Royal Messianism," *CBQ* 19 (1957): 29, n. 15.

the key messianic promises recorded in verses 21–33: (1) God used a vision to speak to his "faithful people" about how he would use David to help them; (2) God discovered David, probably an allusion to Samuel's mission to Bethlehem to find the person whom God had chosen; (3) God "bestowed strength on [David to be] a warrior"; (4) God exalted this "young man" above all the other people and declared that he was "my servant"; and (5) God anointed him as king with the sacred oil administered by Samuel.

Then follows a series of twelve promises made to David in the prophecy given by Nathan:

(1) David and his seed would be given divine assistance (v. 21).

(2) No enemy of David's house would subject him to tribute or be allowed to oppress him (v. 22).

(3) God would mow down the enemies of the Davidic house as their foes advanced against them (v. 23).

(4) The Davidic power ("horn") would triumph because God had set his gracious love on that house (v. 24).

(5) The Davidic kingdom would extend its scope far beyond Canaan (v. 25).

(6) David and his seed would be able to cry out at any time to God as "my Father, my God, the Rock my Savior" (v. 26).

(7) So exalted would David be over the other kings of the earth that he would be known as God's "first-born" (v. 27).

(8) The terms of David's covenant and God's gracious love for him would never fail or end (v. 28).

(9) The line of David's seed and his throne would endure as long as the heavens (v. 29).

(10) God would not renounce his promise to David just because some of his offspring did not follow God's statutes and laws; these descendants might personally fail to participate in the benefits of the Davidic

covenant, but they had to transmit those promises to the rest of the line of David (vv. 30–34).

(11) God took a final oath, based on his holiness, that what he had promised to David was inviolable and unbreakable (vv. 35–36).

(12) God promises one more time that David's line/seed and throne will be as enduring as the sun and moon are in the sky (vv. 36–37).

The dilemma posed in Psalm 89. But times seem to have changed for the psalmist, for in verses 38–45 he is confronted with a situation that appears to contradict what God so clearly announced to David. As previously noted, this may have been a tragedy or an impending disaster. On the other hand, given the fact that the psalmist uses past tense verbs that are called "prophetic perfects" in Hebrew grammar (where the future events are so certain that they may be described as being already complete), the verbs may well describe that the psalmist sees the future so clearly that he depicts it as a past event. This phenomenon is a well-known device that is frequently used by the prophets in the OT.

In any case, the results and effects are devastatingly real. David's house is not the same as the one pictured in Nathan's oracle; instead it is now in a dilapidated condition. God seems to have "spurned" his "anointed one" (v. 38). The covenant appears to have been "renounced" (v. 39) and the crown of David "defiled" (v. 39). The walls of Judah have been "broken through" (v. 40), and the cities are in "ruins" (v. 40). Those passing by join in "plunder[ing]" Judah (v. 41), and the divine assistance appears to have shifted to Judah's enemies (vv. 42–43). David's throne has been "cast . . . to the ground," and his "splendor" has come to an "end" (v. 44). The vigor of David's youth has now been cut short, and the mantle of his office lies covered with shame (v. 45). Surely this depicts some horrendous disaster. Was it the revolt of David's son against his father's government? Or the division of the kingdom that came after Solomon's death? Regardless of the crisis alluded to, the result is that the eternal provisions given unconditionally to David seem defied.

The supplication of Psalm 89. The appeal of the psalmist in verses 46–51 is that God will speedily intervene. God's wrath cannot, nor will it, last forever (v. 46). Since life is so short, help must come quickly if it is going to do any good (vv. 47–48). The sole bases for seeking relief from this situation are God's gracious love, his oath sworn to David, and his faithfulness (v. 49). Thus, for the sake of God's own "anointed one" (v. 51), the psalmist pleads with God to requite those who have been mocking every step of this messianic person. The taunts of all the nations must not be left unanswered (vv. 50–51); otherwise, the oath, the covenant, and the promise made about the coming Messiah and his kingdom, rule, and reign will be worthless and without divine vindication. God must, and will, vindicate what he has promised David.

Psalm 132

Psalm 132 and the house David's Son will build. Psalm 132 belongs to a group of fifteen pilgrim psalms, or Psalms of Ascent.[20] Its theme, like Psalm 89, centers on the promise made to David, especially regarding to the house he wanted to build for God. In fact, the words of verses 8–10 appear in the closing words of Solomon's prayer of dedication of the temple (2Ch 6:41–42).

The structure of Psalm 132. This psalm is divided into two halves, with the break occurring after verse 10. The first half, which is a prayer originally offered perhaps at the dedication

---

[20]For a discussion of how these psalms were used, apparently, as the men of Israel made their way up to Jerusalem three times a year, see especially (on Ps 132) Walter C. Kaiser, Jr., "When You Forget the Past," in *The Journey Isn't Over: The Pilgrim Psalms for Life's Challenges and Joys* (Grand Rapids: Baker, 1993), 129–40.

of the temple, had three subdivisions: (1) verses 1–5 describe how David intended to build a house for Yahweh; (2) verses 6–7 indicate how the people responded when the temple was finally erected; and (3) verses 8–10 reuse that portion of Solomon's dedicatory prayer in which David is mentioned as God's "anointed one." The second half, which contains God's answer to the people's prayer, has two subdivisions: (1) verses 11–12 focus on the covenant God made with David; and (2) verses 13–18 declare why God chose Zion as the city where his temple has been built.

What David longed to see has now been realized: the temple of God. Even though David (hyperbolically) vowed not to let his eyes enjoy sleep until he saw this project completed, God has graciously completed it in his own way and time.

In the meantime, the ark of the covenant has all but been forgotten. In Ephrathah (an older name for David's hometown of Bethlehem), a report was received from "the fields of Jaar" (a shortened form for Kiriath-Jearim, "the city of the woods") that the ark was still in the house of Abinadab (1Sa 7:1–2). Even though David knew about the ark from his youth only on the basis of hearsay, he set out for Kiriath-Jearim to worship God at that place. But now that the temple has been finished, it is time to restore the ark to its central place in the house of God.

The petition addressed to God in verses 8–9 asks that all God's people rejoice in the restoration of the ark back to its rightful place. It also asks that David's desires may likewise be fulfilled. Three of David's requests are fulfilled the day the temple is dedicated: (1) A resting place for the ark is finally provided; (2) a place for the ministry of the priests is likewise provided; (3) the arrival of the next person in the line of the coming Messiah is witnessed.

Based on the teaching of 2 Samuel 7:13, the psalmist finds the answer of God reassuring: God will never change his mind, his plan, or his intention to benefit the whole world through

David's offspring. The conditional "if" of Psalm 132:12 cannot affect the certainty of the promise; it can only affect an individual's participation in the benefits of that promise, while the promise itself remains inviolable.

The ark will find its "resting place" in Zion. It will symbolize the permanent residence of the living God in the midst of Israel and of all who later believe (Ps 132:12–15). As for the priests, God will clothe them with his own righteousness, so that they can minister with joy to the people of God (v. 16).

Psalm 132 ends by taking up the issue of the Lord's "anointed one" (vv. 17–18). Three symbols describe the Messiah: a horn, a lamp, and a crown. The title "lamp" has already been assigned to David in 2 Samuel 21:17 (see also 1Ki 11:36). Just as the lamp keeps burning in the temple in God's presence, so the Davidic line will continue perpetually. It points to the Messiah.

The "horn" that will "sprout/grow" for David is another double allusion to the Messiah. In Daniel 7:7–8, 24, the horn is a symbol for a powerful king. No less mindful of this same fact is Zechariah, the father of John the Baptist, when he prophesies in Luke 1:68–69:

> Praise be to the Lord, the God of Israel,
> because he has come and has redeemed his people.
> He has raised up a horn of salvation for us
> in the house of his servant David.

That "horn/power" will "sprout/branch out," just as the messianic title "Branch" is used of the Messiah (Jer 23:5; 33:15; Zec 3:8; 6:12). Both title of a "horn" and "branching out" once again point to the Messiah.

The third messianic theme depicted in Psalm 132 is the symbol of the "crown." The word *nēzer* is used here and in Psalm 89:39 to mark the anointed one's consecration to the royal office. The word, however, is not only used for the king's crown; it is also used for the diadem of the high priest (Ex 29:6). Moreover, the verb used in Psalm 132:18 with the symbol of the crown ("will be resplendent" [*yāṣîṣ*]) is a cognate to the noun *ṣîṣ*, which was the "plate" of gold worn by the high priest that bore the inscription, "Holiness to the LORD." The crown is unmistakable evidence that the Messiah will be God's future ruler, who will be both high priest and king.

With such high accolades, there can be little doubt that the anointed is not simply one of God's earthly anointed ones in the Davidic line; he has God's heavenly appointed one, Jesus Christ. That is God's answer to the inquiry made by David's son Solomon as to whether God will maintain his promise. He surely will!

APPENDIX: THE MESSIAH IN THE WISDOM LITERATURE

The wisdom books are generally thought to include Proverbs, Ecclesiastes, and a number of selected wisdom psalms. There is little predictive material in these books. However, for our purposes there is one figure that should be discussed in the context of the messianic theme: the figure of wisdom. In the section of the book of Proverbs probably written by Solomon, "wisdom" is represented on three separate occasions as speaking and acting in the role of a person (Pr 1:20–33; 8:1–36; 9:1–12).

It is not easy to decide quickly between "wisdom" being a mere personification of an attribute of God and "wisdom" being a full-bloomed hypostatization[21]—that is, a deliberate "standing under" of a divine quality or function, rising to a separate person of the Trinity.

---

[21]See the important study of Helmer Ringgren, *Word and Wisdom: Studies in Hypostatization of Divine Qualities and Functions in the Ancient Near East* (Lund: Hakan Ohlssons Boktryckeri, 1947); also see the arguments in Walter C. Kaiser, Jr., *Toward an Old Testament Theology* (Grand Rapids: Zondervan, 1978), 175–78.

Some, such as Hartmut Gese, are certain that wisdom is a part of the Christological development of the OT.[22] A. van Roon seems to be more representative of the prevailing sentiment that there was no connection between the wisdom of God in the OT and later Jewish sources for Paul's argument for Christ in the NT.[23]

What is clear from Proverbs 8:22–31 in particular is that wisdom was used by God in creating the world; thus, wisdom was present before the world was here. Wisdom rendered delightful service to the Creator just as she continued later on to be of service to men and women, warning them to use her services in order to live successfully.

The case for wisdom as a messianic theme certainly falls short of being a *direct* argument for the Messiah. And it is not clear that it is an *indirect* argument or a type for the Messiah either. Had it not been for Paul's statement in Colossians 1:16,[24] it is doubtful if any connection would have been made between the coming Messiah and wisdom. Instead, we see wisdom as a personification of a quality or attribute of God. And in every instance where such a personification occurs, it is distinguished from God himself and made more or less an independent reality that is never brought into the kind of association one would see in the passage we have studied thus far concerning the prophetic, priestly, or kingly roles of the Messiah.[25]

---

[22]Hartmut Gese, "Wisdom, Son of Man, and the Origins of Christology: The Consistent Development of Biblical Theology," *HBT* 3 (1981): 23–57.

[23]A. van Roon, "The Relation Between Christ and the Wisdom of God According to Paul," *NovT* 16 (1974): 207–39.

[24]Some, of course, will point to the intertestamental literature and suggest that what the Gospel of John ascribes to Jesus is what *Sirach* and the *Wisdom of Solomon* ascribe to Wisdom and Torah. See Ben Witherington III, *Jesus the Sage: The Pilgrimage of Wisdom* (Minneapolis: Fortress, 1994). I owe this suggestion and bibliographic note to my editor.

[25]Some point to a fourth leader-type in Israel: wise men. In this case, in addition to being prophet, priest, king, Jesus is also the wisest of the wise (cf. Mt 12:42; Lk 11:31; 1Co 1:24, 31; Col 2:3).

◆ 4 ◆

The Messiah in
the Psalms (Part 1)

"The greatest single block of predictive matter concerning the Savior to be found anywhere in the Old Testament," according to J. Barton Payne, is the book of Psalms.[1] He has counted 101 verses of direct prophecies of Messiah, occurring in thirteen different psalms.

Other writers are more conservative in their estimate of how extensive the messianic predictive elements are in the Psalms. Leupold, for instance, limits the number to four (Pss 22; 45; 72; 110); the other messianic psalms are included by virtue of their being types of Christ.[2] The other interpretive extreme is found in St. Augustine, who treated practically every psalm as if it were messianic. Such an approach, however, violates principles of exegesis. It is better to begin with the straightforward claims of the text itself.

Most of the messianic psalms belong to the Davidic period. Among those we would definitely attribute to David are: Psalms 2; 16; 22; 40; 68; 69; 109; and 110. In addition to these are Psalm 72 by Solomon; Psalm 118, not attributed to anyone

---

[1]J. Barton Payne, *Encyclopedia of Biblical Prophecy* (New York: Harper and Row, 1973), 257.

[2]H. C. Leupold, *Exposition of Psalms* (Grand Rapids: Baker, 1974), 21ff.

in its title line; and Psalm 45, a psalm of one of the sons of Korah.

Since all eleven psalms (not counting Psalms 89 and 132, which we have already treated[3]) that we consider messianic appear to belong approximately to the period of the monarchy of Israel, what organizing principle should we use to treat them? Perhaps the best grouping of these psalms is that of James E. Smith,[4] who used the following headings to treat sixteen psalms he regarded as messianic:

David's Greater Son (Pss 89; 132)
The Mystery of the Incarnation (Pss 8; 40)
The Rejection of the Messiah (Pss 118; 78:1–2 [sic])
The Betrayal of the Messiah (Pss 69; 109)
Death and Beyond (Pss 22; 2)
Victory Over Death (Pss 16; 102)
Messiah's Marriage and Ministry (Pss 45; 110)
The Reign of the Glorious King (Pss 72; 68)

Our present discussion will begin with the two jewels in the messianic psalms: Psalms 110 and 2. The former unfolds the prediction of Nathan made by Yahweh concerning David, while Psalm 2 represents the Messiah as already enthroned in Zion on the right hand of Yahweh as his Son, following the investiture scene described in that psalm. Then we will discuss the remaining nine messianic psalms, arranged according to the predictions they made in the life of the Messiah:

The Rejection of Messiah (Ps 118)
The Betrayal of Messiah (Pss 69; 109)
The Death and Resurrection of Messiah (Pss 22; 16)

---

[3]The covenant made with David was highlighted in Psalms 89 and 132; that is why we linked those two psalms so closely with 2 Samuel 7 in our previous chapter. These two psalms point beyond King David to the climactic Son who would arise in his line: the Messiah himself.

[4]James E. Smith, *What the Bible Teaches About the Promised Messiah* (Nashville: Thomas Nelson, 1993), 90–209.

The Written Plan and Marriage of Messiah (Pss 40; 45)
The Triumph of Messiah (Pss 68; 72)

A. THE CONQUERING KING AND ENTHRONED MESSIAH

1. Psalm 110

While the external evidence that this psalm is messianic is large,[5] the internal evidence is just as overwhelming. Consistent with our procedure, we will turn first to the internal evidence, for we are confident that it requires a messianic figure as its ultimate referent.

The plan or argument of this psalm is fairly simple. It is organized around two divine utterances in verses 1 and 4: "Sit at my right hand until I make your enemies a footstool for your feet;" and, "You are a priest forever, in the order of Melchizedek." The same person is addressed in both affirmations; first as king, then as priest. Both statements are directed from Yahweh to David about one whom David calls "my Lord." In other words, three distinct persons are involved in this psalm: Yahweh, the speaker; David, the recipient of the message; and one whom David calls "my Lord" and whom he understands to be his sovereign—indeed, the one to whom he must submit.

That unnamed Lord is a royal person, for he was invited to "sit at [God the Father's] right hand." A sovereign's right-hand seat was reserved for anyone whom a king wished to honor or who was associated with the sovereign in the government of that realm. If the God of the universe invited this

---

[5]This psalm is quoted in the NT more frequently than any other psalm (referred to in Mt 22: 41–45; Mk 12:35–37; Lk 20:41–44; Ac 2:34–36; Heb 1:13; 5:6, 10; 6:20; 7:11, 15, 17, 21). This psalm is also the source for the references in 1Co 15:25; Eph 1:20; Col 3:1; 1Pe 3:22; Heb 8:1; and 10:12.

other Sovereign to take such a distinguished seat alongside himself, then we may be sure he was no one less than the promised Messiah, invited to participate in the divine government of the world. The "scepter" given to him (v. 2) is reminiscent of the promise made to Judah in Genesis 49:10, that the scepter would not depart from Judah until it was given to the one to whom it belonged. That scepter, with the authority it symbolized, now appears in Psalm 110.

The troops that serve in the army of this messianic Sovereign are strangely clothed, to say the least. They are "arrayed in holy majesty." If this expression refers, as many suppose, to priestly garments, then this conflict is indeed extraordinary. Just as their leader in battle will be a king and a priest, so the warriors will be an army of priests, dressed in sacred garments, rather than the usual blood-stained, government-issued, regulation army dress. The priesthood, formerly restricted to the family and tribe of Levi, is now extended to the population at large.[6]

Besides being a conquering king, the Messiah has four other characteristics: he will be (1) a priest, (2) appointed by God, (3) an eternal office holder, and (4) uniquely styled, not after the line of the high priest Aaron, but after the priest-king of ancient Jerusalem, Melchizedek.

The successes of "my Lord" are detailed in verses 5–7. Similar to the statement in Psalm 2:5, this Lord on Yahweh's right hand "will crush kings on the day of his wrath." The Messiah will carry out the judgment against the nations that he has threatened (cf. Ps 72:2, 9–11), to such an extent that the earth will be heaped with the dead corpses. This will be God's final showdown with the forces of wickedness and evil. That is exactly what was promised in Genesis 3:15 and in Numbers

---

[6]This accords well with what Isaiah 66:20–21 will also affirm: "[Some] from all nations . . . I will select . . . to be priests and Levites." What is more, it would be a strange army in Psalm 110 if it were composed solely of Levites, as some might infer.

24:16–19: the serpent (i.e., the devil himself), along with the kings of all the earth, will have their heads shattered and crushed.

The allusion to drinking water from a brook at a wayside in verse 7 has often troubled interpreters, but it seems best to regard this as describing the setting under which Psalm 110 was written. Having just concluded a decisive battle, David pauses beside a running stream to refresh himself physically with the cool water and spiritually by reflecting on what God had done in a similar circumstance for the earlier man of promise, Abraham (Ge 14). Abraham, with as few as 318 hired men, launched a surprise night attack on the four Mesopotamian kings who had raided the five cities of the Jordan Plain, plundered them, and taken Lot captive. Outnumbered and outclassed as they were, God gave them a victory. In much the same way, he has now given David the same kind of overwhelming victory. When the king recalls that he is a participant in the same promise, it is like taking another long draft of cool water after a hot battle that had ended decisively in his favor. And why not? Had not God predicted that this was how he would treat the seed in the line of Eve, Shem, Abraham, Isaac, Jacob, and David?

Psalm 110, then, is a direct and specific messianic psalm for the reasons we have argued above. "My Lord" is a King-Priest, who has a throne appointed by God, a priestly office that no one else has yet fully occupied, which is to be filled by the King-Priest in perpetuity, with a kingdom and sphere of service that is worldwide and that will enjoy a complete, full, and final victory over every form of evil and opposition. Only the Messiah fits that description, judging by what previous messianic texts have detailed for us.

2. Psalm 2

Even though this psalm is not attributed to any author, its contents indicate that it was composed during David's time when he was challenged by the nations surrounding him.[7] Its main theme is found in verse 6: "I have installed my King on Zion, my holy hill." The psalm itself is divided into four strophes of three verses each:

The Rebellion of the Nations (vv. 1–3)
The Reaction of God (vv. 4–6)
The Response of Messiah (vv. 7–9)
The Recommendation to the Nations (vv. 10–12)

The psalmist is shown a host of nations gathering themselves in mad rebellion against God and his Anointed One. That Psalm 2 specifically speaks of two persons as being the object of the hostilities can be seen from the rebel's slogan in verse 3: "Let us break *their* chains ... and throw off *their* fetters" (emphases added). Yahweh and his Messiah are both targeted as the objects of the rebellion. There is little difference between this assault and the series of tirades and attacks that have been conducted all throughout history by those who have opposed God and his Son. That is how Peter, for example, viewed the opposition he faced in Acts 4:27–28: "Indeed Herod and Pontius Pilate met together with the Gentiles and the people of Israel in this city to conspire against your holy servant Jesus, whom you anointed. They did what your power and will had decided beforehand should happen." Such opposition is only a foretaste and a dry run of the enormous climactic battle of history, when God himself will dramatically put down forever all opposition to himself and his Son.

---

[7]Thirty-seven of the forty-one psalms in Book 1 (Pss 1–41) are attributed to David. Thus, it is rare that a psalm in this book should be anonymous. But since Acts 2:30 calls David a "prophet," and since so many other messianic psalms are explicitly attributed to him, it seems fair to regard this psalm as belonging to him as well. It may be that this psalm is without a title and an ascription as to who the author was because Psalms 1 and 2 were seen as a double introduction to the whole Psalter. Acts 4:25 quotes from the beginning of Psalm 2 and ascribes it to David. Other NT uses of this psalm are Acts 13:33; Heb 1:5; 5:5; Rev 2:27; 12:5; 19:15.

With all the wild tumult happening on earth, God is at first amused (he "laughs"; v. 4) by the senseless thrashing about of his creatures against himself and his Messiah, like little children who hopelessly try to resist the announced time for bed only to be picked up and carried off to bed. In like manner, God will act easily to quell the uprising against heaven; he "rebukes them in his anger and terrifies them in his wrath" (v. 5).

Yahweh, too, has a speech: "I have installed my King on Zion, my holy hill" (v. 6). Because the earth belongs to the Lord and all its fullness (Ps 24:1), he will conclude history as he has planned, with his Anointed One installed as King on the throne he promised to David's offspring. All resistance against Yahweh and his Anointed One will be fruitless.

The reason why all efforts to revolt against God and his Messiah are so ridiculous is that the "decree of the LORD" (v. 7) has already been announced. It is an unalterable declaration—the same one that had been given to David in 2 Samuel 7:14: "I will be his father, and he will be my son," only changed here from the first person pronoun to the second person. The time when that will take place is called "today" (v. 7c). Just as there was a certain day when God gave David this promise, so also on the day when God throws down the gauntlet, the full terms of this disclosure will be seen: the Lord will set his King in Zion. Therefore, just as David was installed with the promise of his enduring throne, dynasty, and kingdom, so on another coming day, all that planning will come to final fruition.

Likewise, the clause, "today I have become your Father" (or, as older translations said it, "I have begotten you"), means that the Son will be installed as sovereign on his throne rather than that he will be born. On a particular day in history, God will manifest his Anointed One to be his Son by placing him on the throne, and he will rule over the kingdom of God forever. That throne, of course, is the same as the one given to David. The climactic event it foreshadows is the Second Coming, though when Christ rose from the dead (so argues Paul in Ac

13:33), the end has already begun overtaking the past. The first resurrection Sunday is the "today" in the mind of the psalmist. God has given Christ a name, rank, and authority that correspond to the new turn of events his plan took when he rose from the dead. *Begetting*, in this sense of the term, means the establishment of the official relationship and the installation into a new sphere of service, just as Nathan announced earlier in 2 Samuel 7:11–16 and Moses declared of all Israel in Exodus 4:22.

Sonship also entails being heir of everything. The Son has only to ask for it, and everything is his from the Father. In Psalm 110 God was calling the King-Priest to his right hand as he led an army of priestly attired warriors to victory over the nations. But now in Psalm 2, the Messiah has taken his seat at the right hand of Yahweh as the enthroned Son on Mount Zion, having rebuked his enemies. He is both a Sovereign and a Son. All who have resisted his irresistible power have been subjugated. Their power and authority have been smashed and dashed to the ground like a piece of pottery.

It is therefore recommended that the kings, rulers, and nations (1) get smart, (2) be warned and instructed, (3) serve the Lord with fear, (4) rejoice in who Messiah is and what he will do, and (5) do homage to the Son before it is too late and the Son's anger flares out against them. Indeed, "Blessed are all who take refuge in him" (v. 12), but how silly to think any other posture is plausible in the presence of such a great God and such an awesome Son.

Recall once again that David was also a prophet who could, and did, foresee what he spoke about (Ac 2:29–32). His house and offspring were slated for a destiny that was mind-boggling in its depth and scope. It would have no boundary limitations and no temporal bars restraining it. David may not have had a complete knowledge of all that God was planning to do through the words given to him, but he certainly must have had an adequate idea that went far beyond the bounds of ordinary humanity and typical sovereignties.

B. THE REJECTION OF THE MESSIAH (PSALM 118)

On first reading, Psalm 118 does not appear to be a messianic psalm. Nevertheless, our interest is piqued especially by the presence of verse 22: "The stone the builders rejected has become the capstone."[8] Could the "stone" in this text be another title for the Messiah? And what was the nature of the rejection mentioned here?

No author or title line is given for this psalm, but recent scholarship is returning to the view that it is early enough to fit into the time of David. The accumulation of allusions to events that could only have happened during his lifetime argue for seeing his hand, experiences, and setting as the proper one for this psalm. For example, if the triple refrain in verses 10b–12 (translated in the NIV as "I cut them off") were rendered more accurately as "I circumcised them," the reference could well be to David's killing two hundred Philistines to acquire the foreskins Saul had demanded (1Sa 18:25–27). The distress caused by the enemies that surrounded David in Moab, Edom, Ammon, Syria, Philistia, and Amalek may be another allusion to David. He had faced threats of death, attack from his enemies, and marvelous deliverances from his God (vv. 5–18). David, the representative of that royal person, the Messiah who was to come, could truly say that he had experienced all of these things, both personally and as the office-holder of the Promised One. Thus, a strong case can be made for Davidic authorship.

The structure of the psalm is best viewed as an antiphonal arrangement used as a processional hymn at an occasion such as the Feast of Tabernacles; that is the way both the Talmud and Midrash understood it. Verses 1–19 are sung by the Levites and priests as they joined in the worship of God. At verse 19 they

---

[8]Quotations from Psalm 118:22 abound in the NT. Included are: Mt 21:9, 15, 42–45; 23:39; Mk 12:10; Lk 20:17; Jn 12:13; Ac 4:11; Ro 9:33; 1Co 3:11; Eph 2:20; Heb 13:6; 1 Pe 2:7. Almost all of the allusions or quotations of this verse are put it into a messianic context.

stand at the entrance to the "gate of the LORD"; verses 20–27 are sung by the ministering personnel who receive them. The arriving group sings verse 28, and everyone joins together in verse 29, which in chiastic fashion repeats the call to thanksgiving given in verse 1. Thus, the call to give thanks opens and closes the psalm, while verse 19 contains its central and focal theme: "I will enter and give thanks to the LORD."

Central is the stone spoken of in verse 22, which forms the object of praise for these worshipers. That stone, of course, is symbolic, for as often happens in the course of building, the builders select one stone to be the pivotal stone for the foundation. But in this situation, whether real or illustrative, the stone rejected and set aside by the builders as a foundation stone is later chosen as the capstone for the whole project.

In a similar way, David, the father of the promised heir and coming Messiah, was also rejected. His father, Jesse, did not consider him suitable material for anointing as king (1Sa 16:11). His brothers scorned him and misunderstood him (17:28–29). Saul had tried on numerous occasions to kill him, while his first wife, Michal, daughter of Saul, despised him (2Sa 6:20–23). Only Judah accepted David as king at first, for the northern ten tribes preferred to follow Saul's house, despite all that Saul had tried to do to David (2Sa 1–3). But what human beings had rejected, God designed to cap out what he had planned to do from the beginning: He installed David as his king over the whole kingdom.

The psalm opens and closes with an invitation to praise God for his enduring gracious "love" (*hesed*; vv. 1, 29). This gives the psalm a covenantal setting, for the word *hesed* appears approximately 248 times in the OT, mostly in contexts where God promises his grace, love, and faithfulness in maintaining his covenant. Israel is called upon three times in verses 2–4 to affirm that God's "*hesed* endures forever." The emphasis on the perpetuity of God's covenantal love is reminiscent of Yahweh's covenant with Abraham and David, both of which stressed the eternity of God's promise.

Verses 5–18 refer often to the abiding presence and help of God to the leader of Israel (e.g., v. 6, "The LORD is with me"; and v. 13b, "The LORD helped me"). God's man may feel surrounded by hostile nations swarming around him like angry bees (vv. 10–12), but three times he answers, "In the name of the LORD I cut them off" (or, "I have circumcised them").

Then in the climactic verse 19, three requests are laid at the entrance of "the gate of the LORD": (1) "Open for me the gates of righteousness," (2) allow me to "enter" into the very place from which the blessings we receive from God flow, and (3) allow me to "give thanks to the LORD." So sang the priests and Levites on behalf of the central person in the promise-plan of God.

An antiphonal response that comes from inside "the gate of the LORD" to those who stand at the entrance: this indeed is the threshold through which "the righteous may enter" (v. 20). The use of the personal pronouns "I," "me," and "my" in verse 21 and "us" and "our" in verses 23–25 indicates that the singers have in mind the promised leader of Israel as he becomes the signal of the blessings that are to be passed on to all of them. That person is David in his capacity of being the earnest or down payment for the Messiah who is to come. Therefore, just as David was saved from trouble and was victorious over his enemies, so will the righteous be saved in the future in One who comes in David's line.

God's "salvation" (v. 21) is suddenly described in terms of a rejected stone that has become the capstone for the whole building (v. 22). This act is done by the Lord himself, and it is "marvelous" in their eyes (v. 23). The Hebrew word chosen for "marvelous" must have been deliberate, for it comes from the Hebrew root *pl'*, meaning the God who "does difficult," "hard," or "wonderful" things. That is in fact the name Isaiah gave to Messiah in Isaiah 9:6-7; his name will be "*Wonderful* Counselor" (emphasis added). The word also appears in Genesis 18:14a, when God reassured the laughing Sarah by asking her, "Is anything *too hard* [or too wonderful, too marvelous] for me?" (emphasis added). No wonder the priests conclude by singing, "This is the day the LORD has made; let us rejoice and be glad in it" (v. 24).

This day is the one in which God will install the coming Anointed One on the ancient throne of David and give to him the recognition and esteem he deserves as God's capstone to everything, even though many have pushed him aside—just as David had borne the brunt of being a rejected stone for many years before he was finally installed over the whole kingdom. On that day the children of God will cry, "O LORD, save us [Heb. *hôšî 'â nā'*; i.e., "Hosanna"]; O LORD, grant us success" (v. 25). That same cry rang out on the day of Christ's triumphal entry into Jerusalem on Palm Sunday. The singers and shouters were entreating God for the same thing that Jesus taught his disciples to pray, "Your kingdom come, your will be done on earth as it is in heaven" (Mt 6:10). And so it happened! "Blessed [indeed] is he who comes in the name of the LORD" (v. 26). In sending David and his offspring, especially the last one in that anointed lineage, the Lord God has "made his light shine upon [all of] us" (v. 27).

The psalm concludes with the singers giving thanks (v. 28) as both those within and outside "the gate of the LORD" join in a final doxology (v. 29), using the same words as those with which the psalm began.

C. THE BETRAYAL OF MESSIAH

1. Psalm 69

Psalm 69 is quoted more times in the NT than any other psalm except for Psalm 110.[9] But who does the psalmist depict as suffering here?

---

[9]This psalm is quoted seven times in the NT: Mt 27:48; Jn 2:17; 15:25; 19:28, 29; Ac 1:16–20; Ro 11:9, 10; 15:3.

Whatever else may be said, it is someone who is in great misery, needs help (vv. 2–5), and has been put into these straits because of his zeal for God's service (vv. 6–13). Repeatedly, the sufferer calls for God's help and assistance (vv. 14–19) as his enemies add to his misery (vv. 20–22). If only God would punish and destroy these malicious predators (vv. 23–29)! But the end comes bright with hope, salvation, and deliverance as the sufferer thanks God for his help (vv. 30–34) and invites all creatures to join him in praising God (vv. 35–37).

The successful interpretation of this psalm, then, hinges on our ability to identify the sufferer at the center of this sad description of woe. Since the title ascribes the psalm to David, its circumstances fit David's life, and the psalm in other ways resembles those where David's authorship is assured,[10] this psalm cannot apply to the Babylonian exile or to the suffering the people experienced there. Neither can it apply to some sufferer in general, for such attribution of the sufferings of the righteous in general cannot be affirmed or refuted. But if the psalm comes out of the experience of David, who, as the holder of the office and the benefits that are to come from the Messiah, experiences in miniature form the identical malice that his namesake will experience, then it becomes evident that the suffering is both literal and predictive of the Messiah, or at least is true in a typical sense and therefore predictive.

The main problem with this conclusion is found in verse 5: "You know my folly, O God; my guilt is not hidden from you." Adam Clarke spoke for many when he complained, "How can such words as are in this verse be attributed to our blessed Lord, however twisted or turned?"[11] Some have attempted to evade this objection by limiting the literal references about the Messiah to verses 9–10, 21–22, 25, and 27. But

---

[10] For example, Psalms 16; 22; 35; 38; 40.

[11] Adam Clarke, *The Holy Bible ... With Commentary and Critical Notes,* 5 vols. (New York: Waugh and Mason, 1833): 3:224, as cited in Smith, *What the Bible Teaches About the Promised Messiah,* 133.

such a piecemeal approach is a step backward in the history of interpretation, for it treats the Bible as if it were a mere collection of proof texts that can be associated with later fulfillments in a random way, disconnected from their contexts.

The problem in this text is the same as the one that exists in those texts that contain the Davidic promise, but which also warn that if anyone in the Davidic line sins, they will not participate in the blessings of the promise-plan, even though they are duty-bound by God to transmit those same benefits and office to the coming Messiah (e.g., 2Sa 7:14b; Ps 89:30–34; 132:12). Even the heroic solution posed by A. J. Maas does not solve the problem as well as the distinction just made between the human frailty or sinfulness of the Davidic line through which the Messiah came and the purity of the Messiah. Maas incorrectly concluded:

> We may add here that what the psalmist says of his own sinfulness may apply to Christ in so far as he has taken upon himself the sins of all; at the same time, the justice and righteousness of the sufferer are so much extolled that they cannot fully apply to any one but the Messias [sic].[12]

The sufferer (here, the human Davidic officeholder) petitions the Father to save him, for he is in serious trouble. With two figures, he depicts his plight as being similar to that of a drowning man (v. 1) and to one sinking in deep mire (v. 2). But God knows the real facts of the situation: The psalmist has been hated and accused without cause or reason (vv. 5–6). In fact, the only explanation that makes any sense is the one that notes the sufferer is so zealous for God's house that he is totally consumed by his desire to see God's honor and glory promoted and vindicated (v. 9). Thus, the insults that are thrown up against the owner of the house of worship fall on the suf-

---

[12]A. J. Maas, *Christ in Type and Prophecy* (New York: Bazinger Brothers, 1896), 2:296–97. Note that Ps 69:5 ascribes the "folly" and "guilt" to the individual directly; it is not just "folly," "guilt," and sin that is borne by another!

ferer. Remarkably, both John (Jn 2:17) and the apostle Paul (Ro 15:3) attribute the same motivation to Jesus' actions in the temple and his rule of not pleasing himself but the Father.

The sufferer's tormentors increase their attack by putting "gall in [the sufferer's] food" and supplying "vinegar for [his] thirst" (v. 21). Later, the Romans mixed a little myrrh with sour wine as a means of deadening some of the pain for those condemned to die (as they did in the case of Jesus [Mk 15:23]). Here the sufferer must endure yet another form of abuse, in his act of eating food.

At this point the sufferer breaks out in a series of imprecations (vv. 22–28). Some complain that such imprecations against one's enemies are inadmissible on the lips of Messiah, but the same type of expressions occur in Psalm 16:3 and Isaiah 50:9, 11, and elsewhere in the OT. What must be remembered is that the same curses uttered by the sufferer have elsewhere been decreed as belonging to the justice of God.[13] Therefore, the only thing that the sufferer desires in his prayer is that God's justice may be accomplished in his punishments as well as in his plan of redemption.

The sixth curse of what may be regarded as ten imprecations[14] in these verses is of special interest as it invokes the curse "May their place be deserted; let there be no one to dwell in their tents" (v. 25). In this case, a curse falls on the tormentor's place in society and on their dwellings on the earth. It is small wonder that Judas should have received the judgment listed here as one of the wicked persons who collaborated with the enemy by leading them to Jesus in the Garden of Gethsemane. This is not to deny that other perpetrators of

---

[13]On the imprecatory psalms in general, see Walter C. Kaiser, Jr., *Toward Old Testament Ethics* (Grand Rapids: Zondervan, 1983), 292–97.

[14]David Dickson, *Commentary on the Psalms.* 2 vols. (reprint, Minneapolis: Klock and Klock, 1980), 1:419ff., as cited by Smith, *What the Bible Teaches About the Promised Messiah*, 135–36. He identifies ten "plagues" pronounced against the sufferer's persecutors.

evil, who also conspired against David and his royal line, did not also deserve and receive some of the same treatment that Judas received. There is a line of evil (recall the seed of the serpent in Ge 3:15) that finds its epitome and climactic fulfillment in the representative of the whole group, just as there is a line of righteousness that eventuates in the Messiah. That is why 1 John 2:18 teaches, "The antichrist is coming, [but] even now many antichrists have come." Thus, just as a long line of tyrants and bullies in history qualify as "antichrists," though a final "antichrist" will appear at the end of history, so there was a line of opponents to David and his line, up to the days of Messiah, who would lose their place as a judgment from God until the final wicked opponent came in the form of Judas Iscariot (Mt 26:14–16; 26:47–56; Ac 1:16–20). He, like the others who had given David and his seed grief, will find "his place deserted," for he betrayed God's final anointed king in that same line. In other words, there is a corporate solidarity between the representative of the whole group and the whole group, whether that one or group is allied to evil or to good.

2. Psalm 109

Once again, the psalm title ascribes this lament to David. As in Psalm 69, the psalmist presents some strong imprecations in verses 6–19.

David has suffered physical, social, and spiritual persecution, all of which leaves an indelible mark on him (see 1Sa 19:11, 20; 20:1, 3, 31–33, 41; 23:9, 15; 24:10–15). The identity of the culprit who causes him to lay out his complaint is not known. Perhaps that is best, for in that way the issues raised here may be set forth in principial form, thereby reducing the need for putting them into a universal category before we apply them to contemporary situations.

There are, of course, several who may have been the occasion for the grief that came to David. Many have suggested

Doeg, the Edomite, who reported to Saul that David had stopped off to speak to the high priest, thereby causing the death of that priestly family and depriving David of their godly counsel and friendship (1Sa 21:7; 22:9–23). But it could also have been David's counselor Ahithophel, who joined the revolt against David (2Sa 15:12, 31–34; 17:23), or perhaps Shimei, in this betrayal of David (2Sa 16:5–14). There is no lack of suitable candidates for betrayers. Each had a part to play in the line of opponents to the kingdom of David and hence the kingdom of God. It is best to leave the psalm without any specific identity as to the historical occasion of its writing, for that allows us to focus on the ones who appear as the ultimate and climactic betrayers of the last one who will come in David's house.

The psalm is structured in the following way: The Davidic petitioner cries out for help (vv. 1–5), using plural nouns to describe his persecutors. Suddenly, a shift to the singular describes the opponent of the sufferer (vv. 6–19), with the final verses (vv. 20–31) reverting again to the plural.

Psalm 109 begins with an appeal to God to intervene against ruthless perpetrators of malice and deceit against the sufferer. They have plotted the ruin of this sufferer and repaid evil for good. Ten judgments[15] are introduced against one specific adversary (vv. 6–19):

The enemy will have Satan at his right hand (v. 6).
He will be found guilty when tried (v. 7a).
His prayers will be regarded as sin (v. 7b).
The one opposing God's anointed will die prematurely (v. 8a).
This betrayer's office will be filled by another person (v. 8b).

---

[15]I have modified the list that appears in Smith, *What the Bible Teaches About the Promised Messiah*, 141–42.

His children will be orphaned and his wife widowed (v. 9), while his family is forced to beg for a living (v. 10).

His creditors will seize everything the enemy has worked for (v. 11).

No one will show compassion on the opponent's descendants (v. 12).

The betrayer's sons will die childless (v. 13).

The guilt of his sin and the iniquity of his family will be remembered against them (vv. 14–15).

The reason for such horrendous judgments against one special opponent of the Davidic line, presumably directed against the final one who is to come in the line of David, is because "he never thought of doing a kindness, but hounded to death the poor and the needy and the brokenhearted" (v. 16). He also deliberately chose to follow a policy of pronouncing a curse against the sufferer, who now cries out to God for relief and adjudication.

Having heard the divine pronouncements of verses 6–19, the psalmist resumes the prayer begun in verses 1–5 (vv. 20–31), where he enumerates the grounds on which he seeks God's intervention.

The messianic aspect of this psalm is to be found, as we argued in Psalm 69, in the fact that all the enemies of David, his throne, his dynasty, and his kingdom, are finally epitomized in one final hostile adversary upon whom God's judgment must fall. Is it any surprise that Judas became that opponent of the Messiah? Does not John 13:27 record that Satan entered into Judas as he conceived the plot to betray Jesus, just as Psalm 109:6 declares? And was not the place of Judas taken over by another after he committed his treachery and ended up hanging himself (cf. Ac 1:16–20)?

David, of course, does not know the name of Judas; but that is not the important issue. His role, demeanor, motivating forces, and resulting judgments are all clearly marked out by Psalm 109:6–19. He knows that this enemy is a single individual, that he will have Satan at his side as he performs his deed of opposing the head of the kingdom of God, and that his place will be taken by another. This act of betrayal, Peter argues under inspiration of the Holy Spirit, was spoken "long ago through the mouth of David concerning Judas" (Ac 1:16). Some may argue that it has been more recently read into David's words, but that is not a fair hearing of the claim Peter makes on behalf of this text. And what we have attempted to show is that everything except the name of the betrayer and the time when it happened could have been obtained from this passage of Scripture long before the events take place. Come to think of it, is that not one of the charges that the Lord brings against the two disciples on the road to Emmaus in Luke 24:25–27, 44–45? They could and should have known these things from the Scriptures, but they were "fools" and "slow of heart" when they refused to listen to the OT text itself!

♦ 5 ♦

The Messiah in
the Psalms (Part 2)

D. THE DEATH AND
RESURRECTION OF MESSIAH

The most dramatic predictions the psalmists made occur here. Just as the best overall statement of the Messiah in the Psalms can be found in Psalms 110 and 2, so Psalm 22 played a central role in the passion of Messiah is Psalm 22. And the most startlingly clear statement about the Messiah's resurrection occurs in Psalm 16.

1. Psalm 22

Psalm 22 is one of the most profound psalms in the whole repertoire of passional psalms.[1] Like the majority of the messianic psalms, it is ascribed to David in its title line.

Is David also the innocent sufferer described in this psalm? Clearly David faced much suffering and opposition during his life. In that sense, then, much that is written here fits. But there is also much in the language that exceeds any-

---

[1]Along with Psalm 22, scholars classify Psalms 35; 41; 55; 69; and 109 as passional psalms. It is quoted in Mt 27:35, 46; Mk 15:34; Jn 19:24; Heb 2:12.

thing that appears appropriate to David. For example, what events in David's life might provide the background for the abject status before all people mentioned in verse 6? When were his hands and feet pierced (assuming that is the proper reading of v. 16) and his garments divided among his detractors (v. 18)?

First, let us examine the prevailing opinions as the Holy Spirit gifted the church in former days. John Calvin, for example, commented: "From the tenor of the whole composition, it appears that David does not here refer merely to one persecution, but comprehends all the persecutions which he suffered under Saul."[2] In the same vein, Franz Delitzsch concluded: "David descends, with his complaint, into a depth that lies beyond the depth of his affliction, and rises with his hopes, to a height that lies far beyond the height of the reward of his affliction."[3] Even a contemporary scholar such as James L. Mays opens the door for David's experience both to set the benchmark for the suffering and yet to be transcended by the suffering of another:

> There is, of course, the possibility that this feeling about the scope of the psalm is prompted by its association with the death of Jesus, yet when the psalm is carefully examined in the context of other prayers for help, it becomes clear that the intensity and comprehensiveness is a fact of the psalm's composition; *it is there in the text itself.*[4]

Fair-minded exegetes must come to the same conclusions that Charles Briggs did when he studied the sufferings of verses 12–18:

> *These sufferings transcend those of any historical sufferer,* with the single exception of Jesus Christ. They find their

---

[2]John Calvin, *Commentary on Psalms* (Edinburgh: Clark, 1845), 1:357.

[3]Franz Delitzsch, *Biblical Commentary on the Psalms*, 3 vols. (Grand Rapids: Eerdmans, 1980), 1:306.

[4]James L. Mays, "Prayer and Christology: Psalm 22 as Perspective on the Passion," *TToday* 42 (1985): 324 (emphasis added).

exact counterpart in the sufferings on the cross. They are more vivid in their realization of that dreadful scene than the story of the Gospels. The most striking features of these sufferings are seen there, in the piercing of the hands and feet, the body stretched upon the cross, the intense thirst, and the division of the garments.[5]

James E. Smith adds one more point to clinch the case:

No Old Testament person could have imagined that his personal deliverance from death could be the occasion for the world's conversion. Such a hope must be restricted to the future Redeemer. Under inspiration of the Holy Spirit, David in Psalm 22 saw his descendant resembling, *but far surpassing, himself* in suffering. Furthermore, the deliverance of this descendant would have meaning for all mankind.[6]

That is the position adopted here. David did experience unusual suffering, but under a revelation from God he witnesses suffering of one of his offspring, presumably the last in that promised line, that far transcends anything that came his way.

The psalm consists of two major divisions: verses 1–21 describes the gloom of suffering; verses 22–31 depict the jubilant triumph over death and suffering. The first division is further divided into three parts: verses 1–5, 6–11, and 12–21.[7] In each David expresses his anguish (vv. 1–2, 6–8, and 12–17), but he also replies with confidence in Yahweh's presence and ability to help him (vv. 3–5, 9–11, and 19–21). The second division has two parts: verses 22–26, which speak of the

---

[5]Charles A. Briggs, *Messianic Prophecy* (New York: Scribner's, 1889), 326 (emphasis added).

[6]James E. Smith, *What the Bible Teaches About the Promised Messiah* (Nashville: Thomas Nelson, 1993), 146 (emphasis added).

[7]All of the verse numberings are given as they are in the English Bible; the Hebrew text will always be one number higher since it often, as it did here, counts the title as the first verse. The English text's system of numbering is used here so as not to confuse the general reader.

congregation's reaction to what has transpired in the suffering, and verses 27–31, which address the universal implications of the whole event.

The psalm begins with a cry of anguish addressed to *ʾēlî*, "my God." Only those who have Yahweh as their God can use a pronoun of endearment such as "my" in a situation like this. Most oral interpretations of this passage put the emphasis on the wrong part of this phrase, saying in the public reading of Scripture, "My *God*, my *God*!" But that is to swear against and blaspheme God rather than to show that the speaker still regards God as his very own Father. Instead, the emphasis should fall on "*My* God, *my* God." That is where the emphasis falls in the Hebrew: *ʾēlî, ʾēlî*.

The sufferer is haunted by four questions: (1) "Why[8] have you forsaken me?" (2) "Why are you so far from saving me?" (3) "[Why are you] so far from the words of my groaning?" (4) "You do not answer [me]"; why not? But only those who forsake God need worry about abandonment by God.[9] The sufferer is immediately reassured in verses 3–5 that since God is still the "Holy One," his stainless faithfulness, truth, and character can be counted on in this situation. The sufferer need only recall what God has done in the past. Israel trusted him and were delivered. They cried out to God, and they were not disappointed. Three times David refers to the virtue of trusting God.

In verses 6–8, types of suffering are described: first the gibes and attitudes of the mockers, then the actions of his opponents. Thus, while the fathers trusted and were delivered, the sufferer emphasizes his present situation: "But I." Each

---

[8]In the Gospel record, Matthew explained that Jesus was asking, "For what reason [*hinati*] have you forsaken me?" Mark glossed Jesus' cry this way, "To what end [*eis ti*] have you forsaken me?" Matthew apparently interpreted the Hebrew text of Ps 22:1 as if it read *lammâh*, Mark read it as if it were *lemâh*.

[9]See this truth stated in 2 Chronicles 12:5; 15:2; 24:20.

statement in verse 6 is paralleled by Isaiah in his description of the Servant of the Lord. Here the sufferer says, "I am a worm" (cf. Isa 41:14, "Do not be afraid, O worm Jacob, O little Israel"). The psalmist also cries, "[I am] not a man, scorned by men" (cf. Isa 53:3, where the sufferer is "despised and rejected by men," i.e., lacking in respect and prestige to support him). The psalmist cries: "[I am] despised by the people" (cf. Isa 49:7, which depicts someone "who was despised and abhorred by the nation").

The mocking and insults carry over into actions, for the enemies laugh at him and shake their heads at him, saying sarcastically, "He trusts in the LORD; let the LORD rescue him. Let him deliver him, since he delights in him." Curiously, that is the precise speech that was hurled at Jesus on the cross (Mt 27:39–43).

Once again, the psalmist finds reassurance and an answer (vv. 9–11). He focuses his view on God the Father once more. God has brought him through his birth; he has protected him during his early years; he has always been God for him. Twice he mentions his "mother" (not his father!) as the one bringing forth this descendant in the line of David.

The most intense description of suffering comes in the first part of the third strophe (vv. 12–18). His enemies are like strong bulls (v. 12), raving and roaring lions (v. 13), and vicious wild dogs that prowl the streets (v. 16). He feels exhausted, poured out like water (v. 14a). His bones are out of joint (v. 14b); his heart has turned to wax and melts away (v. 14b); his thirst is raging (v. 15a). He is near to dying (v. 15b). His hands and feet are pierced (v. 16b).[10] His skin has become so taunt

---

[10]This translation is supported by the Septuagint, Vulgate, and Syriac versions. Most [recent?] Hebrew manuscripts read, "like a lion" instead of "they have pierced." However, the evidence is, as E. W. Hengstenberg argued in his *Christology of the Old Testament*, Arnold abridgment (1847; reprint, Grand Rapids: Kregel, 1970), 82, n. 4: "We take . . . the form *kā'arî* as the irregular plural for *kā'arîm*. This form will then be plural participle of *kûr*. Although this participle is properly *kār*, yet the *scriptio plena* is not in other in-

that his bones stick out (v. 17). He watches helplessly as they gamble for his garments (v. 18). This last item is not missed by the evangelists either, for Matthew 27:35 and John 19:23, 24 both note the scene at the cross where the Roman soldiers divide up his clothing into four parts, but when it comes to his seamless robe, they cast lots as to which of the four of them will get it.

Once again, as in each of the previous strophes, the sufferer puts his trust in the Lord who is his strength. He is certain that God has heard him (v. 21b).

The mood suddenly changes in verse 22. The test has been passed and the victory won. First the sufferer announces he will set forth the Father's name among those who believe (the "name" of God embraces all his attributes and qualities). Then the whole congregation of Israel joins in that same praise. The "I" of verse 22 and the plural "you" of verse 23 give way to the reason, "for [God] has not despised or disdained the suffering of the afflicted one; he has not hidden his face from him but has listened to his cry for help" (v. 24).[11] These are the talking points with the congregation at large.

---

stances without example: thus, Hos 10:14. *qā'm;* v. Eze 28:24, 26, *šā'tîm* (despisers). There is everything in favour of giving the verb *kûr* (which is not again found in Hebrew) the sense *to pierce through.* This interpretation is sustained (1) by the Hebrew usage. *kûr* is then synonymous with the verb *kārâh to bore through,* which often occurs. Such a permutation of the verbs *ayin"waw* and *lamad"hah* is common.... (2) The testimony of the Seventy, who translate *ōruxzan cheiras mou kai podas mou* as well as the Syriac version, which has ... *perforarunt. transfixerunt,* and the Vulgate, *foderunt.* This coincidence of the three most important direct translations deserves great regard. (3) And lastly the comparison with the Arabic is decisive. There the agreement of *kûr* with *kārâh* which we have assumed, really exists." There is no justification for the NEB translation, "They hacked off my hands and my feet."

[11]The writer of Hebrews makes the same point: "During the days of Jesus' life on earth, he offered up prayers and petitions with loud cries and tears to the one who could save him from death, and he was heard because of his reverent submission. Although he was a son, he learned obedience from what he suffered" (Heb 5: 7–8).

A second strophe of triumph appears in verses 27–31. Here "all the ends of the earth" are to remember what has been done for them and must turn to the Lord (v. 27). The reason, once again, is signaled by the word "for": "for dominion belongs to the LORD and he rules the nations" (v. 28).

Thus, the death and sufferings of this one who came in David's line and who suffered far more than David ever did is the means by which God will usher in his universal rule and reign over everything. In fact, every kingdom of the world will be given to him; nothing will be left outside of his domain. Even those who have gone down to the dust (i.e., have died) will one day kneel before him (v. 29).

That "posterity" (i.e., the believing offspring begun with Eve and continued in Shem, Abraham, Isaac, Jacob, and David) will serve him. They "will proclaim his righteousness to a people yet unborn" (v. 31) that the sufferer "has done it" (v. 31b).

It is no coincidence that the so-called fourth word on the cross, "*My* God, *My* God, why have you forsaken me?"[12] and the sixth word, "It is finished,"[13] both come from this psalm. It indicates that on the cross the mind of our Lord was instructed, comforted, and encouraged by the contents of this psalm. His use of verse 1 in the fourth word on the cross indicates that the title, not only the theme, is on his mind and tongue. In antiquity, there were no chapter numbers, verses, or even titles of books to refer to or quote from; instead, the first line was generally used to refer to the whole poem. The fact that Jesus' cry of final accomplishment can be attached to the final line of this psalm is further evidence of same argument.

---

[12]See Matthew 27:45–49 and Mark 15:33–37 for the two reports of this fourth word on the cross (emphasis added).

[13]This word is reported in John 19:30, a quote from Psalm 22:31. On two other occasions a word of completion came from the lips of the Godhead: one marking the division between creation and God's work in providence (Ge 1:31); the other coming some day to mark the division between history and eternity (Rev 21:6).

While to a lesser degree it is possible to speak of some of these things happening in the life of David, it is only with that climactic descendant of his, the Messiah, that it is possible to see most of these things fulfilled in detail.

2. Psalm 16

There are numerous points of contact between this psalm and the phrases used in the other well-attested Davidic psalms. They include: verse 1 (cf. Ps 7:1; 11:1, "in you I take refuge"); verse 5 (cf. 11:6, "my portion and my cup"); verse 8 (cf. 10:6; 15:5, "I will not be shaken/moved"); verse 9 (cf. 4:8, "rest secure/dwell securely"); verse 10 (cf. 4:3, "your Holy One/Favorite One"); verse 11 (cf. 17:7, 15; 21:6; 109:31, "joy in your presence" and "at your right hand").[14] This list is a compelling and imposing argument for Davidic authorship.

When the external evidence of the New Testament is added to this, it is difficult to escape the same conclusion reached on internal grounds, for Peter quoted from this psalm in his Pentecost address in Acts 2:27, commenting that David foresaw and spoke about the resurrection of Christ when he sang the words of Psalm 16:10. The apostle Paul likewise used this passage in his message at Antioch (Ac 13:35).

The special event in David's life that occasioned this psalm is difficult to determine and probably never will be known for certain. There are four major suggestions: (1) a severe sickness after he had finished building his cedar palace (F. Delitzsch); (2) his stay at Ziklag among the Philistines in 2 Samuel 27, when he was tempted to worship idols and when his life was in constant danger (Hitzig); (3) his first arrival in Gath (1Sa 21:10–15), while Saul's enmity was implacable and the Philistine King Achish's suspicions about David were at their height

---

[14]This list was compiled by E. W. Hengstenberg, *The Psalms* (Edinburgh: Clark, 1851), 1:231.

(Rosenmüller); and (4) David's word about his future dynasty upon hearing Nathan's prophecy (2Sa 7) about a throne, dynasty, and kingdom (Lange). Because of the scope of Nathan's prophecy and its obvious link with Psalm 16, the last suggestion seems to fit best; however, all four situations may have played a part as David views his whole life in light of the pleasant promises that have fallen out to him as he still struggles with enormous opposition that threatens him, up to the point of death.

As for the contents of Psalm 16, David begins by expressing an exuberant joy and happiness that know few boundaries. He has placed himself under the overlordship of his suzerain, Yahweh (v. 1), whom he describes as his "portion" (v. 5) and his "inheritance" (v. 6). There is no other good he seeks besides his Lord. Accordingly, David delights in the company of fellow believers (v. 3), but he detests all whose lips and lives serve false gods (v. 4). Out of such a fellowship and enjoyment of God comes counsel, admonishment, and protection (vv. 7–9a) .

Suddenly, in the middle of verse 9, David switches to the Hebrew imperfect tense: he who is God's "Holy One" (Heb. ḥāsîd) will rest confidently in the fact that neither he nor God's everlasting "offspring" (here called ḥāsîd) will be abandoned in the grave, but the God who has given the promise will be the same Lord in whose presence he will experience fullness of joy and pleasures forevermore.

This psalm, then, has a direct messianic prediction, though everything depends on how one views the word "Holy One/Favorite One" (ḥāsîd). ḥāsîd occurs thirty-two times in the OT, but only in poetic texts.[15] But there is a major textual problem here. If the Hebrew text is read according to its

---

[15]Besides the twenty-five examples in the Psalms, it appears in Dt 33:8; 1Sa 2:9; 2Sa 22:26 (duplicated in Ps 18:26); Pr 2:8; Jer 3:12; Mic 7:2; 2Ch 6:41 (duplicated in Ps 132:9). In seventeen cases it is in the plural; eleven times it is in the singular; four times there are variant readings.

consonants, it is a plural, "your holy ones." But the vowel points and the Masoretic note require that we read it in the singular. All older versions testify that it is singular in number, just as Peter and Paul argue in Acts 2:27 and 13:35. This last argument is particularly relevant since the apostles appealed to this very fact to demonstrate the case for the resurrection of Christ and that it was anticipated by Psalm 16:10. If their proof could have been invalidated by the response of their Jewish audiences that the text read "holy ones," this would have been most damaging to their case. However, the silence of the Jewish sources in that era was striking. The singular is also attested in the oldest and best Hebrew manuscripts.[16]

So conclusive are the arguments raised for the singular reading that even the defenders of the plural reading, "your holy ones," attempt to defend it on the supposition that the plural here stands for the singular. Whether the plural reading is the more difficult reading (a principle that is generally preferred when making textual decisions) depends more on which side of the argument one stands. Apparently, the plural reading is not attested until well after the Christian era, thereby suggesting that its appearance is motivated more by reason of refuting the Christian claims for a resurrected Messiah than they are by hard textual evidence.

Despite skepticism among current scholars, ḥāsîd is best rendered in a passive form, "one to whom God is loyal, gracious, or merciful" or "one in whom God manifests his grace and favor," rather than the currently preferred active form, "one who is loyal to God."[17] It is the context, not just the form, that finally decides whether it is active or passive in meaning.

---

[16]See E. W. Hengstenberg, *Christology of the Old Testament*, 76. He mentions 156 codices of Kennicott and 80 codices of de Rossi.

[17]The noun and adjectival pattern, according to Hupfeld on Psalm 4:4, is like 'āsîr, "one who is bound, a prisoner," or qāsîr, "what is gathered, the harvest"; so BDB, 339.

Clearly, David claims to be Yahweh's ḥāsîd, as Psalm 4:4[3] declares: "Realize that Yahweh has set apart for himself a Favorite One (ḥāsîd); Yahweh will hear when I call to him" (pers. tr.). It is this confidence that comforts David when others attempt to frustrate him with their evil deeds and attacks. As David affirms in Psalm 18:25 (cf. 2Sa 22:26), "With a Favorite One (ḥāsîd) you [O Lord] will manifest yourself graciously/favorably [ḥāsîd; a hithpael form from the same root as the noun]" (pers. tr.). Accordingly, the "Favorite One" is a person in whom God's gracious ḥesed is specially manifested. More often than not, the special covenantal love implied in this noun is what was first announced to Abraham, Isaac, Jacob, and the dynasty of David in the unconditional covenant God made with them.

A key passage in this whole discussion of the meaning of ḥāsîd is Psalm 89:19–21[18–20]:

> Indeed, our shield belongs to the LORD, our king to the Holy One (qedôš) of Israel. Once you spoke to your Favorite One (ḥāsîd)[18] in a vision and said: I have set the crown on a hero, I have exalted from the people a choice person. I have found David my servant [a messianic term in Isaiah] with my holy oil and I have anointed him [another messianic allusion]. (pers. tr.)

We conclude that the ḥāsîd is David. Yet as part of the ongoing line and offspring of the woman Eve, Shem, the patriarchs, Judah, and David, the ḥāsîd is the Final One who will embody all that the promise-plan of God has entailed: the Messiah himself. That Holy One/Faithful One/Favorite One will live and rule forever.

Beyond the question of the identity of this Favorite One is his character, nature, and work. He will not suffer corruption or

---

[18]Most manuscripts also read the singular here as well, even though modern scholars lean toward the plural reading, as do many translations, such as the NIV, "your faithful people." But the problem here is exactly as it is in Psalm 16:10.

decay; God will not abandon his royal offspring in the tomb, nor will he let him decay. He will come forth from the tomb: "you will not abandon me to the grave/Sheol." And in his coming back from the grave, he will thereby make known to David the "path of life," a phrase that the psalmist often uses for *eternal life*.[19] Little wonder, then, that David rests secure in this hope. Certainly he will die at some time in the future, but that will not end it all: David will experience "eternal pleasures at [the] right hand [of Yahweh and his *ḥāsîd*]." That is why David's "body also rest[s] secure" (v. 9b).[20]

The Messiah will come out of the grave/Sheol. How, when, and under what circumstances, the text does not elaborate. It is enough for David to realize that one of his relatives, who will live forever, will triumph over death. Thus David and all who belong to that spiritual offspring will likewise be raised to eternal life and eternal pleasures at God's right hand. No wonder the apostles Peter and Paul used this passage so boldly in front of their Jewish audiences! And no one appears to have challenged them or refuted their appeal to this text.

Perhaps this is one of the passages that the disciples learned firsthand from Christ as he talked with those two disciples on the road to Emmaus. If he showed them that his resurrection was in the book of Psalms, then this must have been the passage, for after his ascension, we find them appealing with great emphasis to this text.

---

[19]See the argument for this equivalency in Mitchell Dahood, *Psalms*, 3 vols. (Garden City, N.Y.: Doubleday, 1965), 1:91.

[20]For a more detailed statement of the exegetical features of this text, see Walter C. Kaiser, Jr., "The Promise to David in Psalm 16 and Its Application in Acts 2:25–33 and 13:32–37," *JETS* 23 (1980): 219–29. It has been reprinted as chapter 2, "Foreseeing and Predicting the Resurrection," in *The Uses of the Old Testament in the New* (Chicago: Moody Press, 1985), 25–41.

E. THE WRITTEN PLAN AND MARRIAGE OF MESSIAH

1. Psalm 40

The heading of this psalm attributes it to David,[21] though most modern scholars prefer to place it in the post-exilic era[22] because it uses vocabulary such as the "slimy pit" and "mud and mire" (cf. Ps 40:2)—phrases usually compared with Jeremiah 38:6 and Isaiah. But some of the same terminology can be found elsewhere in the Davidic psalms (e.g., Pss 32; 51).[23]

Psalm 40 consists of two divisions: verses 1–11 bring thanksgiving and gratitude to God for deliverance; verses 12–17 form a lament in which the psalmist prays for a speedy deliverance from his foes. It is true, of course, that the second division appears with only slight textual variations as Psalm 70. But some scholars have correctly argued that the psalm is a unity in that a past deliverance often serves as a basis for expecting or requesting relief in one's present situation. Perowne[24] added three more reasons why the unity of the psalm should be maintained. (1) The two parts are found together in all manuscripts and ancient versions. (2) It is easier to explain

---

[21]For an argument for the originality of these headings, see Robert Dick Wilson, "The Headings of the Psalms," *PTR* 24 (1926): 353–95. For a more recent argument against their originality, except in a half-dozen cases or so of the seventy-three Davidic psalms, see Sigmund Mowinckel, *The Psalms in Israel's Worship*, trans. D. R. Ap-Thomas (Nashville: Abingdon, 1967), 2:98–101.

[22]Charles A. Briggs, *A Critical and Exegetical Commentary on the Book of Psalms*, 2 vols. (ICC; New York: Scribner's, 1906), 1:351.

[23]For a more detailed defense of Davidic authorship and other points on this psalm, see Walter C. Kaiser, Jr., "The Abolition of the Old Order and the Establishment of the New: Psalm 40:6–8 and Hebrews 10:5–10," in *Tradition and Testament: Essays in Honor of Charles Lee Feinberg*, ed. John S. Feinberg and Paul D. Feinberg (Chicago: Moody Press, 1981), 19–37; reprinted in idem, *The Uses of the Old Testament in the New*, 123–41.

[24]J. J. Steward Perowne, *The Book of Psalms*, 2 vols. (reprint of 4th ed.; Grand Rapids: Zondervan, 1966), 1:332.

the textual variations in Psalm 70 on the supposition that it was detached from Psalm 40 than on the reverse hypothesis. (3) There is a play on the words appearing in the second half of Psalm 40 with the words in the first half, such as "be pleased" (v. 13) with "your will" (v. 8; a word omitted in Ps 70:8). Most significant of all is the fact that "verse 12 of Psalm 40 is not a natural ending to the Psalm, for [it] seems to require a prayer to follow it."[25]

It is impossible to say what circumstances caused David to compose this psalm. Some suppose that it was written when he fled from his son Absalom. Nevertheless, it is possible to understand the psalm as it stands.

The psalmist begins by describing some great danger he was experiencing when the Lord rescued him. So grave was the situation that he felt as if he were sinking into a miry pit (v. 1). However, he has been rescued, and his feet are now set on a solid rock (v. 2). This evidence of God's grace puts a "new song" into his mouth (v. 3) and is the source of encouragement to all who believe in the Lord. Such persons are happy ("blessed," v. 4). This fact forms the transition as the psalmist next mentions the incalculable multiplicity of God's miraculous works and his incomparable plans for the believing community (v. 5).

What adequate response can the psalmist make for such unbounded goodness from God? Surely, God is best thanked not by external ritual offerings (v. 6); instead, more appropriate is voluntary obedience to do his will, the very will that is written "in the scroll" (v. 7). That is what the psalmist, along with all who love the Lord, proposes to do.

Precisely at this point the messianic implications arise. To be sure, the psalmist does not reject sacrifices as such, any more than do the prophets who follow him (Isa 1:11–18; Jer 7:21–

---

[25]S. R. Driver, "The Method of Studying the Psalter," *Expositor* 52 (1910): 355.

23; Hos 6:6; Am 5:21; Mic 6:6–8). The same sentiments appear in the Psalms (50:8, 14; 51:16; 69:30–31) and Proverbs (15:8; 21:3), not to mention those that have preceded the psalmist (Ex 15:26; Dt 10:12, 20; 1Sa 15:22). Sabourin labels this form of the psalmist's statement "dialectical negation"[26]; that is, the ceremonial practice is held in tension until the ethical and spiritual preparation for the performance of that practice is met. The effect is to speak in proverbial form: "I do not desire this so much as I desire that," or "without this there is no that."

Between the two pairs of sacrificial terms is the middle clause, "but my ears you have pierced" (v. 6). Initially, this unique biblical clause suggests the well-known custom of boring a slave's right ear to denote that his voluntary dedication of himself in perpetual service to his master (Ex 21:6; Dt 15:17). But this otherwise suggestive explanation has two main drawbacks: (1) the technical term for "bore" is not *kārâ* ("to dig") but *rāsâ'* ("to bore"), and (2) only one ear was bored, not both ears, as in this verse (*'oznayim*). The clause refers, then, to the fact that the instruments for obedience, the ears, have been made by God (Ps 94:9); hence, the ability to obey has been given by God.

Instead of connecting verse 7 in a temporal sequence, the psalmist emphasizes the internal connection between the declaration of the preceding verse and this one. "Then" marks the consequence of the announced obedience that has been contrasted with mere external ritualistic offering of sacrifices. The form of the obedience that David talks about is one where he places himself at the service of God. "Behold, I come [*or* have come]" (NASB). These are the words of a servant who answers the call of his master (Nu 22:38; 2Sa 19:21; Isa 6:9). What

---

[26]Leopold Sabourin, *The Psalms: Their Origin and Meaning*, 2 vols. (New York: Society of St. Paul, 1969), 2:48.

David has come to do, however, is what has been written in the scroll "of, concerning, about, or for" David (v. 7).

Some wish to restrict David's reference to "the scroll" to the law of the king found in Deuteronomy 17:14–20. But it is better to understand it as referring to God's will as expressed to him by Nathan the prophet in 2 Samuel 7. This can be demonstrated by the fact that in verse 8 David delights to do God's "will"—a word similar to the word for God's "plan," although it stresses the aspect of pleasure and favor connected with that plan.

Psalm 40, then, is David's presentation to God of his willing and obedient spirit to carry out what is written of him "in the scroll." Since he is the promised offspring and line through whom God's plan will unfold, climaxing in a Son who will live and reign eternally, he carries in his person, as does each favored descendant in that line, everything that God is going to do for all the nations of the earth. Therefore, what has been written thus far about the coming Messiah and his work is written, in effect, about David. David delights in everything he finds written therein, for God has dug out his ears, as it were, and given him a willing heart and mind to follow what is written. Such also, in light of David's most recent escape from danger, is the substance of the good news that he will herald forth in the midst of God's gathered congregation.

Many have objected that the writer of Hebrews, following the Septuagint, has changed the Hebrew reading of "my ears you have pierced" to "a body you have prepared for me" (Heb 10:5). But the Septuagint expresses the same sentiment as the original, giving it a dynamic equivalent rather than a word-for-word rendering, since the Hebrew metaphor does not appear among the Greeks. Thus, the idea that the Greek translators gave it was something on this order: "You, O Lord, have required nothing outward but myself for sacrifice, and that I freely offer to you." This paraphrase yields the correct sentiment because to dig the ears is a figurative expression for imparting certain precepts and for rendering others willing to follow them.

The psalm concludes with a prayer that God will answer the psalmist once again as he has in the past. The references to his sinfulness are to be explained just as we have argued earlier: the Davidic line will be judged for their sin, but they are still the channels by which God will transmit the blessing of the promise-plan, since it depends on God's work and not their own.[27] The psalmist enthusiastically enjoins his readers: "May all who seek you rejoice and be glad in you; may those who love your salvation always say, 'The LORD be exalted.'"

2. Psalm 45

Psalm 45 is a marriage or wedding song. Its language and attributions made of the king and his bride far transcend any legitimate words that could be used of the best earthly kings. Occasionally the language is drawn directly from the promise made to David (e.g., v. 2, where the king is said to be "blessed ... forever," as 2Sa 7:13, 16 predicted).

In spite of the elevated language, some have viewed this psalm as one of David's marriages—perhaps to Saul's daughter Michal, or to Maacah of Geshur, or even to Bathsheba. But none of these suggestions work, for David was not a king when he married Michal, nor was he king over all Israel when he married Maacah; and Bathsheba was not from a royal line (as the bride in this psalm, v. 9). Another popular opinion claims that it represents Solomon's marriage to the Egyptian princess. But Solomon was no warrior, like the king depicted here (vv. 3, 5), nor were his sons made princes over the whole earth (v. 16). Moreover, his marriage was not approved by God (1Ki 11:1–13).

---

[27]See our discussion of Psalm 69:5 for a fuller explanation.

None of these persons embody all the elements found in this psalm. Any other nominees for the identity of this king have likewise fallen short of the description given in this psalm. Spurgeon's comment is one of the best I have seen on this matter:

> Some here see Solomon and Pharaoh's daughter only— they are short-sighed; others see both Solomon and Christ—they are cross-eyed; well-focused spiritual eyes see here Jesus only.... This is no wedding song of earthly nuptials, but an Epithalamium for the Heavenly Bridegroom and his elect bride.[28]

As to the content of the psalm, an illustrious king is introduced to us briefly. He is distinguished as a most remarkable person: handsome, gifted in speech, heroic, and righteous. His kingdom is everlasting and enhanced with the highest dignity and honor. His achievements are awesome, for he is a "hero" (Heb. *gibbôr*)[29] in battle and victorious in his cause. He has triumphed over all his enemies as he marches forth for truth, meekness, and righteousness.

This king/bridegroom is identified in verses 6–7 with four facts that forever close off the possibility of equating this royal person with an earthly king.[30] (1) Most importantly, he is a *divine ruler*. He is addressed in the vocative as "O God" (v. 6). Though several have tried to take *Elohim* as a genitive rather than a vocative, clearly none of the ancient versions ever treated it that way. Others try to take *Elohim* as in the nominative case: "Your throne is God for ever and ever"; i.e., God will forever sustain your throne. But when one compares 2 Samuel 7:13 and Psalm 89:29, it is clear that "for ever and

---

[28]C. H. Spurgeon, *Treasury of David*, 7 vols. (New York: Funk and Wagnalls, 1892), 2:351, as cited by James E. Smith, *What the Bible Teaches About Prophecy*, 176.

[29]The word *gibbôr* by itself does not necessarily indicate deity, but when it is joined with the divine name *El* ("God"), as it is in one of the four names Isaiah 9:6 gives to the Messiah, it is a title of majestic proportions.

[30]See Smith, *What the Bible Teaches About Prophecy*, 180–81.

ever" must be an attribute of the kingdom, not of God.[31] (2) This ruler's kingdom is an *eternal kingdom*. That is what Nathan promised David in 2 Samuel 7:13, 16. (3) He is an *anointed ruler*, for God "anoint[ed him] with the oil of joy" (v. 7). That anointing (if the Messiah is the one intended here, as we believe) must have come when Jesus was anointed with the Holy Spirit during his baptism (Lk 4:18). (4) The bridegroom is a *righteous ruler*; he will wield the scepter of justice— the scepter of his kingdom (v. 6b-c).

The joyous festivities connected with the divine ruler's reign are set forth in verses 8–9. His garments are fragrant, woven (as if it were possible) from myrrh, aloe, and cassia. His palace is either made of ivory or inlaid with ivory panels, and the music played for the wedding is on stringed instruments.

Verses 9b–15 describe the bride. If the Messiah is the bridegroom, then the bride must be his people, the believing body of the ancient offspring mentioned since the days of Eve, Shem, Abraham, Isaac, Jacob, and David. She is a royal bride attired in gold, even as the royal priesthood of Exodus 19:5–6 had predicted. She must leave her home, presumably in the world, and sever her ties with her past. Now she must "listen," "consider," "give ear," "forget [her] people and [her] father's house," and "honor" the one who is her Lord (vv. 10–11).

The psalm ends by describing the marriage attire (v. 13), the marriage procession (v. 14), the joy of the marriage (v. 15), and the fruit of the marriage (v. 16). This psalm will help to perpetuate the memory of the king throughout all generations so that other people besides Israel may praise him (v. 17).

---

[31]E. W. Hengstenberg, *Christology*, 53, makes an especially fine technical point after noting that *Elohim* is used of judges and kings in Ex 21:6; 22:7– 8 and Ps 82:1. "No where, however, is *any single magistrate* called *Elohim*, but always only the *magistracy* as representing the tribunal of God" (emphasis his).

F. THE TRIUMPH OF MESSIAH

1. Psalm 68

Almost every commentator begins this psalm by complaining that it is the most difficult of all the psalms to interpret.[32] What is most elusive about it is its structure. The title ascribes it to David, though frequently this is denied by scholars without much external or internal evidence. The most that can be said in favor of a non-Davidic date is that some of the phrases in this psalm are shared with those in Isaiah 40–66. But that only introduces the question as to which is prior, Psalm 68 or the sections in Isaiah 40–66.

If one must depend on evidences of borrowing in order to set the date, there is an abundance of evidence in Psalm 68 to show that the language of this psalm borrows heavily from events prior to David's time, including the Song of Moses (Ex 15), the shout of Numbers 10:35, the Song of Deborah (Jdg 5), Israel's experiences in the desert, their entry into Canaan, and their occupation of Mount Zion or Jerusalem.

The setting of this psalm is probably one of David's victorious returns from battle (e.g., after his defeat of the Syro-Ammonite coalition, 2Sa 10). David surveys in verses 7–17 what God has done in the past. On that basis, the rest of the psalm looks forward to what God will do in the future. This makes verse 18 both the pivotal and climactic verse. It is the grand messianic verse of the psalm as well.

---

[32]Smith, *What the Bible Teaches About Prophecy*, 198, quotes the sentiment of Simon De Muis on the difficulty of this psalm: "In this Psalm there are as many precipices and labyrinths as there are verses or words. It may not be improperly termed the torture of critics and the reproach of commentators" (Smith found this quote in Adam Clarke, *The Holy Bible ... With Commentary and Critical Notes*, 5 vols. [New York: Waugh and Mason, 1833], 3:217). Charles A. Briggs, *Messianic Prophecy*, 428. n. 1, also concludes that "there is no psalm which has troubled critics so much as this psalm. The history of its interpretation is a marvel of errors and contradictions."

The psalm begins with the ancient shout that accompanied the lifting up of the ark on the shoulders of the priests as the men in the forces of Israel went out to battle: "God will arise,[33] his enemies shall be scattered" (v. 1, personal translation). What is expected is the magnificent coming and appearance of God in one of his theophanies, or as we shall see, a Christophany. This coming will mean that the wicked and all their opposition to God will be as useful as wax is before a fire: they will be blown away like smoke is dispersed by the wind. God will come in his chariot supplied by the clouds (v. 4). The defenseless will suddenly sense that their champion has intervened on their behalf. In the past, this was the day of God's visitation; but it is also, by the same token, a harbinger of the final day of the Lord in the end times.

In verses 7–17, the past becomes the lens through which David catches a glimpse of the future. Did not God lead his people in the desert (vv. 7–10)? Did he not give them the land of Canaan (vv. 11–14)? And did not God lead David's troops to conquer Mount Zion (vv. 15–17)? In language styled after the rebuke of the lazy and slothful in Judges 5:16, warnings are raised lest any should neglect to enter in to take each one's share of the spoil of this battle (vv. 12–13, 16).

The heart of this psalm is verse 18, which depicts the theophanic person ascending into heaven. There are five important things to note in this verse: (1) The psalmist suddenly turns to address someone in the second person; (2) this person "ascends," rather than processes in some line of march on earth; (3) the place this person ascends to is "on high" (Heb. *mārôn*, a term that never means anything less than heaven); (4) in the train of his ascension, this theophanic person takes captives; and (5) after having ascended, the theophanic person both receives and gives gifts, which in this case are men and

---

[33]Despite the prevalence of the translation, "Let God/ May God arise," in most ancient and modern translations (e.g., AV, RV, RSV, NRSV, NIV, etc.), the Hebrew verb *yāqûm* is not a jussive but an indicative.

women! This is a most exalted declaration worthy of further inspection.

Verse 18 addresses someone, using the second person pronoun. It celebrates that time in the past at Mount Sinai when God came down on the mountain to meet with Moses and to speak with him face to face. Whether it depicts a theophany or a Christophany may be debated, but since there is conversation with God the Father, it seems that an appearance of the Messiah on Mount Sinai is what is being hailed and celebrated.

One cannot refer to the incident of Moses' being on Mount Sinai for forty days without also remembering the incident about the golden calf (Ex 32–34). When Moses asked the idolatrous Israelites, "Whoever is for the LORD, come to me" (32:26), only the Levites rallied to his side! The rest of the people stood fixed and unmoved! Because of this, God set the Levites "apart to the LORD [that day]" (32:29). Numbers 8 and 18 is a divine commentary on just what that setting apart meant for the Levites and for the service of God. The Levites were "given wholly to [God]" (Nu 8:16; 18:24) after they were "taken" (8:18) and treated as "gifts" (8:19; 18:6) to God in order to carry out the ministry at the tabernacle. Thus, it is not a long leap in logic to argue that, just as the Messiah in a preincarnate form had come down from heaven to meet with Moses face-to-face, so he will return to the Father because, in the meantime, he has taken captives in the form of Levites, whom he now offers to the Father as gifts to carry out the work of the ministry in his absence.

The apostle Paul draws the same inference from this psalm in Ephesians 4:8, "When he ascended on high, he led captives in his train and gave gifts to men." Only here it is no longer Levites whom God is using, but prophets, apostles, evangelists, and pastor-teachers, who have been given to the Father as gifts in order to equip the saints for the same work of the ministry as previously he had left to the Levites (4:11–13).

The captives, then, are first the Levites, but eventually all those called into the equipping ministry of outfitting all God's people to do the work of the ministry. Paul did not spiritual-ize, allegorize, or supply a *pesher* meaning to the text; he gave the straightforward grammatical-historical sense of Psalm 68:18, which depends in turn on the theology of Numbers 8 and 18.[34]

The ultimate goal of the Messiah's advent, ascension, and endowing his people with gifts is that all may enter into his final victory over the rebellious—increasingly as the ages move on and finally in that last day, when the grandest of all victories is consummated in Christ's second coming. At that time he will come to dwell among mortals in Zion.

The psalm concludes on an even more dramatic note of triumph as the Lord speaks out directly for the only time in this psalm (vv. 22–23). The people of Israel will be retrieved from Bashan, from nearby frontiers, and from as far away as the depths of the sea. In front of King Messiah and his con-quering army will come singers with damsels playing tam-bourines (v. 25), followed by the tribes of Israel. As the Messiah is ensconced in Jerusalem, the Gentile nations of the world will send their tribute to him at his temple (v. 29).

The last verses of the psalm are a prayer that Zion will be strengthened and all Messiah's enemies destroyed (vv. 28–35). The whole world is invited to acknowledge that the God who appeared in the past and who appeared on Sinai is the God who rules over all, and the nations declare that God is indeed an "awesome" God (v. 35).

2. Psalm 72

This psalm is a direct messianic prediction because it uses the future tense throughout and because not even Solomon in all his glory could have fulfilled what is said here. Solomon is

---

[34]I am indebted to my student Gary V. Smith for pointing out to me the basic lines of argumentation in this text. See his article "Paul's Use of Psalm 68:18 in Ephesians 4:8," *JETS* 18 (1975): 181–89.

given credit in the title line of this psalm for writing it, but his reign supplies only the imagery, language, and line of descent through which the peaceful and prosperous reign is to come.

Psalm 72 represents the Messiah as ruling in righteousness, justice, and peace as he receives the homage of the nations of the world. According to Charles Briggs, the psalm consists of three strophes, each of which begins with a prayer that corresponds, in part, to the prayer offered by Solomon for wisdom at Gibeon and at the dedication of the temple. This structure has not always been observed since many versions failed to notice that the verbs in verses 8 and 15 are jussives, not imperfects.[35]

The first strophe (vv. 1–7), describing the Messiah's righteous reign, opens with the request that God endow the king, his son, with such judicial powers that can come only from God himself. As a result of such a fair and righteous reign, the kingdom will experience peace and prosperity in perpetuity. In fact, the advent of the Messiah's reign will be like fresh rain falling on earth (v. 6), a messianic figure of speech that occurs elsewhere (e.g., Hos 10:12; Joel 2:23).

The second strophe (vv. 8–14) opens in verse 8 with a second petition, "Yes, let him rule from sea to sea, and from the river to the ends of the earth" (pers. tr.). What began as an allusion to the description of the projected boundaries of the Promised Land surpasses it by stretching those boundaries to the ends of the earth. The Messiah's enemies will "lick the dust" (v. 9), an obvious allusion to the Edenic promise given to Eve in Genesis 3:15. Believers will come from all over the globe to worship the Messiah, to bring him gifts and tribute, and to honor him (vv. 10–11). The worldwide government of the Messiah will be marked by its impartial justice for all. Those who had relied on bloodshed, violence, and pillage in

---

[35]Charles A. Briggs, *Messianic Prophecy*, 138, n. 1.

the past must now reckon with a kingdom that totally removes that from its sight (vv. 12–14).

The third and final strophe (vv. 15–19) begins once again with a prayer: "Long may he live! May the gold from Sheba be given him. May people ever pray for him and bless him all day long" (v. 15). The Messiah's kingdom, the psalmist assures us, will be exceedingly prosperous, with plenty of gold, grain, fruit, and a population as thriving as "the grass of the field" (v. 16).

Following that is a prayer that the "name" of the Messiah may endure forever and "continue as long as the sun" (v. 17). The same prayer entreats God that "all nations [may] be blessed through him" and that "they [may] call him blessed," a word that strikes the note of the gospel with its call for all to believe in God's Man of Promise who is to come. This prayer is clearly based on the Abrahamic promise of Genesis 12:3; 22:18; and 26:4. One promise-plan has been in effect in David and Solomon's day. Ever since God announced it almost one millennium before to the patriarchs, it has not changed in its basic thrust. Its focus and center is on the Anointed One, the Messiah, who will come in the line of Abraham, Isaac, Jacob, Judah, and David; but its benefits are to be made available to all the families of the earth.

The psalmist closes with a doxology (vv. 18–19). As Isaac Watts sang, based on this psalm,

> Jesus shall reign where'er the sun,
> does its successive journeys run.
> His kingdom spread from shore to shore,
> till moons shall wax and wane no more.

◆ 6 ◆

The Messiah in the Ninth- and Eighth-Century Prophets

The promise-plan of Messiah was not concluded when the days of the covenant promises made to Eve, Shem, Abraham, Isaac, Jacob, and David were over. On the contrary, these same promises began to proliferate and blossom beyond anything anyone could have imagined once we arrive at the writings of the sixteen "Latter Prophets."[1] In their writings, the doctrine of the Messiah and his work, as outlined in the writings already covered, became the constant basis of their appeals for what God was doing and was going to do.

That is why the promise-doctrine had a twofold character: It was a standing prediction for what God was going to do in the future, but it was also a doctrine by which men and

---

[1]The four major prophets (Isaiah, Jeremiah, Ezekiel, and Daniel) and the twelve minor prophets (called minor not for their importance, but for their bulk and size in comparison with the major prophets; Hosea, Joel, Amos, Obadiah, Jonah, Micah, Nahum, Habakkuk, Zephaniah, Haggai, Zechariah, and Malachi) made up the sixteen writing prophets of the Hebrew canon. These prophets are contrasted in the Hebrew canon with the "Former Prophets," consisting of Joshua, Judges, (1, 2) Samuel, and (1, 2) Kings.

women lived in their contemporary situations. In fact, for the contemporaries of David and the prophets, it was just as much, if not more importantly, a doctrine for the present as a forecast for the future. As Willis J. Beecher described it:

> ... [T]his messianic doctrine [was] preached by the prophets, sung in the Psalms, built into the temple, [rose] with the smoke of every sacrifice, [was] the quickner of Israel's conscience, the bulwark against idolatry, the protection of patriotism from despair, the comfort under affliction, the warning against temptation, the recall to the wandering; in short, [it was] a doctrine of salvation offered to Israel and every Israelite; more than this, [it was] Israel's missionary call to the nations, inviting all without exception to turn to the service of Yahaweh [sic].[2]

Before we examine a wide sampling of some fifty major treatments of the coming Messiah in the Latter Prophets, we must remind ourselves of two important hermeneutical principles for interpreting them.

(1) The first principle is the concept of *inaugurated eschatology*,[3] in which the writers of Scripture embody a "now" along with a "not-yet" aspect to many of their predictions about the future. They often encapsulate contemporary fulfillments of their predictions into the ultimate and final fulfillment of the climactic work of God in the last day. They can do this because they see many of these events as belonging to a series of causes that are generically related to the final effect—especially in the case of the coming Messiah. Thus, each chosen son of each of the three patriarchs and each successive king in the Davidic line of Judah is at once a fulfillment of the promise of the Messiah (in the sense that he is an earnest and down payment on what God will ultimately do) and a further prediction that the Messiah will yet come.

---

[2]Willis J. Beecher, *The Prophets and the Promise* (Grand Rapids: Baker, 1975 [reprint of 1905]), 243.

[3]See above, ch. 3, n. 8.

(2) Another hermeneutical concept was that of *corporate solidarity*,[4] wherein there is an oscillation and a reciprocity between the whole community and the individual. For example, the very name "Israel" raises a wide variety of meanings. Sometimes we mean the ancient political organization, sometimes the country, sometimes the Jewish people, sometimes the religious body, sometimes the spiritually minded among them, sometimes the NT believers, and sometimes the heavenly body of believers poetically called Zion. Each context must be carefully examined to determine which of these referents is in the mind of the writer.

The prophets are in the habit of regarding Israel as the people of promise. As such, they can be addressed together as one whole group or through the representative of the larger whole. This is especially evident when the prophets use corporate terms (often words that are neither singular nor plural, but collective singular terms) such as *offspring (seed)*, *son*, *chosen one*, *holy one*, *servant of the Lord*, *branch*, *anointed one*, and the like.

The scope of the messianic doctrine in the prophets is large. In some ways, the only fair treatment of this doctrine is to give an exposition of all sixteen prophets, for it belongs to the warp and woof of all their writings. However, for the purposes of this study of messianic prophecy as a part of a biblical theology, we will treat the subject diachronically, grouping the prophets roughly into the ninth, eighth, seventh, sixth, and fifth centuries. Probably only Joel and Obadiah are included in the ninth century,[5] though both are often dated as late as the fall of Jerusalem in 586 B.C., even by conservative scholars.

---

[4]See above, ch. 2, n. 15.

[5]Since 27 of Joel's 72 verses have literary parallels with Isaiah, Ezekiel, Amos, Micah, Nahum, Zephaniah, and Malachi, it raises the question of Joel's integrity if his book is placed after these prophets; if that were the case, almost one-half of his book would be taken from his colleagues, thus making him most unoriginal.

The eighth century was an active period of prophetic activity, with Hosea, Micah, Amos, Jonah, and Isaiah all preaching and proclaiming the message of God. The seventh century featured Habakkuk, Zephaniah, Nahum, and Jeremiah as its prophets. Then, during the Exile, Ezekiel and Daniel ministered in the sixth century from their places of captivity in Babylon. Finally, in the late sixth and fifth centuries of the postexilic times, Haggai, Zechariah, and Malachi complete the prophetic picture of the OT. Not all of these prophets include a direct messianic prediction in their works, but all of them include at least something that pertains to the messianic era in the broad sense. For our study here, we will focus on those passages that have direct messianic references, as we have done thus far.

A. THE NINTH CENTURY:
THE MESSIAH AS A TEACHER (JOEL 2:23)

Both Joel and Obadiah speak of a future time when the regal and judicial acts of Yahweh will climax in what they refer to as "the day of the LORD." This day is depicted as a period when the Lord will conclude his work of salvation and judgment on a universal and cosmic scale. In both books the topic of that day is introduced by means of a contemporary calamity: in Joel's case, a severe locust plague; in Obadiah's case, an event in which Edom stood on the side and refused to come to rescue Judah when it was attacked.

Joel's prophecy begins by describing the onslaught of a devastating locust plague. Twice he issues his call for repentance and a return to the Lord (Joel 1:13–14; 2:12–14). Then, suddenly and dramatically, the prophet changes direction by using four past tense verbs (2:18; contrary to the NIV and NASB renderings[6]), indicating that his audience has finally heeded

---

[6]The Hebrew verbs used in Joel 2:18 are *waw* conversives with the Hebrew imperfect tense—verbs that are universally translated as the narrative past tense. The verbs are: *wayeqannē'* ("And [the LORD] was jealous"),

the call for a spiritual response to the events of that day and his pleas for a change. This action has possibly come in response to the revival led by Jehoiada the priest during the time of King Joash.

Then follows a prediction that involves the principle of an inaugurated eschatology: there is both a near and a distant fulfillment to the prophet's words about this coming "day of the LORD." In Joel 2:19–27 the immediate effects of the people's repentance can be seen in the restoration of the produce of the fields, orchards, and the pastures. But in 3:1–4:21[2:28–3:21] there are long-range fulfillments that will come as a result of the predictive word of God in the end times.

In the midst of the immediate effects of this work of God comes the startling prediction that God will give "a teacher for righteousness" (Joel 2:23b; cf. NIV note).[7] Here Joel is giving a threefold word of encouragement to the "land" (v. 21), the "wild animals" (v. 22), and the "people of Zion" (v. 23) to "be glad" and to "rejoice in the Lord [their] God." The people of the covenant are to join in celebrating with the animal and vegetable kingdoms because the Lord is sovereign over all. Therefore, whatever else happens by way of calamities to these three entities, they all can endure because God has maintained (and will continue to do so) the messianic hope that is basic to everything else. To reinforce that promise, God declares that he will give them a "teacher for [i.e., who gives, or who acts in accordance with] righteousness."

This "teacher" must be the Messiah for several reasons. (1) The Hebrew text uses the definite article with "teacher"

---

wayyahmol ("and he had pity"), *wayya'an* ("and he answered"), and *wayyo'mer* ("and he said").

[7]See G. W. Ahlström, *Joel and the Temple Cult in Jerusalem* (Leiden: Brill, 1971), 107–9, who makes a strong case for the personal interpretation of *môreh*. Also see O. Sellers, "A Possible Old Testament Reference to the Teacher of Righteousness," *IEJ* 5 (1955): 93–101; J. Weingreen, "The Title Moreh Sedek," *JSS* 6 (1961): 169–75; C. Roth, "The Teacher of Righteousness and the Prophecy of Joel," *VT* 13 (1963): 91–95.

(*hammôreh*); Joel has a distinct person in mind. (2) The term *môreh*, which appears in the singular eight times in the Bible, is rendered "teacher" in all cases and is translated that way in several ancient versions: the Vulgate, the Targum, and the Greek translation of Symmachus.[8] (3) What clinches the identity of the Messiah as a teacher is the connection of the word "righteousness" with the preposition "to" or "for" (*lisdāqâ[h]*). God the Father will give to the people of Zion a teacher who is the personification of righteousness. As James Smith has noted, "Later prophets will refer to him as the righteous servant (Isa 53:11), and as one who will usher in everlasting righteousness (Dan 9:24)."[9] This term *righteousness* cannot be applied as a quality of "rain," for it is an ethical and moral term. In one OT passage, God himself is called the teacher, *môreh* (Job 36:22), but more frequently the function of teaching is connected with the priests (e.g., 2Ki 17:28; 2Ch 15:3).

The blessing of God in sending his Messiah as a teacher is again depicted in terms of the coming of rain and the fruitfulness of the land (Joel 2:23c). This verse is the only passage where *môreh* (its second appearance in this passage, now without the article) means "rain." The usual word for "rain" is *yôreh*); thus, the writer deliberately plays on the word *môreh* meaning "teacher" *and* "rain" to indicate that the coming of God's Teacher will signal, as one mark, the coming of the autumn and spring rains in their season: at least, that is what will come "at first" (*bāri'šôn*) (2:23d; pers. tr.). "And afterward" (*'aharê kēn;* 2:28 [3:1]) God will send a "downpour" (pers. tr.) of his "[Holy] Spirit" on his people "in those days" (2:29 [3:2]). Thus, rain is connected with the Messiah's role as teacher of

---

[8]Only in Psalm 84:6 does the KJV and the NIV render it "rain," but it could be rendered "teacher" there as well. The word *môreh* appears in the plural form seven times; four times it is rendered "archers" and three times "teachers." In none of the cases is it rendered "rain."

[9]James Smith, *What the Bible Teaches About the Promised Messiah* (Nashville: Thomas Nelson, 1993), 222.

his people, because rain is used metaphorically to describe the coming of divine righteousness on the land.

That same connection between rain and righteousness is seen in Psalm 72:5–7, for the Messiah is the One who gives life and produces the abundance of grain and fruit.[10] But his coming will also be linked (speaking of rain) with a mighty downpour of the Holy Spirit in the distant future. Pentecost, of course, signaled another earnest or down payment of that promise, but the mighty force of it still awaits a final enactment by God.

The Messiah, then, will be a teacher who introduces justice, righteousness, and prosperity of the soil by means of the coming of the rain that was withheld during the nation's disobedience and turning away from God. Again, there are both near (Joel 2:19–27) and distant (2:28–3:21) effects of what lies ahead for God's people. What teacher can compare to the teaching that the Messiah himself will give?

B. THE EIGHTH CENTURY: THE MESSIAH AS THE SECOND DAVID (HOSEA 3:4–5)

While Joel focuses on the role of Messiah as teacher, Hosea zeroes in on the Messiah's role as king, the one who will come in David's line, throne, dynasty, and kingdom. Hosea's marital problems become the basis of an object lesson whereby God instructs his people and all future generations on how he will provide for them. Subsequent to Hosea's marrying Gomer, she abandons him and the three children[11] she bore in order to

---

[10]Ibid., 224, notes how Jesus applied to himself Isaiah 54:13 in John 6:45. Smith also calls attention to the fact that Jesus was called a teacher by his disciples as well as his opponents (227–28). Of the sixty instances of the word *didaskalos* ("teacher") in the NT, thirty are directed to Jesus. John 1:38 equates the term "Rabbi" with *didaskalos* (all the Gospel writers except Luke refer to Jesus as "Rabbi").

[11]For a more extensive defense of the fact that all three children were fathered by Hosea and that his wife turned adulterous after they had been mar-

give herself over to sacred (pagan) or professional prostitution. After a long separation, God instructs the prophet to buy Gomer back, even though she has committed adultery and has given herself in prostitution to others. The prophet does just that (Hos 3:1): he pays a total of thirty shekels of silver for her (the going price of a slave, for Gomer is no longer of any use to those who have prostituted her body).[12]

Hosea is ordered to allow for a period of purification when Gomer returns to him in (3:3). That time becomes the basis for another messianic announcement in Hosea 3:4–5. In a similar manner,

> the Israelites will live many days without king or prince, without sacrifice or sacred stones, without ephod or idol. Afterward the Israelites will return and seek the LORD their God and David their king. They will come trembling to the LORD and to his blessings in the last days.

Just as Hosea could not overlook his wife's time of sowing wild oats, God cannot overlook the nation's apostasy and idolatry. The disobedient nation of Israel will live for many days without the advantage or security of a king, prince, sacrifices, or even the idolatrous forms of worship. That has been the case from the days that the northern kingdom was carried off in captivity in 722 B.C. by the Assyrians up to today. The prophet also seems to anticipate Israel's move to an almost overwhelmingly secular state of existence since the Babylonian exile, for it will not even have a stomach for idols in her new religionless state of being, much less for God and the ritual connected with his worship. Neither will Israel have a king, a prince, or the sacrifices that provided for her reconciliation to God.

---

ried for some time, see Walter C. Kaiser, Jr., chapter 62, "Go, Take to Yourself an Adulterous Wife," *Hard Sayings of the Old Testament* (Downers Grove, Ill.: InterVarsity Press, 1988), 216–19.

[12]Hosea 3:2 informs us that it was "fifteen shekels of silver" and a "homer and a lethek of barley," a commodity that many equate with being worth about another fifteen shekels of silver.

But that is not where things will end, for God will remember his covenant with Eve, Shem, Abraham, Isaac, Jacob, and David "in the last days"—a phrase repeatedly used to point to the eschatological times when Messiah arrives as King over all. Five specific aspects of the promise are made here. (1) The Messiah will return when Israel returns to their Lord. Only when they come "trembling to the LORD" with full repentance will he come in his second advent.

(2) The Messiah will be a descendant of David, for he is called "David their king" (v. 5). That is because he is the culmination of the Davidic line, the one promised to David in 2 Samuel 7, 1 Chronicles 17, and Psalm 89. He is David's greater son (Jer 30:9; Eze 34:23–24; 37:24–25).

(3) He will be a great king who will rule over those who fear him.

(4) The northern house of Israel that broke away from Judah after the days of Solomon will render allegiance to someone in the line of David, only he will be far greater than David ever was. They must return to the united kingdom that was split apart in 931 B.C. because God has promised the whole kingdom to David as an everlasting gift.

(5) Most preeminently, the Messiah is closely identified with Yahweh, yet at the same time distinguished from him. The Israelites will turn and "seek the LORD their God *and David their king*" (v. 5, italics added) in that future day. The reference must be to the new David, the Messiah. Thus, any return to God the Father likewise entails a returning to the Messiah, since he is uniquely linked with Yahweh. The prophet does not fully equate the human Messiah, the second David, with Yahweh, even though they are so closely linked that a returning to the one is thereby a returning to the other. The coming of this second David will take place in the latter days, the days of Messiah.

C. THE EIGHTH CENTURY: THE MESSIAH AS THE RAISED HOUSE OF DAVID (AMOS 9:11–15)

The prophet Amos also appeals to the ancient promise made to David as the basis for his teaching about the coming Messiah. In his prophecy, it is the restoration of David's "house" (2Sa 7:5, 11), viewed here as a "booth [NIV tent]" (*sukkâ*) that is in such a dilapidated state that it is "the one falling down" (the Hebrew participle with the definite article, *hannopelet*).[13] In other words, when the prosperity of David's family is spoken of, the phrase is "the house of David," but when its demise is indicated, the less dignified term "booth" is called for. A *booth* was a temporary shelter that each Israelite pilgrim "wove together" (the root meaning of the noun *sukkâ*) from branches at the time of the celebration of the Feast of Booths or Tabernacles, which commemorated their lives in the desert for forty years (Lev 23:40, 42; Dt 16:13). The present active participle stresses the fact that either its *present* state ("falling") or its *impending* state ("about to fall") indicates a demotion of the once glorious dynasty of David in the days of Amos.

But God says he will "raise up" or "restore" (*'āqîm*) what is currently falling (or is about to fall)—a verb often used at critical moments when God intervenes to demonstrate his glory and his salvation (e.g., in the messianic prophecy about "raising up" a prophet in Dt 18:15). The time when God raises up this messianic king will be "in that day" (*bayyôm hahû'*), an expression referring to the eschatological times that began in the New Testament era and will climax in the second coming of Christ.

The suffixes on the three expressions in Amos 9:11 are of special interest. If the Masoretic text is correct (and there is no

---

[13]See Walter C. Kaiser, Jr., "The Davidic Promise and the Inclusion of the Gentiles (Amos 9:9–15 and Acts 15:13–18): A Test Passage for Theological Systems," *JETS* 20 (1977): 97–111 now reprinted in idem, *The Uses of the Old Testament in the New* (Chicago: Moody Press, 1985), 177–94.

good reason to suspect it), then the suffixes on the phrase "*its broken places*" (*pirsêhen*, feminine plural suffix), "*its* ruins" (*harisōtāyw*, masculine singular suffix), and "build it" (*benîtîhā*, feminine singular suffix) are of major significance in interpreting this passage, in spite of the fact that almost all modern translations hesitate to render them accurately.

The feminine plural suffix must refer to the two kingdoms of northern and southern Israel that were divided since 931 B.C. until the present moment of this chapter. God will "wall up their rents" or divisions by bringing the northern ten tribes back into the fold of the Davidic kingship (this unification is later pictured by Ezekiel in Eze 37:15–28). In the days of the Messiah the nation will be restored as a single entity again—something that has not yet happened.

The masculine suffix must refer to David, not to his "hut" or "booth" (which is feminine). But David is dead; therefore, it must refer to that "second David," mentioned in Hosea 3:5. God will raise up from the ashes of "destruction"[14] the new David, even Christ, the Messiah.

Only after these two acts of reconstruction are discussed does the third clause appear. The verb "to build" may well mean here "to finish building, to carry on, enlarge, and beautify the building."[15] Naturally, the feminine suffix must refer to the "fallen booth." But it is also important to notice the phrase that completes this clause: "as it used to be," or "as it was in days of old." Here is one of the keys to the passage, for it points back to the promise of 2 Samuel 7:11, 12, 16, where God promised to raise up one of David's seed after him and give him a throne and a dynasty that would endure forever. Accordingly, the resurrecting of the dilapidated Davidic fortunes will involve a *kingdom*, a *seed*, and a *dynasty*.

---

[14]For this meaning of *harîsâ*, cf. Isaiah 49:19.

[15]C. F. Keil, *Biblical Commentary on the Old Testament: Minor Prophets* (Grand Rapids: Eerdmans, 1954), 1:330.

The purpose for God's raising up this fallen booth is clearly indicated: "so that *they* may possess the remnant of Edom, *even* all the nations that bear my name" (italics added; epexegetical "and" is translated here as "even"). The subject of the first clause is clearly the people. Therefore, what is decisively taught here is the fact that the people and a Gentile remnant are indissolubly linked together; one stands or falls with the other.

Can we be more precise who the people are and who the remnant is? The remnant is called "the remnant of Edom." This is not an offensive reference or even a retaliatory one. On the contrary, Edom, along with the other Gentile nations, will come under the reign of this coming Davidic King—the Messiah. This non-Jewish remnant must share in the covenant promise made to David and his people Israel!

Gerhard Hasel has pointed out that the remnant theme appears in Amos in three different ways: (1) "to refute the popular remnant expectation that claimed all of Israel as the remnant" (Am 3:12; 4:1–3; 5:3; 6:9–10; 9:1–4, all of which are bleak descriptions of doom with little hope for Israel); (2) "to show there will indeed be a remnant *from* within Israel" (5:4–6, 15, in an eschatological sense); and (3) "to include also the 'remnant of Edom' among, and with, the neighboring nations as a recipient of the outstanding promise of the Davidic tradition"[16] (9:12).

Edom, then, is singled out because of her marked hostility toward her blood relative, Israel, regarded here as the people of God. Edom's role is similar to that of the Amalekites, the earliest nation to represent those human kingdoms (Ex 17:8–16; Dt 25:17–19) who violently opposed God's kingdom. Moreover, Edom's representative role can be seen by the epexegetical clause that follows in verse 12: "and/even all the

---

[16]Gerhard Hasel, *The Remnant* (Berrien Springs, Mich.: Andrews University Press, 1972), 393–94.

nations [Gentiles] that bear my name." The point here is not about David's, or Israel's, subjugation of Edom or the Gentiles; instead, their spiritual incorporation into the restored kingdom of David is in view here. Indeed, that was the mediated promise God made to Abraham and David, that the "blessing" would come to the Gentiles as a result of God's using their off-spring as a channel.

Even the verb "to possess" is deliberately chosen, for it preserves the prophecy made by Balaam in Numbers 24:17–18. There it was predicted that a "star" and a "scepter" would arise (or be "raised up") in Israel "to take possession of Edom . . . while Israel did valiantly." This "one from Jacob would exercise dominion" over all (pers. tr.). He was the Messiah.

Amos's prediction is used by James at the Jerusalem Council to stop a squabble between Jewish and Gentile believers about who actually belong to the kingdom of God and who do not. James mentions that Peter has just related how God first visited the Gentiles "by taking from the Gentiles a people for himself" (Ac 15:14). But that action, James insists, is in precise agreement with what the prophets announced. He then quotes Amos 9:11–12, with its identical concept of "the Gentiles who bear my name."

Thus, what once was a dilapidated "booth" of David will one day mean the restoration and unification of the northern and southern kingdom into a single kingdom under the one house of David, but it will be a kingdom that incorporates both believing national Israel and believing Gentiles from all the world.

D. THE EIGHTH CENTURY: THE MESSIAH AS THE BREAKER (MICAH 2:12–13)

Micah ministered in the eighth century to the southern kingdom of Judah, though toward the end of that century. During his days as a messenger of God's revelation to his people, he saw the northern kingdom of Israel fall to the Assyrian conqueror Sargon (722 B.C.). Indeed, even his own country of Judah was later overrun by the Assyrian armies (701 B.C.), though a sudden intervention by God saved its citizens from Sennacherib's armies and from their becoming a similar casualty.

But none of these threats by the Assyrians, or by anyone else for that matter, will be the way that God concludes the history of the people to whom he has solemnly promised his provision of an Heir, the inheritance of the land, and the heritage of the good news that in Abraham's offspring all the nations of the earth will be blessed. God will answer all such invasions on his people by sending his royal scion from the house of David, who will ultimately have a kingdom that will rule over all without exception.

The book of Micah divides easily into three major blocks of material, each beginning with the call to "hear" or "listen": Micah 1:2–2:13; 3:1–5:15; and 6:1–7:20. The first section opens the series of proclamations with a declaration of God's judgment on his covenant people as a result of their unmitigated sin against him and his law.

Suddenly, like a bolt out of the blue, a word of hope is interjected into that series of declamations (Mic 2:12–13). Such an interruption of a series of denunciations is not unusual for the prophets, even though many modern scholars view these abrupt reversals in the prophetic flow as so intrusive that they do not belong to the original message of the prophet. However, this pattern is so common to Hebrew literary style and to the nature of OT revelation that the problem is with Western criteria of what should or should not be included in a writing, rather than from what is in the Semitic mentality. These two verses, then, paint a rosy-tinted picture of what God is going to do in the last days as his final answer to the failures and sins of the people. He will judge the sin on the current scene, but in no way will that sin ultimately frustrate his promise to carry out the provisions of his covenant. That decision will remain despite every failure in Israel.

Micah 2:12–13 focuses on two key participants in the messianic era: (1) the remnant of Israel, depicted as sheep in a pen waiting to be released to go out to pasture (v. 12), and (2) the "One who breaks open the way" out of the pen for his sheep (or, as other translations have it, the "Breaker"; v. 13).

(1) As for the first participant, we encounter a theme often found in the prophets, who refer to the work of regathering the nation of Israel so frequently that one cannot avoid the topic and still be faithful to their message. While this regathering may have had a number of fulfillments in the past (such as Jerusalem's deliverance from Sennacherib's siege or Judah's restoration from the Babylonian captivity), these are clearly only earnests or down payments on what God is going to do in the final day on a much larger and grander scale. Once again, then, there is a now and a not-yet aspect to God's work of fulfillment. Even more convincing is the fact that after the nation did return from Babylon under Zerubbabel in 536 B.C., the same promise about Israel's restoration from many distant lands is repeated by Zechariah in 518 B.C. (Zec 10:6–12). Thus, none of the previous returns can be what the prophets ultimately have in mind.

(2) The second participant enters the scene: this flock needs a leader, who will free his penned-up sheep. Thus the grand messianic aspect of this text is unveiled. Three titles are given to this leader. (a) He is the "Breaker," the "One who breaks open the way" (v. 13). The picture of the Breaker suggests a couple of pictures. If the sheep metaphor is being carried over, then the Breaker is the Good Shepherd who lies down in the doorway to the sheep pen to keep the sheep from straying outside and to prevent wild animals from coming in to harm them. When the time is right, he will open the passageway so that the sheep can break forth into the pastures. Or perhaps Micah is thinking of the Messiah as someone who will smash through the ranks of the besieging army that has surrounded the remnant of Israel. In that case, we have a picture of a conqueror—the Messiah, who will come and rescue his people.

(b) This Breaker was also known as "their king." The royal theme of the Messiah is again drawn to the foreground. Of course he has the right to be King since he created everything and is the Lord of the whole universe. By the phrase "their king," Micah is alluding to the ancient promise made to Judah, Balaam, and David.

(c) The third title used for this coming leader is Yahweh. The Hebrew parallelism of the lines and terms in verse 13 requires that the "king" and "the LORD" be regarded as one and the same person. Accordingly, not only will the Messiah be the Breaker who bursts the bands restricting his flock and a King who sovereignly exercises a universal dominion over everything, he will also be a divine person who will go before his people into battle ("at their head," v. 13c). In that sense the Messiah will be the liberator and champion of all who are oppressed, downtrodden, abused, hurt, and left defenseless. This person will himself personally take up the cause of his flock and lead the charge as he sets his people free. Then all God's sheep will "break through the gate and go out" (v. 13b), frolicking and gamboling like animals pent up all winter, awaiting the first day they can go out to pasture. The one who smashes through the gate and makes the release possible will be the Messiah.

E. THE EIGHTH CENTURY: THE MESSIAH AS THE COMING RULER (MICAH 5:1–4)

In many ways, the theology of and situations faced by Micah match those of his contemporary, Isaiah. This point is illustrated in his prophecy in chapter 5.

The messianic predictions of Micah that pyramid to the surprise announcement of a coming Ruler (5:1–4) mount up in three stages.[17] (1) Micah first envisions a day when the

---

[17]So argued Charles Briggs, *Messianic Prophecy*, 216–17.

mountain of the house of the Lord will be established above the highest mountains. This is in direct juxtaposition with his earlier prediction that Jerusalem will be a heap of ruins and the mountain of the house of God a forest (3:21), but that is not how things will remain.

(2) The tower of David that lost its ancient dominion will recover its former position. Micah 4:8 addresses the people of Micah's day at two sites: the "watchtower of the flock" (*migdal 'eder*) and the "stronghold [lit., Ophel] of the Daughter of Zion." The former alludes to Genesis 35:16–21, where the patriarch Jacob returned from burying his wife Rachel just north of Jerusalem to a place about a mile from Bethlehem called "Tower of the Flock."[18] If this identification is accurate, then the Tower of the Flock (Migdal Eder) refers to David's birthplace, marked by a tower out in the field among the flock where he once pastured. Ophel ("stronghold"), on the other hand, is the well-known acropolis on the eastern slope of the old city of Jerusalem (2Ki 5:24), the city also known as "the Daughter of Zion." Thus, both Bethlehem and Jerusalem are put on notice that their former dominion and prominence will be restored. Micah christens the Tower of the Flock as the emblem of the future kingdom for the new David who is to come. It will also be the symbol of the royal house of David, since he was a resident of Bethlehem and kept the flock there as well. Jerusalem will again turn to David's heir, at the same time as the nations of the earth turn to Jerusalem to worship the King.

(3) The greatest stage in this build-up of messianic promises will be achieved when the predicted Ruler comes from Bethlehem in that future day. At the same time as the prophet sees Zion in difficult straits, besieged and captured and her ruler treated shamefully, then the royal line of David will recommence its ancient rule and return to its original home.

---

[18]The church father Jerome, who lived in Bethlehem in the fourth century A.D., declared that Tower of the Flock was near to Bethlehem.

The description of sorrows begins in Micah 4:11, where the theme of many nations' being gathered together against the nation Israel parallels events often described as the final eschatological battle. That the nations will initiate that eschatological battle to settle the so-called "Jewish Question" appears in such passages as Ezekiel 38–39; Joel 3; and Zechariah 12 and 14. Micah notes the purpose of this international assembling of nations against small Israel: "Let her be defiled." It will be as if Israel were a virgin daughter whom the nations lustfully attempt to seize, only to hand her over to international genocide as the world stares insultingly at this outrage with little regard except that of a voyeur.

Zion is then told in Micah 5:1 to "marshal [her] troops," for their king will be insulted with a smarting slap across his cheek. The great day of the Lord is on. But whereas the final king of Judah will suffer such a humiliating and degrading insult, the world had better sit up and notice what God is going to do to make amends. Soon after Jerusalem has labored and her birth pangs have ended, God will give a son to the family of David from the ancient city of Ephrathah,[19] now known as Bethlehem. The ancient promises will be fulfilled.

Micah's prophecy of the Messiah affirms at least three things about him. (1) He will be an ancient Ruler, even though he arrives on the scene in times that are closer to our own day than Abraham's day. The clause, "his going forth is from the beginning" (or, as the NIV has it, "whose origins are from of old"), attests to the fact that he is eternal and not merely temporal. Modern translations and scholars are loathe to render *ûmôṣā'otâw miqqedem mîmê 'ôlām* straightforwardly as "whose going forth is from of old, [even] from the days of eternity." The Messiah only has two goings forth: one at the Incarnation

---

[19]Ephrathah was either the ancient name for Bethlehem (David's father was known as "an Ephrathite from Bethlehem in Judah," 1Sa 17:12; cf. Ge 35:19; 48:7; Ru 4:11) or the district in which Bethlehem was located.

and the other applied to his eternal generation. Since the temporal birth of the Messiah is still represented as being future to the time when this prophecy is given, the present clause must refer to his eternal generation. This, of course, harmonizes with other prophecies of the Messiah, where he is said to be God (Ps 2:7; 45:7; 110:3; Isa 9:6).

(2) This Ruler will be a unique person, for he will come forth "*for me.*" This new David will not only be a man after God's own heart in a way that even surpasses David, he will do absolutely everything that the Father wants him to do.

(3) His birth and coming will signal a new day for God's people (Mic 5:4). His birth will mark the end of the days of abandonment (v. 3). When the woman who is with child (a reference that parallels Isa 7:14) gives birth, that coming Ruler will bring unity to his people as he stands and rules in their midst. The nation can count on peace, security, and success after he is installed as king over both his "brothers" and all "the ends of the earth" (vv. 3–4).

The Messiah is the great Ruler who will come one day. According to his human heritage, he will descend from the family of David who lived in Bethlehem and will be born in that same town, even though he has a divine line of descent that takes him clear back to eternity. He will be both human and divine. What a mystery!

The Messiah in the Eighth-Century Prophets (Isaiah)

Isaiah is one of the most prolific announcers of the Messiah and his times among the OT prophets. Probably for this reason he has sometimes been called "the fifth Evangelist," along with Matthew, Mark, Luke, and John. According to some counts, the NT has over four hundred allusions to this book, and parts of forty-seven chapters of Isaiah's sixty-six are either directly quoted or alluded to in the NT. This means that Isaiah is second only to the book of Psalms as the favorite OT book from which the early church drew its predictions of what happened to Christ.

According to J. Alec Motyer, it is possible to organize the expansive description of the Messiah given by Isaiah under three basic portraits: (1) as King (Isa 7:10–15; 9:1–7; 11:1–16; 14:28–32; 24:21–25; 32:1–8; 33:17–24); (2) as Servant (42:1–4; 49:1–6; 50:4–9; 52:13–53:12); and (3) as anointed Conqueror (55:3–5; 61:1–6; 63:1–6).[1] To these fifteen passages

---

[1]J. Alec Motyer, *The Prophecy of Isaiah: An Introduction and Commentary* (Downers Grove, Ill.: InterVarsity Press, 1993), 3–16.

must be added 4:2 (as "Branch"), 28:16 (as "Foundation Stone"), and 30:19–26 (as "Teacher").

In this chapter, we will treat thirteen of these eighteen texts as direct references to the Messiah and his times, under the three rubrics suggested by Motyer.

A. THE MESSIAH AS KING

It is impossible to avoid the regal theme of the Messiah, for since its first appearance in the promise given to Judah, it reappears with high frequency over the centuries. But in Isaiah it comes into full flower as various facets of the royal motif of the Coming One are described.

1. The Branch of the Lord (Isaiah 4:2)

The title "branch" or "shoot/sprout of the LORD" is one of the most beautiful descriptions of the Messiah in the OT. This botanical figure of speech probably had its origins in 2 Samuel 23:5, where David uttered these sentiments as part of his last words:

> Is not my house right [or: established] with God?
>> Has he not made with me an everlasting covenant,
>> arranged and secured in every part?
> Will he not bring to fruition [or: cause to sprout, branch out,
>> shoot] my salvation
>> and grant me my every desire?

What was a verb in David's last words, "bring to fruition/sprout/branch out," now in Isaiah becomes a proper noun and a designation for the Messiah.

Three prophets exhibit four marvelous pictures of the Branch—pictures that are often likened to the emphases given to Jesus the Messiah in the four Gospels.[2] They are as follows:

---

[2]See David Baron, *Rays of Messiah's Glory: Christ in the Old Testament* (1886; reprint, Grand Rapids: Zondervan, n.d.), 71–128.

The Branch of *David*: Jeremiah 23:5–6 (likened to
  Matthew's presentation of Jesus as the Davidic Messiah [Mt 1:1])
My *servant*, the Branch: Zechariah 3:8 (likened to Mark's
  presentation of Jesus as the Servant [Mk 10:45])
The *man* whose name is the Branch: Zechariah 6:12
  (likened to Luke's presentation of Jesus in his manly
  and human aspects [Lk 23:47])
The Branch *of the Lord*: Isaiah 4:2 (likened to John's presentation of Jesus as from God [Jn 20:31])

Whereas the first three of these Branch passages focus on the
royal, servant, or human aspects of the Messiah's character,
Isaiah highlights his deity.

The reason that a divine character is called for in Isaiah
4:2 is clear from the context. The prophet has declared that Israel must be cleansed from her sin and have the stains of that
guilt washed away (Isa 2:5–4:1; 4:3–4). But who can forgive sin
but God alone? Thus, even though the Messiah may be the Son
of David, he must be the Son of God if he is to deliver humanity from the bondage of sin. Therefore, it is important to note
that the genitival relationship expressed by the word *of* denotes
source or origin: He is the Branch that came *from* Yahweh.

But the Messiah's humanity is also included in Isaiah's description, for under a second botanical figure, he declares that
the Messiah is from "the fruit of the land" (Isa 4:2b). This expression is no doubt borrowed from Numbers 13:26 and
Deuteronomy 1:25, where the spies returned with some of "the
fruit of the land." Thus, the Messiah will come, in one sense
(i.e., according to his human descent), from the land of
Canaan, just as the samples of the fruit came from there. Hebrews 7:14 later declares that "he descended/sprang forth out
of Judah." Since he is also from God, he is thus divine at one
and the same time.

For Isaiah the coming of the Branch will be regarded as:
(1) "beautiful," because of his character and life, (2) "glorious,"

because all that any people ever had to boast about is this one in whom everything has its completion, and (3) a moment for "pride," because by comparison, everything else is only "rubbish" (Php 3:7–8). The Branch's subjects will be those who have escaped the judgment of God and who form the remnant of Israel (Isa 4:2c-3). The Lord counts them as holy (v. 3), for they have their sins forgiven and their guilt removed.

In the same day when the Branch returns, his judgment and fires of wrath will purge the land of its bloodshed, violence, and accumulated sin (v. 4). Then it will be possible for him to set up his personal protective presence as a shelter and refuge for his people. Indeed, his presence will act as a canopy over those assembled on his holy mountain of Zion to worship him, just as he sent the cloud by day and the pillar of fire by night when the Israelites were moving through the desert.

As divine Lord, he is at once the King of kings and Lord of lords. No one else can compare to him.

2. The Virgin Birth (Isaiah 7:1–16)

Mastering the occasion of this messianic prophecy is important for understanding the uniqueness of this word from God. The occasion begins with an alliance between Rezin, king of Aram (i.e., Syria), and Pekah, king of Samaria (i.e., the northern ten tribes of Israel). They have marched against Judah with every intention of overthrowing her, deposing the house of David, and setting up "the son of Tabeel" (Isa 7:6) in place of the former Davidic line. All this is in retaliation for Judah's refusal to join their alliance against the Assyrian menace.[3]

It is no wonder, then, that so much is on the line, for were Pekah and Rezin successful, everything that God incorporated into his ancient covenant with Israel would be lost—not to

---

[3]For a more elaborate discussion of this passage, see Walter C. Kaiser, Jr., "The Promise of Isaiah 7:14 and the Single-Meaning Hermeneutic," *Evangelical Journal* 6 (1988): 55–70.

speak of the cancellation of the impending events of Christmas and Easter. That is why verses 2, 13, and 17 address the whole "house of David." King Ahaz, the current ruler on the throne of David, is more than a pawn in a game that has high theological stakes: He embodies all that God is presently doing to fulfill his promise and all that God will do in the future for the whole world!

In the midst of this national crisis, God directs Isaiah to go with his son Shear-Jashub (meaning "a remnant will return"), to meet the Judean King Ahaz as the king inspects the water reserves to determine how long he can last in what certainly will be a siege of Jerusalem. God's word to Ahaz is, "If you do not stand firm in your faith, you will not stand at all" (Isa 7:9b). Furthermore, the prophet invites Ahaz to ask God for a "sign,"[4] i.e., a "miracle," either from heaven or earth (v. 11). But Ahaz, depending more on his alleged savvy as an international politician, protests that such a request will "put [God] to the test" and tempt him (v. 12)—a deed that he claims the Bible forbids him to exercise (presumably Dt 6:16). It makes no difference to him that God himself is the one inviting him to prove that he will maintain his ancient promise regardless of the circumstances. The truth of the matter is that Ahaz has probably already sent off messengers to the king of Assyria with tribute and a request to put pressure on the two kings allied against him.

In spite of that reluctance, Isaiah proceeds with the sign the Lord himself has given, which indicates that the Lord will deliver Ahaz in spite of the fact that the present house of David does not merit any consideration, much less a divine prophecy or a miracle.[5]

---

[4]A sign might be a predictive word about the future or a miracle, as it is in Ex 4:8–9; 7:8–12; Dt 13:2–5; Jdg 6:36–40; 2Ki 20:8–11; Isa 38:7.

[5]Some have incorrectly conjectured that a period of time elapses between the encouragement of Isa 7:9b and the words that followed in 7:10–14, but the verb yôsep (in the Hiphil form of the verb "to add") marks the pericopes as being together without a break.

Isaiah 7:14 begins with a "therefore" (Heb. *lālēn*), indicating that what precedes is the reason for what follows. That is, the divine word is not separate from what has triggered it in this episode:—both externally and internally. Isaiah begins: "The Lord [*Adonai*, the name signifying that Yahweh is Lord and master over all] himself will give you [Ahaz; "you" is plural, since it refers to the whole house of David; cf. NIV note] a sign," even though he refused to request it in his unbelief: "Behold [untranslated in NIV, but a term that calls special attention to a particular fact] the virgin [Heb. *hā'almâ* "will be with child and will give birth to a son, and will call him Immanuel [i.e., God with us]."

The word *hā'almâ* ("the virgin") has caused much debate. The Septuagint (as did Mt 1:23) chose the Greek noun *parthenos*, a word that has the specific meaning of "virgin." When all the passages in the OT with *'almâ* are investigated, the only conclusion one can arrive at is that it means a "virgin" here.[6] To date, no one has produced a clear context, either in Hebrew or in the closely related Canaanite language from Ugarit (which uses the cognate *ǵlmt*), where *'almâ* can be applied to a married woman. Moreover, the definite article on this word does speak not of any virgin, but of "*the* virgin"—a special one whom God has in mind. Given the frequency with which OT and NT prophecy have both a now and a not-yet aspect to their predictions, Ahaz is granted evidence of this sign in his own day, even though the full impact of all that God has in mind will not be realized until the Messiah himself is born in a unique manner in fulfillment of this passage.

What is the near fulfillment? Simply this: Hezekiah, Ahaz's son and the next in the Davidic line, is born not long

---

[6]*'almâ* is used of Rebekah (Ge 24:16, 43), Miriam (Ex 2:8), and of the way of a man with a maiden/virgin (Pr 30:19); but it also appears in the plural form in Song of Songs 1:3; 6:8; also Ps 46:1; 68:26[25]; 1Ch 15:20. Thus, the word appears nine times; four times in the singular and five times in the plural form.

after this prophecy. But this interpretation raises at least two objections. (1) Hezekiah's birth was not as a result of a virgin birth. That is true, of course, but emphasizing this misunderstands the connection that usually exists between the near and distant fulfillments of a prophecy. Rarely does the near event meet most, much less all, the details and expectations that the ultimate event completes. For example, five prophets in four different centuries declare that the crisis they are undergoing is in fact the "day of the LORD"; yet that in no way embraces all that God will do in his final day of judgment.[7] Nor do any of the "antichrists" that have already appeared in history (note the plural in 1Jn 2:18) depict in a full measure what that final "antichrist" will be like in all of his fury! Likewise, John the Baptist only exhibits the "spirit and the power" (Lk 1:17) of Elijah, the prophet who is to come before the great and notable day of the Lord (Mal 4:5).

(2) Others insist that Hezekiah is about ten years of age when Isaiah gives this prediction; but that overstates the case. In fact, the one remaining problem in the chronology of the kings of Israel and Judah, along with all their synchronisms between the two kingdoms, is a ten-year problem during the life and reign of Hezekiah. We believe that that can be accounted for in this prophecy as well as by a reexamination of the date for the Syro-Ephraimite War.[8]

Therefore, as the Syrian and northern Israelite kings threaten to destroy the Davidic royal line in order to place the son of Tabeel (a name distorted, no doubt, by the prophet from something like Tabel or Tabiel, "[my] God is good," to Tabeel, meaning approximately, "good-for-nothing") on the throne, God announces the next installment of that son of David who will continue the promise until the ultimate Davidic son

---

[7]That is, in no way does Joel's locust plague, Isaiah's Assyrian threat, or Jeremiah's fall of Jerusalem exhaust all that God plans to do in the last day.

[8]For suggestions on the revision of this date, see my article, "The Promise of Isaiah 7:14."

comes. And before Hezekiah is old enough to know right from wrong (the age of accountability?), both kings harassing the house of David will be removed. If that is the marker for the near fulfillment, much more awaits God's ultimate work: the sign value of a virgin birth still to take place in times "not yet" known to any mortals.

Furthermore, Isaiah 7:15–17 cannot be separated from 7:14, as some have attempted to maintain, for everything in the context demands that the description of this son continue throughout the so-called "Book of Immanuel" (7:1–12:6).

In conclusion, we are once again confronted with another insight into God's coming Davidic king who will rule over all. Not only will his birth be a miraculous sign; even his name will indicate an altogether different kind of king than has ever been known before: He will be Immanuel–"God with us."

3. The Wonderful Ruling Son (Isaiah 9:1–7)

The context for this announcement is still the same as in Isaiah 7:1–16: the Syro-Ephraimite threats of extinction against the Davidic dynasty. But the gloom and distress that this day, and all similar challenges, have signaled will come to an end; yes, even Zebulun and Naphtali, the two northern parts of Israel that were always the first to be exposed to invasion, will rejoice because of the great light rising over the land. In place of the gloom and distress will one day come great joy (9:3).

Isaiah gives three separate reasons for rejoicing, with the third one being the most powerful of all. These reasons form the heart of this messianic passage. (1) The nation will be delivered from the oppressor by God's hand, just as God delivered Gideon from the Midianites in days long ago (v. 4). Each oppressor down through history (the Assyrians of that day, or the Babylonians, the Persians, the Greeks, and the Romans of the future), used the rod or staff on the shoulders of this oppressed nation of Israel. But that will be shattered in the messianic era.

(2) The age of Messiah will be characterized by a lasting universal peace (v. 5). No longer will the government have to issue military uniforms, nor will the paraphernalia of war be needed. All remembrances of war can be tossed into the fire, for they will be useless and outmoded.

(3) The best reason of all for rejoicing before the Lord is that a new leader will be born. This child will have earthly or human origins, for he will be "*born*" to oppressed Israel. And he would be a *male* child, "a son," just as God promised Eve, the patriarchs, and David. The persons who will benefit from his birth are the people of God: "*us*" (v. 6).

The significance, dignity, and importance of this child and his birth continues to increase with each new word in verses 6–7. This child will be a *king*, for the "government" will rest on his shoulders. This government, contrary to all earthly governments, will *never end*. And it will be a rule of perfect and complete "*peace*"—a marvel unequaled in history. The most startling aspect of the child's incomparable greatness is in his *titles*. Since names in the OT designate a person's character or nature, it is no wonder that when the meaning of these names is understood, they confer such superiority and excellence to this coming child that no other child in history can ever compare with him. Four names are cited: "Wonderful Counselor," "Mighty God," "Everlasting Father," and "Prince of Peace."

(1) The Hebrew root for the word *wonderful* is *pele'*, meaning "one who does difficult, hard, or even miraculous things" (cf. Ge 18:14a; Jer 32:17). Nothing will be too difficult for the coming Messiah. One aspect where his working of hard or miraculous things is evident is the area of his wisdom or "counsel." "The Spirit of wisdom" will rest on the Messiah (Isa 11:2).

(2) This child is also the "Mighty God." If his birth indicates his human descent, this title indicates his divine nature. Accordingly, just as his first title stresses the wonder of his wisdom and counsel, this title stresses his might and power.

(3) He will also be known as the "Everlasting Father." Here the mystery of the Godhead stretches our human understanding almost to the breaking point. This newborn child is not only eternal, with an existence that never had a beginning, but he is also addressed as "Father." The term *Father* is regularly used to address Yahweh and to denote his relationship to his people. Thus, the one who will arrive later is one who has been here from the beginning of time and more! He is also the one who has brought into existence the very people he calls to himself.

(4) Finally, the child is the "Prince of Peace." His rule and reign will be marked by both the absence of war and hostilities and by every blessing that accompanies times of peace.

One can expect that his government will increase continually (v. 7). In fact, the kingdom he sets up will never be destroyed. The throne he occupies will be "[David's] throne" (2Sa 7:16), and he will rule over David's "kingdom" (v. 7c; 2Sa 7:13, 16). Thus, everything promised to David will be fulfilled in this coming scion of David.

4. The Reign of Jesse's Son (Isaiah 11:1–16)

Unfortunately, the stately tree of the Davidic dynasty will be cut down while the world waits for the Messiah to arrive, leaving for the time being only the "stump" of the original dynasty (Isa 11:1). The reference to the cutting down and the stump may have been to King Ahaz himself. But that is not how things will end, for a "shoot" (or a twig or small branch; Heb. *ḥōṭer*) will come forth from what appears to be a dead stump. That is because Yahweh is the one who has planted the tree and who has not forsaken it even when the tree cut itself off from the Lord. God's covenant is an unconditional and unilateral covenant that he himself promised to Abraham, Judah, and David. The shoot who will come forth from this cut-down stump will be the son of the virgin named Immanuel (7:14), even the child whose titles are "Wonderful Counselor, Mighty God, Everlasting Father, Prince of Peace."

The Davidic descendant will succeed in his tasks because he will be endowed with the Spirit of Yahweh (Isa 11:2). This will not be a temporary endowment on the Messiah, but the very presence of God himself in his life. This abiding work of the Spirit in his life qualifies him for his messianic mission as both the Son of God and the son of David.

Isaiah notes three pairs of gifts for this shoot. (1) He will have the intellectual gifts of wisdom and understanding. He will know what decisions to make and his appraisal of all situations will be correct. (2) He will have administrative gifts. Rather than attaching to his government a string of advisors and handlers, he will not need such services. He can formulate his own plans for the future and has the power and authority to make them happen and to bring them into fruition. (3) He will possess spiritual gifts. Just as Proverbs 1:7 declares that the "fear of the LORD" is the basis for all knowledge, so this coming son of David will demonstrate the heart of all knowledge of God and all other things. He will be rightly related to God the Father. And any knowledge worth knowing will begin with a knowledge of God. These three sets of attributes are given to the Messiah to indicate to us that he knows how to carry out so massive and so impressive a rule and reign.

Verses 3–5 describe the Messiah's regal conduct. Negatively, he will not make decisions on the basis of what he sees or hears; instead, he will demonstrate true piety and skill as he renders his decisions according to the standard of righteousness and justice. No mortal has yet been able to render perfect justice, but the Messiah will be able to; and he will demonstrate it before all peoples as he champions the cause of the poor and the oppressed. Moreover, he will spill his wrath over on the wicked as they are dealt the stinging blow of his judgments. Just one word from his mouth will be enough to slay them. Thus, there will be no pulling back from dealing with evil and no opposition to his government. The armor he uses will be this: righteousness/fairness as his belt, and faithfulness/consistency as the sash around his waist (v. 5). He will be called "Faithful" and "True," and he will make war and render judgment in righteousness/fairness (see Rev 19:11).

Isaiah then describes the realm over which Messiah will reign (vv. 6–9). It will be a peaceable kingdom, in which nothing will "harm nor destroy on all my holy mountain" (v. 9). Not only will hostility between mortals be eliminated, but nature itself will be transformed as the wolf, leopard, calf, lion, cow, and bear lie down together with a little child playing alongside them; indeed, the infant will even play with what were formerly deadly serpents and not be harmed.

Finally, Isaiah depicts the coming reign of the Messiah (vv. 10–16). Clearly, it will be a universal reign that embraces all the nations. The old stump, with what many thought were dead roots, will be a banner or an ensign to the nations. In fact, in that day, the northern ten tribes (Ephraim) will no longer be jealous and opposed to Judah, nor will Judah be hostile to Ephraim (v. 13). Thus, the ancient schism between the two nations that has existed since 931 B.C. will be dropped and replaced by fraternal relations and a reunited people.

God will reassemble his people Israel "from the four quarters of the earth" (v. 12). This will be the second great exodus that all the prophets have been talking about as Jews return from Assyria, Ethiopia, Egypt, Iran, Iraq, Syria, Lebanon, and the far-flung countries of the earth (routinely called in Isaiah, "the islands of the sea"; v. 11b). How will Israel fare against her traditional enemies in that messianic era? Concertedly, Israel will swoop down over the Gaza Strip (ancient Philistia; v. 14a) and will also subjugate the people to the east of their nation (presumably those in the Golan Heights; v. 14b). They will also lay hands on the ancient territory of Edom, Moab, and Ammon. And God will make a path through the Euphrates River, just as he dried up the "gulf" (or tongue) of the Egyptian Sea (i.e., Red Sea) during the first exodus to allow his people to return to their homeland (v. 15). The end of the matter will be mind-boggling, for with a highway now between Israel, Egypt, and Iraq, the remnant of the three nations will come together to worship the Lord as one people (v. 16)!

5. The Universal Triumph of Messiah
(Isaiah 24:21–25)

The cycle of prophecies that begin with chapter 24 and extend to chapter 27 have few parallels in the OT. Only Zechariah 9–14 comes close to equaling the eschatological and apocalyptic nature of the subjects found here and the treatment given to them. After taking their rise in the sharply defined historical circumstances of Isaiah 13–23, these vanish as the prophet lays hold of the radical idea that carries out the implications of God's work far beyond any outward historical enactments seen up to that time or ours. Thus, the historical forms are mere emblems of the events of those far off days of the Messiah's rule and reign. Any and all individual judgments predicted of the nations in chapters 13–23 flow into the last judgment; and any salvation and deliverances seen in piecemeal fashion in history are now concentrated *en masse*. Thus, what a finale does for a piece of music, so chapters 24–27 do for the scattered themes mentioned in chapters 13–23, as it brings everything into a grand climax.

First, there is an announcement of a future global judgment (Isa 24:1–3); it will extend everywhere without religious, social, or economic distinctions. Next, verses 4–6 explain that all the earth, its inhabitants, and especially the proud, the haughty, and the aristocracy, will be affected by this coming judgment of God. The reasons are clear: humanity has transgressed God's law, changed his statutes, and attempted to frustrate his everlasting covenant, but these efforts will be judged.

The earth will be cursed, the population reduced, and only a remnant will remain (v. 6).

The enactment of this prediction of a universal upheaval on earth is described in verses 14–23. First is universal praise for the majesty and glory of the Lord (vv. 14–16a). This is followed by a description of how inescapable, global, and real the judgment of God will be as the earth breaks apart, splits asunder, totters, trembles, and rocks back and forth like a drunkard (vv. 17–20). It will be so dramatic that it leaves the prophet reeling in his own mind (v. 16b).

The grandest part of this awesome prophecy is 24:21–23, which declares that the "LORD Almighty will reign on Mount Zion and in Jerusalem, and before its elders, gloriously" (v. 23). This person can be no one else but the Messiah, for he is described elsewhere as ruling and reigning on Mount Zion in Jerusalem (see 2:1–4; Mic 4:1–4).

The time of this reign is also given, for it is "in that day" when Yahweh "will punish the powers in the heavens above and the kings on the earth below" (v. 21a). That will be the day when God executes his judgment against the unrighteousness of all kings, governors, justices, and mortals in his second advent.

"The powers in the heavens" is probably an allusion to Satan and all his supernatural hordes, for they "will be herded together like prisoners bound in a dungeon," where they "will be shut up in prison" (v. 22b). Evil will finally be contained and sealed off from its former freedom to effect its will.

However, "after many days," these powers of heaven and their leader will "be released" (v. 22c; cf. NIV note). The verb we have translated "released" is *pāqad*, a verb that sometimes means "visited" or "punished." The context here, however, favors "released." If this rendering is correct, we have here an early anticipation of Revelation 20:2–3, 7–10.

> [The angel] seized the dragon, that ancient serpent, who is the devil, or Satan, and bound him for a thousand years.

He threw him into the Abyss, and locked and sealed it over him, to keep him from deceiving the nations any more until the thousand years were ended. After that, he must be set free for a short time. . . .

When the thousand years are over, Satan will be released from his prison and he will go out to deceive the nations in the four corners of the earth . . . to gather them for battle. . . . But fire came down from heaven and devoured them. And the devil, who deceived them, was thrown into the lake of burning sulfur . . . [to] be tormented day and night for ever and ever.

Accordingly, what Isaiah only knows as "many days," John on the island of Patmos gives in more detailed revelation as a "thousand years." Both, however, know that these evil hordes will be bound in prison before they are released in the final day of the Lord. That will also be a day, according to Isaiah, when great cosmic convulsions will accompany the forthcoming reign of the Messiah. The moon will be abashed and the sun ashamed of shining in that terrible day of God's judgment and appearance (Isa 24:23a). But the Lord God, in the second person of the Trinity, will come as the earth's final Messiah, and he will reign gloriously over all the earth.

6. The Foundation Stone (Isaiah 28:16)

In this fifth section of the book of Isaiah (chs. 28–33, the so-called Book of Woes), the messianic prophecy of the tested and precious cornerstone dominates. The first of the six woes is addressed to Ephraim because of her two sins: drunkenness and mockery of the messengers who bring God's word to the people. Since the people of Samaria are so high and mighty that they no longer listen to God's word, they can be spoken to through the Assyrian conqueror, whose language they do not comprehend (v. 11). In the meantime, the northern kingdom continues to mock the repeated message of the prophets as the drunkards of Israel demean God's message with their slurred aping of what they think the prophets are saying: "Watch your p's and q's, your p's and q's; here a little, there a little,"[9] they jeer amidst their hiccups.

Rather than trusting in God, their leaders have taught them to trust in a security pact negotiated with Assyria or Egypt (v. 15). But such confidence and assurances are misplaced and devoid of any real protection, for they bypass the great promise-plan of God.

This plan is introduced in verse 16 with a "therefore" (Heb. *lākēn*). The insubstantial alliances and schemes of mortals are tissue-paper thin in comparison to what the "Sovereign LORD" designed to do long ago in his covenant with the patriarchs and David. That plan is introduced with "See" (or "Behold"; Heb. *hinnê*), just as Isaiah introduced the shocking announcement of Isaiah 7:14. However, this word has the personal pronoun "I" attached to it here, even though the verb has a third person pronoun attached to its "perfect" tense. Consequently, the thrust of the action is: "Behold: I am the He/The One who has founded/established in Zion a tested stone, a precious cornerstone for a sure foundation" (pers. tr.). In God's eyes that Stone/Rock has already been laid even at the time that Isaiah is writing, for what God has devised to do long before the earth was founded will indeed take place, regardless of what mortals do or do not do.

The figure of a stone or rock as a messianic title has had a long history of use in Israel by Isaiah's time. For example, when Jacob blessed his son Joseph, he referred to "the Mighty One of Jacob" as the "Rock/Stone of Israel" (Ge 49:24). Like-

---

[9] The usual translation fails to capture the fact that the words here are not *do* and *do*, *rule* and *rule* (NIV), or the KJV, "Line upon line, rule upon rule"; instead, it is the Hebrew abbreviation for the Hebrew letters *ṣade* and *qôp*, each followed by *waw*, presumably with the abbreviation marker (") between them. They function, then, just as we say, "Watch your p's and q's [i.e., your pints and quarts]." All of this is said as they reel forward and backward and then fall over after covering the table with vomit from their excessive drinking (vv. 8, 13c).

wise, Moses frequently referred to his Lord as his "Rock" (Dt 32:4, 15, 18, 31). And even Isaiah used this same designation of the Lord earlier in his book, when he referred to him as "a stone that causes men to stumble and a rock that makes them fall" (Isa 8:14).

But whereas the Stone was God in the above passages, here in Isaiah 28:16 it is separate from him, for the Father is the one who lays the Stone in Zion.[10] There is no doubt about who the NT church thought that Stone/Rock is: He is the Messiah, Jesus Christ.

Several descriptions are given of this Stone. (1) He is a "tested stone." He can be trusted, for he has been tested and approved by God. While some, like the builders of the temple, have rejected this stone and set it off to one side (Ps 118:22), and while others have stumbled over it (Isa 8:14; cf. 1Pe 2:8), yet this is the Stone God has chosen to be both the "capstone/keystone" (Ps 118:22) and the "foundation" stone (here in Isa 28:16).

(2) This Stone is also "precious," for it is valuable and has the same value that precious stones have today. What makes this Stone so costly is what it cost God to put this Stone in place for us. The Stone as God's Son must first temporarily empty himself of his glory, come to this earth, and die for us (cf. Php 2:6–8) before his value can be fully realized.

(3) Finally, this Stone is the "cornerstone" or "foundation stone" that ties the building together. That is why it makes such "a sure foundation" (v. 16c). It cannot be wiggled back and forth; it is immovable and secure. And all who believe in this Stone by accepting him as their Messiah "will never be dismayed" (v. 16d). He will prove himself dependable, reliable, trustworthy, and foundational for everything else in life!

---

[10]Notice the various places where the Stone is referred to in the Bible: Ps 118:22–23; Da 2:35, 45; Mt 21:42; Eph 2:19–22; 1Pe 2:6–8.

7. The Messiah As Teacher (Isaiah 30:19–26)

In the midst of the threatened judgment to be administered by the Assyrians as the third woe pronounced over this obstinate nation (Isa 30:1), the word of God's grace comes about Israel's "Teacher," who will be available for those who dwell in Zion (30:19–20). It is true that the NIV translates the word in 30:20 as "your teachers" (Heb. *môrêkā,* a plural), but the verb it agrees with is singular: "*he* will be hidden"! This suggests that the noun *môreh* is the plural of majesty or excellence. In that case, the "Teacher" is God's Messiah, not human teachers who instruct the people. When Israel calls for help, God will answer them. No longer will that nation be served "the bread of adversity and the water of affliction." Her Teacher will "be hidden [from her] no more" (v. 20). This prophecy, then, is similar to and parallel to the provisions given in Joel 2:23.

One day this Teacher will come and be visible so that everyone can see him (v. 20c). He will teach his people how they are to live: "This is the way; walk in it" (v. 21c). How the nation can see him with their own eyes and yet hear his voice behind them is problematic. Perhaps the point is that after a period of seeing him, he will be gone, yet his voice will still be heard through the teaching he leaves behind. Under the tutelage of this Teacher all idolatry will be abandoned and disposed of like filthy rags from another time (v. 22c).

Similar to the promise in Joel 2:23, this messianic Teacher will dispense gifts, such as "rain for the seed you sow" and "food that comes from the land" (v. 23). Paradisal conditions will prevail in that day. But these benefits will only come about after a day of war and great slaughter (v. 25b). What event Isaiah has in mind cannot be determined here, but it no doubt harmonizes with the great judgment to fall on all the unrighteous in the final day.

The final day of the Teacher will be a day of unusual brightness, for "the moon will shine like the sun, and the sunlight will be seven times brighter, like the light of seven full days, when the LORD binds up the bruises of his people and heals the wounds he inflicted" (v. 26). Thus, the Teacher will also be the Healer of the wounds accumulated in Israel's history.

B. THE MESSIAH AS SERVANT

The dominant figure of Isaiah 40–53 is the "servant of the Lord." Up to chapter 53, the term *servant* occurs twenty times in the singular. Thereafter it appears eleven more times as "servants."

The question of the identity of this servant has always been perplexing. It is clear that God's servant is often the nation of Israel (twelve instances in eight verses: Isa 41:8–10; 44:1–3, 21; 45:4). But it is just as certain that the servant is an individual who has a mission to Israel and the nations (42:1–4; 49:1–7). When all these passages are put together, that individual turns out to be the Messiah. Therefore, the Servant is best identified as John Bright has noted:

> The figure of the Servant oscillates between the individual and the group. . . . He is the coming Redeemer of the true Israel who in his suffering makes the fulfillment of Israel's task possible; he is the central actor in the "new thing" that is about to take place.[11]

It is in light of the Servant's identification as a single individual who has a ministry and mission to Israel and the world that we will investigate the four messianic passages that follow—often referred to as the four "Servant songs."[12]

---

[11]John Bright, *The Kingdom of God* (Nashville: Abingdon, 1953), 150–51.
[12]See Henri Blocher, *Songs of the Servant* (London: Inter-Varsity, 1975), and F. Duane Lindsey, *A Study in Isaiah: The Servant Songs* (Chicago: Moody, 1985).

1. The Servant's Ministry (Isaiah 42:1–7)

John Calvin noted that whenever the prophets mention something that is hard to believe (such as the prediction just given in Isa 41 about God's raising up the man from the east [King Cyrus of Medo-Persia] as his servant), they often immediately follow with a promise about Christ, since in him all the promises are ratified (2Co 1:20).[13] Thus, Isaiah breaks off his prediction about the man coming from the east and interjects a new word with his attention-getting term in 42:1 (NASB): "Behold" (Heb. *hēn*).

The prophet first introduces us to the special relationship that this "servant of the LORD" has with the Father: he is "my servant" (Isa 42:1a), a designation that marks his willingness to carry out the Father's will and one that we later learn he voluntarily takes upon himself. His second title is "my chosen one" (v. 1b), indicating that he is accepted by God for a special purpose. He will be endowed with God's Spirit in order to carry out an absolute rule for all that God assigns him to do (v. 1c).

Likewise, his manner will be extraordinary. He will be a gentle, quiet, humble servant, without the pomp and loud bragging that go with human conquerors (v. 2). There will be no proclamation of his miracles and accomplishments in the streets, nor will he seek his own will. Instead, he will support the weak and feeble and save those who are not obstinate and bold. The bruised he will not abuse by breaking them off, as one breaks off a bruised reed. And those who are like smoking wicks he will trim, but he will not snuff them out (v. 3).

The Messiah will soothe and uphold the weak without falling into the excesses of encouraging evil with smooth words or using excessive severity to crush those already weak. His goal will be to establish the rule and kingdom of God on the

---

[13]John Calvin, *Calvin's Commentaries: Isaiah* (Grand Rapids: Associated Publishers, n.d.), 566.

earth (v. 4). The standard he will use to bring about his kingdom and rule will be his truth (v. 3c). "His law" will be what the nations of the world must come to terms with if they are going to participate in that kingdom (v. 4c).

In bringing all this about, his zeal will not flag or falter, nor will his strength suddenly abate. For God has called him in righteousness and given to him the necessary power to perform his task (v. 6a-b). God's plan is to appoint his servant "a covenant [belonging to] ... the people" (v. 6c) and as a "light for the Gentiles" (v. 6d). Thus, all the blessings of the covenant are resident in the Messiah, just as the salvation God wants the Gentiles to receive is also in him. He will open the eyes of the blind and set the captives in the dark prison houses free (v. 7). He is God's Servant *par excellence.*

2. The Servant's Mission to the World (Isaiah 49:1–6)

Isaiah now speaks about one who has been sent and who demands to be listened to (v. 1). This person is neither the prophet nor Yahweh, but One whom Yahweh calls from the womb and whose name Yahweh causes to be remembered since the day he came forth from his mother (v. 1c-d). Thus, the speaker talks about his human birth, the womb from which he came, and the name by which he will be known. In so doing he reflects many of the same themes that Isaiah 7:14 has already mentioned.

Two metaphors arise in verse 2: the "sharpened sword" and the "polished arrow." Accordingly, the speaker's mouth will be prepared to be both incisive and piercing. Nevertheless, he will be preserved and protected by Yahweh.

Yahweh greets him in verse 3 as "my servant" and also as "Israel," for this Servant has so identified himself with the nation that at times the oscillation back and forth between himself as an individual and himself as the nation of Israel is inevitable. Has he not taken his human origins from within this nation? Has he not also performed the function of being a light to the nations on behalf of the nation (Isa 42:6)? He is named "Israel" because his seed is from the seed of the patriarchs, from David and his line. He will labor as their head, their representative, and their ultimate realization of everything that the nation can ever become.

The Servant, however, realizes that in many ways he has labored in vain for Israel (v. 4). Not only was Isaiah told earlier that he would have little success (Isa 6:10–13), but so has God's Servant, the Messiah. What brings satisfaction to the Servant is that Yahweh knows his work and the results that come from it, and he pronounces them acceptable and according to his will.

What is the Servant's task? It is to "bring Jacob back to [Yahweh]" (v. 5). The verb used here (a Hebrew *polel, lešôbēb*) represents an intensive action in the present and speaks of both a physical and a moral and spiritual return. The ancient promises of the covenant are inseparable, for they carry promises relating to their land, their prosperity, the man of promise who will come, and the good news of the gospel—all in one promise-plan.

The assigned task of the Messiah, then, is the deliverance of Jacob's offspring and their complete restoration to Yahweh. But the Messiah will also be a "light for the Gentiles" (v. 6d), just as 42:6 noted. Isaiah has already described how the peoples sat in darkness in 9:1–2, but there too a child appeared as the light for them (9:1–3). Similarly, in this context of 49:6, the Servant will serve as Yahweh's light and salvation for the peoples of the world. That is how God's "salvation" will be brought "to the ends of the earth" (49:6e).

3. The Servant's Gethsemane (Isaiah 50:4–9)

It is amazing how clearly the Servant perceives the humiliation, scourging, and suffering that awaits him at the trial and cross. Christopher North is the first scholar who called this third in the series of the Servant songs "the Gethsemane of the Servant."[14]

The Servant has a majestic view of God, for he addresses him as *Adonai* in verses 5, 7, 9: God is his master, his sovereign, and his Lord. Yet this awesome God has not remained aloof from the Servant, for he has taught him as one teaches a disciple.[15] During this period of instruction, the Servant is sustained morning after morning as he awakens with a reassuring word from the Father. Instead of stubbornly closing his ears to what he is being taught, as the nation of Israel has done, his ears are open (v. 5a). He has not been a rebellious learner or a stubborn pupil.

But beyond learning, the Servant also bears the sufferings that have been assigned to him, for "the Sovereign LORD" has helped him (vv. 7–9). The suffering will be intense and brutal. He will experience flogging by the smiters, and his beard will be yanked out—a degrading and painful insult in a culture where the beard was a symbol of manhood. He will be unable to hide from those mocking him. Their gibes and taunts will be venomous, and they will spit on him.

But the Servant is determined to be faithful to what God has called him to do. He will "set [his] face like flint" (v. 7c), for he knows that he "will not be put to shame" ultimately in the plan of God (v. 7d). God will be near to vindicate him (v. 8). Who, given God's mighty presence and word of approval, can bring a charge against him? Let the accusers come forward now, if they dare (v. 8).

God will intervene to vindicate his Servant and help him, and his enemies will decay like some old moth-eaten garment (v. 9). They should fear what will happen to them on that final day of judgment. But God's Servant, his Messiah, will come

---

[14]Christopher North, *The Suffering Servant in Deutero-Isaiah* (London: Cumberlege, 1956), 146.

[15]The Hebrew has *lešôn limmûdîm*, literally "the tongue of those who are taught [*or* instructed]," i.e., "disciples."

out of this Gethsemane experience approved by God and triumphant in God's plan.

4. The Servant's Atonement (Isaiah 52:13–53:12)

Polycarp the Lysian called this fourth Servant song the "golden *passional* of the Old Testament evangelist." Franz Delitzsch, after reporting this estimate, exceeded it by saying:

> In how many an Israelite has [Isa 52:13 –52:12] melted the crust of his heart! It looks as if it had been written beneath the cross upon Golgotha, and was illuminated by the heavenly brightness of the full šĕb lîmînî. It is the unravelling of Ps. xxii. and Ps. cx. It forms the outer centre of this wonderful book of consolation (ch xl.– lxvi.), and is the most central, the deepest, and the loftiest thing that the Old Testament prophecy, outstripping itself, has ever achieved.[16]

Undoubtedly, this is the summit of OT prophetic literature. Few passages can rival it for clarity on the suffering, death, burial, and resurrection of the Messiah.

The suffering and triumphant Servant of the Lord is narrated in five strophes of three verses each.[17] The prophet, using an inclusio, begins and ends his description with assurances that the Servant will triumph and be successful. He begins with these words: "Behold/See, my servant will have success" (52:13; pers. tr.),[18] and concludes with the Servant's receiving a portion with the great ones (53:12) and with his soul's being satisfied with what his death and resurrection have accomplished (53:11). In other words, the agony of this song is bracketed by the news of the Servant's success and triumph.

---

[16]Franz Delitzsch, *Biblical Commentary on the Prophecies of Isaiah,* 2 vols. (Grand Rapids: Eerdmans, 1954), 2:303.

[17]For an excellent discussion of the outline presented here, see Robert D. Culver, *The Sufferings and the Glory of the Lord's Righteous Servant* (Moline, Ill.: Christian Service Foundation, 1958).

[18]The same word, "have success/be successful," is used in Joshua 1:8.

In the first strophe (52:13–15), Isaiah details the *mystery* of the Servant. It is based on the comparison that Isaiah draws between verse 14 ("just as") and verse 15 ("so"). In verse 14, "many" are appalled at one who can be so disfigured and marred that he does not even look like a man anymore. But in verse 15 he will so "shock/startle"[19] the nations that even kings "will shut their mouths" when they see him—so stunning will he appear in all his power and glory. That is what makes this Servant such a mystery. The solution comes in its fulfillment: the Messiah's first advent is described in verse 14, but his second advent is described in verse 15.

The second stanza (53:1–3) describes the *rejection* of the Servant. Not only are his words and message rejected, but his deeds ("the arm of the LORD") are also tossed aside (v. 1). Furthermore, his person is rejected (v. 2), for most consider the Servant only as a country bumpkin with rustic roots, humble appearance, and no royal presence or carriage. Five sad statements follow, summarizing the nature of the Servant's rejection (v. 3). He is (1) rejected, (2) forsaken by men, (3) thought to be an offense, (4) despised, and (5) estimated to be of little or no value to anyone. This second stanza, like the fourth, states the facts, while the third and the fifth supply the meanings and explanations for what is going on in this drama on the cross.

The *atonement* of the Servant is given in the third stanza (53:4–6). First is the human occasion (v. 4), stating the objective side of the reason for the Servant's suffering: He is bearing our infirmities and sin in his body. But there is a subjective and emotional side as well: He is bearing our griefs and sorrows. Then a terrible thing happens: We add it all up and conclude that the Servant must have done something enormously wrong to be put on the cross. Instead of realizing that it is for us and

---

[19]The Hebrew word *nāzâ* is usually translated by most modern versions as "sprinkle." It appears twenty-three times in the OT (e.g., Lev 4:6; 8:11; 14:7). A possible Arabic cognate means "to leap," or in the causative form, "to cause to leap" or "to startle."

for our sins that the Servant has died, we conclude that it is for the Servant's own sin that he is smitten and stricken.

But verse 5 warns us that God thinks differently. Note that all the verbs in this verse are passive; thus God is emphatically the actor as he does four things to the Messiah: (1) he allows him to be pierced by the nails on the cross; (2) he allows him to be slapped and bruised by the soldiers, to bear the weight of the cross, and to endure the shot of pain from the thrust of the spear on the cross; (3) he allows the punishment due to us to be carried out by the Servant so that we will not need to face the firing squad, the electric chair, or the gallows; and (4) he allows the wounds and stripes that Pilate's men administer to the Messiah and that should have come to us to be the means by which we are healed.

Verse 6 is the central verse in this narrative of the suffering of the Servant, for it voices the great confession of the vicarious and substitutionary nature of the Servant's work. We have all gone astray like sheep. This is the herd instinct in all of us (otherwise known as depravity). But there is also individual guilt, for we are all sinners by choice; each of us has turned to his or her own way.

The *submission* of the Servant followed in the fourth strophe (53:7–9). The Messiah submits in verse 7 to his suffering and trial, in verse 8 to his death, and in verse 9 to his burial. There is not a word of complaint to Herod, Caiaphas, or Pilate. He is "yanked/snatched or taken away" and hurried off to a kangaroo court. The treatment is rough and uncalled for. Five speedy trials are arranged, each one illegal: (1) an interrogation by Annas, (2) another in the high priest's palace before the Sanhedrin, (3) one before Pilate, (4) one before Herod, and (5) the final one, a judgment and sentencing to death. The heartbreak of it all is this: Who cares or gives a hoot? (v. 8b). They assign him a grave "with the wicked" ones (Heb. plural), for he will be crucified between two thieves (v. 9a), though he is actually put in the grave of "a rich man" (Heb. singular; cf. NASB): as it turns out, Joseph of Arimathea (v. 9b). All of this happens even though he has done nothing wrong, nor is "any deceit [found] in his mouth." Above all, it is this statement that rules out the possibility that Isaiah or the Spirit of God means the servant is equated with the nation of Israel. It can never be said that the Israelites in general had done no violence or had any deceit in their mouths. Thus Israel cannot lay claim to being the servant spoken about in this passage. Only the Messiah can lay claim to that praise.

Finally, the *exaltation* of the Servant comes (53:10–12). He is exalted to prosperity (v. 10), to satisfaction (v. 11), and to compensation (v. 12). He will have numerous offspring and long days, and he will see the plan of God successfully completed (v. 10), for he will not remain dead and abandoned in the grave. Rather, he will be resurrected by the Lord. Because he poured out his life in the sweat of accomplishing redemption, he can thereby justify many and bear the sins of those who claim his provisions. The death of the Servant is no misadventure or accident; it is the deliberate plan and will of God (v. 10a). The very life of Messiah constitutes a guilt offering (v. 10c).

Verse 12 gives four reasons why the divine seal of God's approval is placed on this Servant of the Lord: (1) because he poured out his life unto death; (2) because he allowed himself to be counted among the transgressors; (3) because he bore the sins of many; and (4) because he kept on making intercession for transgressors, just as he did on the cross itself when he said, "Father, forgive them, for they do not know what they are doing" (Lk 23:34; cf. Heb 7:25). What a magnificent Servant of the Lord! And what a gracious atonement for our sins!

C. THE MESSIAH AS ANOINTED CONQUEROR

The third and final section of Isaiah presents the Messiah as the one who is anointed by the Lord to be his conquering hero over all opposition and over all sovereignties.

1. The Messiah's Unfailing Gifts
Promised to David (Isaiah 55:3-5)

What the Servant of the Lord has provided for and accomplished by his great act of suffering in Isaiah 52:13–53:12 is now offered in 55:1–13. All these benefits, however, flow from the ancient covenant God enacted ages ago—here called "an everlasting covenant" (v. 3). Its provisions are eternal, not provisional or temporary.

The content of the covenant centers on what God promised King David in 2 Samuel 7:16: a throne, a dynasty, and a kingdom that would be eternal in its scope and universal in its range. Isaiah knows these promises are so certain that he can call them "the sure mercies" made to David and God's "sure mercies" (KJV) promised to him (v. 3).[20] In fact, this phrase, God's "unfailing graces" (pers. tr.), are directly applied to Christ in Acts 13:34.

This grace of God includes the following gifts—all essential points of the gospel and Christian faith: (1) the gift of *Messiah himself*, for God has given him as a gift to the people (v. 4a); (2) the gift of the Messiah as a *witness*, who will testify to the truth of God (cf. Jn 18:37) and will be a witness to the Gentiles (called God's "faithful witness" in Rev 1:5); (3) the gift of the Messiah as a *leader*, a title used of his princely functions in Daniel 9:25; Acts 3:15; Hebrews 2:10; and Revelation 1:5; and (4) the gift of Messiah as a *commander*, i.e., as a *teacher of the commandments* (Heb. meṣawwēh, "the one issuing commandments"), thereby calling attention to his doctrine and his role as a teacher.

Once again the text focuses on the person and work of a personal Messiah who completes the line, tasks, and hopes initiated by those who preceded him in this messianic lineage.

---

[20]For more details on the exegesis of this passage, see Walter C. Kaiser, Jr., "The Unfailing Kindnesses Promised to David: Isaiah 55:3," *JSOT* 45 (1989): 91–98.

2. The Messiah As Proclaimer of Good News (Isaiah 61:1-3)

Isaiah 61:1-2a is the portion from Isaiah that Jesus read when he was called upon to give the reading for the synagogue in Nazareth (Lk 4:16-22). Isaiah first supplies the credentials of the coming Messiah. He will be endowed with the Spirit of the Lord so that he can carry out his role as a prophet (cf. Isa 11:2; 42:1; 49:8; 50:4-5, where the prophet predicted that the Messiah would be gifted with the Spirit of God).

Here the anointing is made the central act in his installation as the Anointed One. Curiously enough, Yahweh appoints the Servant and the Spirit anoints him, thereby making one of the earliest constructs of the doctrine of the Trinity. Rather than being anointed with oil as many the priests and kings in the OT, this Servant is anointed by the Holy Spirit himself.

The mission of the anointed Servant is multiple: (1) he will proclaim the good news of the gospel to the poor; (2) he will bind up and heal the hearts of those who have been broken and burdened; (3) he will proclaim freedom for the captives that sin has taken hostage; (4) he will release the prison doors and set free those bound by spiritual darkness and guilt, and (5) he will proclaim the year of the Lord's favor, including all the blessings of the messianic age.

At this point in his reading, Jesus began his exposition, "Today this scripture is fulfilled in your hearing" (Lk 4:21). In an inaugurated eschatology, these five things were already fulfilled during our Lord's first advent, at least partially, though their full realization awaits his second coming. But our Lord deliberately appears to have avoided two more aspects of his mission as included in Isaiah 61, since he could not say that they were being even initially fulfilled : (6) the proclamation of the day of the Lord, and (7) the comforting of all who mourn. "The day of the vengeance of our God" will be the final period of history when God judges evil and concludes history with a bang as he introduces his eternal rule and reign on earth. And those who mourn should remember that there will be an ultimate blessing for them, for one day they too will be comforted (Mt 5:4; cf. Rev 21:3–4).[21]

3. The Messiah As Conqueror (Isaiah 63:1–6)

The one whom Isaiah describes as coming from Edom with garments stained in crimson attracts his interest. He is a person who exudes confidence and who gives the impression of being great in his person and full of strength. But the question remains: Who is this person? The answer comes from the person himself: "I am he that speaks in righteousness, mighty to save" (v. 1e; pers. tr.). What he means is that he threatens judgment on all perpetrators of evil, but offers salvation for all the oppressed.

Why are his clothes stained crimson? It is because he has been trampling out the grapes in the winepress (v. 2a-b), so that the juice of the grapes have saturated and stained his clothes. But when he adds that he has been working the winepress alone and that no one of the nations has been assisting him, it is clear that the winepress is only a figure of speech. The red on his clothes is the "blood" of the nations, not mere grapes (v. 3).

His is the work of wrath on "the day of vengeance" promised in other texts (v. 4a). But it will also be the day of redemption for those who have prepared for it (v. 4b). But no one helps; he has to tread the winepress alone (v. 5). Thus, he tramples the nations in his wrath and pours out their blood on the ground (v. 6).

This section refers not to the first coming of the Messiah but to his second advent (the NT counterpart is Rev 19:11–21,

---

[21]One could argue that there is initial fulfillment of comfort for all who mourn in connection with the first five mission statements (e.g., in connection with the resurrection of Christ; cf. 1Th 4:18). But final comfort can only come after the day of vengeance of our God.

where the Antichrist and his army are finally destroyed). The one who sits on the white horse in John's vision is the Messiah, who makes war on all who oppose him. He will strike down the nations with the sharp sword that comes forth out of his mouth. "He will rule [these nations] with an iron scepter" (cf. Ps 2) and "treads the winepress of the fury of the wrath of God Almighty" (Rev 19:15; cf. Isa 63:1–6). The Messiah will be the conqueror of all that is evil, for he has been designated as such by the Father.

◆ 8 ◆

The Messiah in the Seventh- and Sixth-Century Prophets

The seventh-century prophets who ministered in Judah are Nahum (whose message focuses on the destruction of Nineveh), Zephaniah (who announces the coming day of the Lord), Habakkuk (who has one brief reference to the "anointed one" in 3:13), and Jeremiah. Only Jeremiah gives what may be termed direct messianic prophecies (three of them), even though there is much discussion about the messianic era itself in his contemporary colleagues. During the Exile, however, Ezekiel gives four direct prophecies about the coming Messiah, and Daniel gives two. These nine prophecies will be our focus in this chapter.

A. THE MESSIAH IN JEREMIAH

God called Jeremiah when he was still a teenager—as best we can tell, in the year 627 B.C. Together with a number of reforms introduced by young King Josiah (especially those inaugurated five years later, after the Book of the Law of Moses was found in the temple), Jeremiah ministered in great hopes that the people would repent and that a national revival would take place, thereby preserving the gains begun by Josiah.

Things turned out differently, however, for as the early years of Jeremiah's ministry rolled on to his later years, not only were his words rejected, he himself became *persona non grata* to the general population. During the reigns of Jehoiakim and Zedekiah, Jeremiah suffered great abuse for his preaching. His only consolation during this period was found in two things: God's personal presence with him and the hope that God's word about the future signaled for him and the Jewish remnant who believed.

1. The Messiah As "the LORD Our Righteousness" (Jeremiah 23:5-6)

In Isaiah 4:2 we discussed the Messiah's title as "the Branch." Jeremiah 23:5-6 adds more to our knowledge of the Messiah than his merely being the Branch that comes out of David, for he is called here, "The LORD Our Righteousness." The name surely signifies that the Messiah is divine. Many have tried to avoid the force of this argument by inserting the verb *is*, making it a statement about God the Father rather than the coming Messiah (i.e., "The LORD *is* our righteousness"). But this will not hold up in the context for several reasons.

(1) The "righteous Branch" (*ṣemaḥ ṣaddîq*) promised by Jeremiah was already promised by Isaiah 4:2 as the "Branch of the LORD" (*ṣemaḥ YHWH*), a genitive of source or origin that declares his divine roots. Since what lies behind the idea of "branch" or "sprout" also appeared in 2 Samuel 23:5 ("Will not God *cause to sprout* [*yaṣmîaḥ*] all my salvation and all [my] desire?—pers. tr. and emphasis) and in Psalm 132:17 ("I will make a horn *sprout* [*'aṣmîaḥ*] for David; I will set up a lamp for my Messiah"—pers. tr.), Jeremiah is certainly developing an accepted concept, not a new one.

(2) The one speaking here is not an ordinary human being, as is true when other symbolic names are given in the

OT,[1] but is Yahweh himself. In addition, note that the introductory formulas that lead up to the name are unique. Rather
than saying, "Call his name" (cf. Ge 16:11, 13; 21:3; 22:14; Ex
17:15), or "Call him" (cf. Ge 16:14; 33:20; 35:7; Jdg 6:24), or
even "His name will be" (cf. Ge 17:5b; Eze 48:35), the text of
Jeremiah 23:6 states two things: "This is [his] name (i.e., his
name will describe the very nature and essence of the
"Branch"), and "This is the name by which he will be called"
(i.e., the name is given to him *by the Lord God himself*).

(3) Finally, the tradition of the Masoretes indicates that
the best translation is, "The LORD Our Righteousness," because the conjunctive accent called a *mêrekā* under Yahweh
connects that word with ṣidqēnû ("our righteousness") without
interjecting the verb "is" between the two nouns. Moreover,
the dividing line (*pāsēq*) in the Masoretic punctuation after
Yahweh indicates that "our righteousness" should not be regarded as a predicate of Yahweh (i.e., "The Lord *is* our righteousness"); instead, "Our Righteousness" is a second name.
Yahweh, then, denotes his *nature*; *Our Righteousness* signifies
his *work*. This Masoretic reading is all the more remarkable
when one remembers that the Christian church had been appealing to this passage to demonstrate the deity of Jesus for
centuries.

The time when this will take place is stated in verse 5:
"The days are coming," that is, during the messianic age. What
will the Messiah do? He will reign as king, indeed as the new
David, with a throne, a scepter, and a kingdom that God
promised to give him. His reign will be characterized by justice
and righteousness in all its aspects. Moreover, he will rule
"wisely," or, as the word can also be translated, it will be a
"prosperous" reign. He will also unite "Judah" and "Israel" so
that they can "live in safety" in that day.

---

[1]Compare the time when Abraham declared "Yahweh-yirah" in Genesis
22:14, Jacob announced "El Elohe Israel" in 33:20, or Moses explained
"Yahweh my Banner" in Exodus 17:15.

Interestingly enough, the title given to Messiah here is similar to the name of the last king of Judah, Zedekiah, which means "Yahweh is righteousness." But Zedekiah was nothing like the Messiah in character or in action, nor did he accomplish anything like the program outlined for the coming Messiah at his second advent.

2. The Messiah As the Priestly King
(Jeremiah 30:9, 21)

Jeremiah's so-called Book of Comfort (Jer 30–33) contains some of the finest statements of any prophet on what God is going to do in the future day. His most outstanding prophecy in this section is that of the "new covenant" (31:31–34). The first half of the Book of Comfort has six sections: (1) the great day of Jacob's distress in the day of the Lord (30:1–11); (2) the healing of Israel's incurable wound (30:12–31:6); (3) God's firstborn restored to the land (31:7–14); (4) Rachel's weeping for her children in exile (31:15–22); (5) the new covenant (31:23–34); and (6) the inviolability of God's covenant with Israel (31:35–40).[2]

The combined functions of priest and king come from the first two of these sections in the Book of Comfort. In Jeremiah 30:9 it is clear that the Lord will raise up for Israel "David their king" (v. 9) "in that day" (v. 8). This does not mean that David will be reincarnated as king once again. Instead, the Messiah will come in David's line and fulfill everything that has been promised to him. He is called the new David (Eze 34:23; 37:24; Hos 3:5).

The Messiah will come as the conqueror who will break the nation's yoke and release her from bondage to other lords (v. 8). While the first David may have liberated the nation from

---

[2]This outline was suggested by Charles A. Briggs, *Messianic Prophecy* (New York: Scribners, 1889), 246–47. Essentially the same outline is given by George H. Cramer, "Messianic Hope in Jeremiah," *BSac* (1958): 237–46.

the Philistines, the second David will free that nation and the whole world from a tyranny that is far greater than anything the first David ever witnessed.

God himself will "raise up" (v. 9c) this king Messiah to carry out this final work of judgment and adjudication. When the peoples serve this king, they "will [thereby] serve the LORD their God" (v. 9a). Here, then, is another indication that the future Davidic king is a divine king. He is also one to whom his subjects will be loyal.

Jeremiah 30:21 continues the description. He will be a "Glorious One" (Heb. *'addîr*; NIV "leader").[3] This title indicates his divine origin, since it is used four times of either Yahweh or God. Nevertheless, this coming divine king will "be one of [Judah's] own" (v. 21a). That is, he will come from the Jews, just as Deuteronomy 18:15 predicted and as a number of Davidic prophecies promised. He will be a "ruler" (Heb. *môšēl*), for the governing of all things will come from him personally, not from a stand-in or from some other figure. This "ruler will arise from among them" (v. 21b). The text is most anxious to stress his human connection and origin, even though great attention has been given to his deity.

Most surprising of all is the fact that this king will also be a priest, for verse 21c specifically declares God's promise, "I will bring him near and he will come close to me." To "come near" or "approach" God means to engage in the work of the priest (see Ex 24:2; Nu 16:5). The prerogative of drawing near to God in the technical sense denoted here belongs only to those persons whom God has consecrated for this task. Jeremiah goes on to ask, in effect, who would risk death and gam-

---

[3]James E. Smith, *What the Bible Teaches About the Promised Messiah* (Nashville: Thomas Nelson, 1993), 349 notes that the Hebrew word *'addîr* appears nine times in the singular in the OT. "Twice it is used as a proper name for Yahweh (Isa 10:34; 33:21). Twice it is used as an adjective descriptive of God (Ps 76:4; 93:9). In the singular, the word is never used of a man. The use of *'addîr* in Jeremiah 30:21 points strongly to the deity of the coming Ruler."

ble with his life to approach God if he were not certain he would be accepted, as the Messiah will be. Thus, the picture is of a "Glorious Ruler-Priest," who performs both political and priestly duties—a well-known concept in the ancient Near East.[4]

3. The Inviolable Promise about the Messiah (Jeremiah 33:14-26)

The prediction in Jeremiah 33:15–16 repeats 23:5–6, which we have already treated. But this repetition adds a good deal more to what the earlier text reported. For just as David will never lack a man to sit on his throne forever, so the priests and the Levites, who serve at the altar and in God's house of worship, will never be without representatives to fulfill this function (33:17). So certain is God of this promise that it can only be broken if God's covenant with day and night can be broken (vv. 20–21, 25–26). However, all one has to do is to look outside. If one can see day or night coming and going in their normal rotation, then one had better believe that God is still maintaining his covenant with David, the priests, and the Levites.

Thus, the royal line and the priestly role will continue in the coming days when the Messiah himself appears. God's covenant with David first appeared in 2 Samuel 7:12–16, whereas his covenant with Levi was probably first made with Phinehas, the grandson of Aaron, in Numbers 25:13 and was repeated in Malachi 2:4–5, 8.

---

[4]J. A. Thompson, *The Book of Jeremiah* (Grand Rapids: Eerdmans, 1980), 562. Thompson agrees with this picture, but then has second thoughts as he says, "The picture is of a ruler-priest performing both political and priestly duties. But this may be to press the picture too far. The passage may mean simply that only one upon whom Yahweh had set his approval would dare to take up the onerous task of leading a nation in the days of restoration."

B. THE MESSIAH IN EZEKIEL

Ezekiel was a younger contemporary of Jeremiah, though he ministered in Babylon where he had been taken as a captive in 598 B.C. along with many of his fellow Israelites. He proclaims five direct prophecies of the Messiah in his book, written after his thirtieth birthday (some five years after being taken captive).

1. The Messiah As the Tender Sprig (Ezekiel 17:22–24)

Shortly before the fall of Jerusalem (587 B.C.), the prophet Ezekiel sets forth the allegory of the two eagles and the vine (Eze 17:1–10); his interpretation follows (vv. 11–21). In the allegory, a great eagle comes to Lebanon, plucks off the top of a cedar tree, and carries it to the land of the merchants, where he plants it. The eagle also takes some of the seed from Judah's land and plants it, where it grows into a vine. However, another great eagle comes along, and the vine stretches out its roots toward it from the land where it has been planted. The allegory closes with a question: Will not this vine wither away, even if it is transplanted? (vv. 2–10).

As to the interpretation, Nebuchadnezzar, the king of Babylon, has gone to Jerusalem and carried off Judah's king and her nobles to Babylon (vv. 12–13). The cedar tree, then, is the royal family, and the top of the cedar is King Jehoiachin, who has been carried off to Babylon (598 B.C.). In his place, Nebuchadnezzar has installed Zedekiah as king in Judah.

Zedekiah, however, foolishly makes overtures toward Egypt. But Pharaoh's army will be of no help in this time of crisis (vv. 15–17). Zedekiah will not escape the trap the Babylonians have set for him (vv. 20–21). He will be taken to Babylon after all his fleeing troops are slain (v. 21). It will not end happily for this Davidic king.

On the heels of this tragic announcement, God informs the prophet that he himself will "take a shoot from the very top of a cedar and plant it" (v. 22). This shoot will, of course, be from the house of David. God will break off this "tender sprig," just as Nebuchadnezzar broke off another sprig from the same stock. God's Sprig, however, will be the Messiah.

The growth of this tender Sprig will be sensational. "It will produce branches and bear fruit and become a splendid cedar" (v. 23b). The kingdom of the Messiah will be as stately as the cedar tree itself. The tree will also be a nesting place for "birds of every kind" (v. 23c). Presumably the birds represent people from all the nations of the earth. So spectacular will be the growth of the cedar tree (i.e., of the kingdom of the Messiah) that "all the trees of the field will know that I the LORD bring down the tall tree and make the low tree grow tall" (v. 24a). In other words, the royal house of David, of which the Messiah will be the climax, will so outstrip all the royal trees of the earth that all other sovereignties will have to acknowledge that the growth of this tender Sprig simply must be the work of God. What was a dry tree (the Davidic line) will flourish by the power of the promise-plan of God, and the green trees (all the governments of the world) will dry up under the condescension and judgment of the living God. The Sprig of David, the Messiah's rule and reign, will grow and prosper for all eternity.

2. The Messiah As the Rightful King (Ezekiel 21:25–27)

This passage is a twin text to Genesis 49:8–10 with its reference to "Shiloh." However, rather than using the word *Shiloh* in Ezekiel 21:27, the prophet substitutes what amounts to a translation of that word, "to whom it rightfully belongs" (*'ad bô' 'ašer lô hammišpāt*, with the addition of the word *rightfully* that was not in Genesis' cryptic *Shiloh*).

The backdrop for this prophetic word is the advancing march of the conquering Nebuchadnezzar, king of Babylon. As he approaches from the north, he stops at a fork in the roads where he has to decide whether to take the one side of the fork that leads to Rabbah of the Ammonites or the other fork that takes him against Jerusalem (Eze 21:19–20). In order to determine which route to take, the king cast lots by shaking his arrows, consulting his idols, and inspecting the livers of animals (v. 21). The message he receives from this pagan wizardry is that he should take the right-hand fork to Jerusalem. However, Yahweh has already decreed that he should proceed to Jerusalem (v. 22).

Meanwhile, the time for the wicked Davidic prince, Zedekiah, has come, for his sins and those of the nation have reached a point where divine judgment must fall (v. 25). Accordingly, the prophet orders the king: "Take off the turban, remove the crown" (v. 26). The crown, of course, means the removal of the king, but the turban (*'atārâh*) is the miter worn by the high priest. Thus, the kingdom and priesthood, as experienced up to that point in Israel's history, will be removed and abolished, suffering an interruption for a period of time. Both will remain in ruins ("A ruin! A ruin! I will make it a ruin!") until the advent of the One appointed by Yahweh "to whom it rightfully belongs" (v. 27).

When David and Aaron's lineage fail to carry out their divine mission, then those who are only "earnests" and "pledges" of what God is going to do in the future must cease operation until the One to whom kingship and the priesthood *together* belong will come to claim and exercise those functions. When the Messiah appears the second time, then the crown and the miter will be given to him, for he will be the new and final King-Priest, the Messiah.

3. The Messiah As the Good Shepherd
(Ezekiel 34:23–31)

The same figure of the tender Shepherd appears in Psalms 78:52–53; 79:13; 80:1; Isaiah 40:11; 49:9–10; Jeremiah 31:10; and later in Zechariah 11. But it is here in Ezekiel 34 that the theme receives its fullest expression. No doubt, this is the chapter that served as the background for our Lord's message on the Good Shepherd in John 10.

By the time Ezekiel gives this message, Jerusalem has already fallen (587 B.C.). During the long nights of that siege, Ezekiel concentrated on prophesying against the foreign nations (Eze 25–32). But now that the nation has fallen, as numerous prophets sent from God warned, it is time to focus on what God will yet do in spite of human failures. Thus, Ezekiel turns to discuss the last days, when Yahweh will wrap up the historical process (chs. 33–48).

To head up this discussion of what will take place in the future days, Ezekiel prophesies about the coming Good Shepherd. At first the announcements are made only about the Sovereign Lord, who will "search for [his] sheep and look after them" (v. 11). He will "bring them out from the nations and gather them from the countries, and ... will bring them into their own land" (v. 13). He will "search for the lost and bring back the strays ... bind up the injured and strengthen the weak, but the sleek and the strong [he] will destroy" (v. 16). Indeed, he will also "judge between one sheep and another, and between rams and goats" (v. 17; cf. vv. 20–22). No longer will the tyranny of the oppressors be tolerated anywhere in God's kingdom.

Suddenly, without any warning, God announces his plan to introduce his royal Shepherd to tend his flock (v. 23). The term *shepherd* is used for more than pasturing flocks and herds; frequently it refers to the work of ruling and governing. In all its uses, it embraces the idea of tenderness and responsible caring for what happens to the people, rather than the mere exercise of brute power.

God's new Shepherd will be "*one* Shepherd" (v. 23), as distinct from the many leaders that the nation has had up to this point. God will "raise up over them" (Heb. *haqimōtî 'alêhem*; NIV "I will place over them") this Shepherd, just as he earlier promised to "raise up … a prophet" (Dt 18:15) and the "off-spring/seed" of David (2Sa 7:12). Thus, the range of meanings for "raise up," as determined by the scope of OT use, means that the Shepherd will be *exalted* to this post, *established* in that role, and *confirmed* as God's appointee for this royal engagement. His appointment does not depend on the popular will or the force of a military coup, but rests on God's authority.

The Shepherd is called "my servant" (v. 23), a messianic term we already met in Isaiah. He is in the line of David (v. 23), just as Hosea 3:5 and Jeremiah 30:9 promised. God will be the people's God (cf. the tripartite formula, "I will be your God, and you will be my people, and I will dwell in the midst of them"),[5] and "my servant David will be prince among them" (Eze 34:24b). The Shepherd, then, will be a ruling and reigning prince in the line of David.

In the messianic age, this Shepherd "will make a covenant of peace with them" (v. 25), which will ensure their safety. Furthermore, the flock of God, his people, will be blessed with showers in their season as well as with crops and fruit in abundance (vv. 26–27). In so doing, the Shepherd will be recognized as the Messiah and their Lord (v. 27c). "No longer [will the flock] be plundered by the nations" (v. 28a), and "no one will make them afraid" (v. 28d). No longer will they "be victims of famine in the land or bear the scorn of the nations" (v. 29), for the Messiah has come to shepherd "the sheep of [his] pasture" (v. 31). At last, Judah will find the rest she has longed for throughout her history. It will only come when the Messiah comes back again the second time. Then Judah will be able to lie down in green pastures and have her soul restored to her by the one Shepherd, God's Servant David.

---

[5]Beginning with the announcement of the first part of the formula in Genesis 17:7–8 and 28:21 and continuing almost fifty times until it is announced at the start of the new heavens and the new earth in Revelation 21:3, this formula bridges both Testaments. See Walter C. Kaiser, Jr., *Toward Rediscovering the Old Testament* (Grand Rapids: Zondervan, 1987), 83–100, esp. 94.

What a fantastic "covenant of peace," a covenant that functions and parallels exactly what Jeremiah called the "new covenant"! But notice how the spiritual and material aspects are all included as one whole in its contents. Note also how it has a national aspect with the regathering of Israel and Judah, yet is simultaneously a cosmopolitan and transnational covenant and promise for the whole world and its peoples!

4. The Messiah As the Great Unifier of the Nation (Ezekiel 37:15–28)

God brings Ezekiel down to possibly the same valley where he received his first vision (Eze 3:22). If so, then the book is bracketed in a unique way with these two revelations. In this valley, the prophet observes bones scattered all over the landscape. When he is asked if these bones can live again, he declines to answer the Lord, "You alone know" (37:3).

God then orders him to preach/prophesy to these bones. When he does so, the bones come together from all over the valley floor. Tendons and flesh form on the bones, though there is still no breath or life in them. Ezekiel is then ordered to preach to them one more time, and the breath of God enters into these recreated zombies who stand lifelessly on the valley floor.

What was the point of this? "These bones are the whole house of Israel" (v. 11). That house of Israel may have wrongly concluded that their hope was gone when Jerusalem was destroyed and the temple burnt down. But God is "going to open [their] graves and bring [them] up from them" (v. 12).

How will God accomplish this? The word of the Lord comes again to Ezekiel to take two sticks of wood and to write on the one, "Belonging to Judah," and on the other, "Belonging to Joseph" (v. 16). Then he is to "join [the two sticks] together into one stick so that they will become one in [his] hand" (v. 17). Verse 21 goes on to explain the purpose for doing this: "I will take the Israelites out of the nations where they have gone. I will gather them from all around and bring them back into their own land." This regathering cannot be the one conducted by Zerubbabel in 536 B.C., or the one overseen by Ezra in 457, or the one led by Nehemiah in 445, for these three are only a prelude to a worldwide regathering that God himself will conduct in that final era of history when there will be "one king" over his people and they will again be "one nation" (v. 22), without the northern and southern divisions that have existed since 931 B.C.

But who will be able to pull off this great act of unification of the nation? As in chapter 34, this person will be known by the name "my servant David" or the "one shepherd" (v. 24). He will not be David in the flesh, but the scion of David, the final one in that promised dynasty.

In that day when there is one nation with one king over all of them and one God, all Israel "will follow my laws and be careful to keep my decrees" (v. 24—all of which we have never seen in history so far). At that time "they will live in the land I gave my servant Jacob, the land where [their] fathers lived" (v. 25). This is the ancient promise made to the patriarchs concerning the land of Canaan; God will end history by completing in space and time what he promised at the beginning. This promise of a reunited nation in the land of Canaan was not fulfilled according to the terms of this prophecy in David and Solomon's day, any more than it was fulfilled in the days of Zerubbabel, Ezra, and Nehemiah—unless someone wants to argue for an unusual period of obedience to God's law in Israel and for a temporary unification of the nation when presumably the Messiah came down to rule and reign in the postexilic days—an event that never took place!

We must then still look for these conditions to take place when Messiah returns again and fulfills his "covenant of peace" (see our discussion of Eze 34:23–31), even his "everlasting covenant" (37:26). At that time God will multiply his people and grant them security from all attackers and enemies. He will put his sanctuary in the midst of them forever; he will become their God, and they at last will become his people (vv. 26–28) in a sense never before enjoyed. Then it will be known that he is the one and only Shepherd, the Messiah, who has restored his people Israel to their land and unified them again—but this time it will take place directly under the personal rule and reign of the Messiah when he returns a second time.

C. THE MESSIAH IN DANIEL

Like Ezekiel, Daniel was carried off captive to Babylon. However, he and his three friends, Meshach, Shadrach, and Abednego, were removed in the first captivity that Nebuchadnezzar, king of Babylon, conducted (606 B.C.). But even in his captivity, Daniel rose to the top with God's help. His work in the foreign governments of two successive empires, Babylon and Medo-Persia, stretches out over some seventy years.

Two passages in Daniel speak directly of the Messiah and his coming, even though much of what he says pertains to the messianic times: Daniel 7:13–14 and 9:24–27.

1. The Messiah As the Son of Man (Daniel 7:13–14)

The vision of Daniel in chapter 7 parallels the interpretation of Nebuchadnezzar's dream that God gave Daniel in chapter 2. Both dreams relate to a succession of four world empires: (1) the Babylonian empire, (2) the Medo-Persian empire, (3) the Greco-Macedonian empire, and (4) the Roman empire (including Western empires) as the epitome of what human kingdoms can achieve over against the kingdom of God. And whereas in chapter 2 a "rock [symbolizing the kingdom of God] was cut out, but not by human hands" (2:34), striking the base of this giant statue and crumbling it, and expanding until it filled the whole earth, here in 7:13 "one like a son of man" comes, to whom is given all "authority, glory and sovereign power; all peoples, nations and men of every language worship ... him." Therein lies the messianic figure of Daniel 7.

But this is getting ahead of our story. In Daniel 7, the prophet sees one beast after another rising from the sea. These are clearly the same four world empires that troubled Nebuchadnezzar in chapter 2. First is Babylon, represented by a lion with the wings of an eagle on its back (v. 2). Then arises the Medo-Persian empire, represented as a bear raised on one side (just as Persia was dominant over Media) and with three ribs in its mouth—apparently the three countries it has already devoured (this empire is later identified in 8:20 as the ram with two horns, the empire of the Medes and Persians). The Greco-Macedonian empire is the third animal in Daniel's dream, the leopard with the four wings like a bird (7:6). This empire is also explained in 8:21–22, where it is depicted as a rough goat with four little horns sprouting up from its head, just as Alexander the Great's four generals succeed him. Finally, there is an awful beast that is beyond description (7:7), which is generally equated with the Roman empire.

As Daniel continues to look at all that is happening in his dream vision, he suddenly sees "the Ancient of Days" (i.e., God the Father) take his seat on a throne, flaming with fire (7:9b). "His clothing was as white as snow; the hair of his head was white like wool" (v. 9c-d). "A river of fire was flowing" forth from in front of him as "thousands upon thousands attended him" and "ten thousand times ten thousand stood before him" (v. 10). It is an awesome sight as the God of the universe moves to render worldwide judgment while receiving the praise of millions of the redeemed who are already at home in his presence and who await the climactic event of history.

But the most significant person who comes before him is "one like a son of man" (v. 13). This "son of man" is another messianic title, for he is a human being (cf. v. 14). Furthermore, "all rulers will worship . . . him" (v. 27d); he must therefore also be a divine individual. This "son of man's" divine nature is also suggested by the fact that he comes from "the clouds of heaven" (v. 13c). If any doubt remains about the identity of this "son of man," one need only look at what "the Ancient of Days," the Father, hands him: "authority, glory and sovereign power," along with "all peoples" and "nations" (v. 14a-b). This "son of man" will have a dominion that will never pass away (v. 27). The glory and splendor of his kingdom will be unequaled. No earthly sovereign power can begin to rival what his sovereignty will be like in that day.

Those who belong to the "son of man's" kingdom will become partakers of a kingdom that will never pass away (v. 18). When will these people receive this kingdom? It will come after the Ancient of Days pronounces judgment on all human kingdoms, but has given favor to "the saints of the Most High" (v. 22). In the interim will be a period of three and a half years when the saints will be handed over to the Antichrist for severe persecution (v. 25). The full identity of these "saints" is a matter of debate. Some think they are all believers, Jews and Gentiles, while others restrict this category only to Jewish believers in Israel. Regardless, after this period of intense persecution, that "little horn" (the Antichrist) will be stripped of his power and be "completely destroyed forever" (v. 26). Then the Messiah, the Son of Man, will begin his uninterrupted rule and reign forever and ever.

2. The Messiah As the Anointed Ruler Who Will Come (Daniel 9:24–27)

Daniel has been having devotions on the recent writings of Jeremiah (Da 9:2) when he realizes that God said that Judah must go into captivity for seventy years. Now that that time has almost expired, Daniel turns to God in prayer and fasting, "confessing [his] sin and the sin of [his] people Israel and making [his] request to the LORD [his] God for his holy hill" (v. 20).

God then instructs Daniel that he sent an answer to his requests as soon as he began to pray, because Daniel is "highly esteemed" (v. 23). God has set aside "seventy 'sevens'" for Daniel's people and for his holy city of Jerusalem to do six things: (1) "to finish transgression," (2) "to put an end to sin," (3)"to atone for wickedness," (4) "to bring in everlasting righteousness," (5) "to seal up vision and prophecy," and (6) "to anoint the most holy [Place or One; cf. NIV note]" (v. 24). That is a stupendous program that embraces everything from Daniel's day to eternity.

The "seventy 'sevens'" are usually understood to be "weeks" of years (the word "seven" can also mean "week"; cf. NIV note), but the usual feminine form for "week," which occurs elsewhere in the OT, is not used here. Moreover, in accordance with the use found elsewhere in this book, what Daniel means by these seventy "heptads" is seventy units of seven years, or "seventy" times "seven" years (i.e., 490 years). These years have been "decreed" by God's predetermined plan for the ages and are now being announced to Daniel in one of the most amazing disclosures into the future to be found in the OT. But note that the "heptads" are for Daniel's people of *Israel* and for their capital city, *Jerusalem*.

God uses six infinitives to describe his divine purposes for Israel during these 490 future years for the nation (cf. above on v. 24). All the transgressions against God must be completed. The final sacrifice that will put an end to sin has to be offered so that atonement can be made. God will need to bring in everlasting righteousness during this period, and the visions and prophecies about the future will remain enigmatic to the Jewish people. Finally, the most holy person, the Messiah himself (or does it refer to the temple as the Most Holy *Place*?) will need to be anointed somewhere during this same 490 years.

God's agenda for the future becomes even more detailed than that listed in the six infinitives. These 490 years will begin with "the issuing of the decree to restore and rebuild Jerusalem" (v. 25). This beginning date has been variously placed, but most prefer to begin with the twentieth year of Artaxerxes' reign in 445 B.C. (Ne 2:1–8).[6]

Two segments of times are mentioned as extending from the going forth of this "word" or "decree": "seven 'sevens'" (49 years) and "sixty-two 'sevens'" (434 years). During the first period, the streets and city of Jerusalem will be restored again; but after that time another sixty-two sets of seven years will follow (i.e., a total of 483 years) until something significant happens.

At this point, "the Anointed One, the ruler" will come (v. 25b). Some feel that it is possible to give the exact date for the announcement of the Messiah's kingdom by presupposing that a "prophetic year" consists only of 360 days (instead of the solar 365¼ days), since during Noah's flood 150 days equaled five months.[7] However, there is no reason to make such an extrapolation. It is enough to know that there are some 483 years between the time that God began to fulfill this word mentioned to Daniel and the time of the first advent of Messiah, without trying to nail down the precise day and month.

Thus far, almost all conservative interpreters agree on the larger meaning of the passage, even though many differ in the degree of specificity that is found here (i.e., which date is forecast here, and does it designate the date of the Messiah's birth, baptism, crucifixion, and/or resurrection?). A wide divergence of opinion, however, comes at verse 26. The expression "After the sixty-two 'sevens'" seems to suggest a gap between the "sixty-nine 'weeks'" and the final seven-year period of the

---

[6]Others begin it during the days of Jeremiah, when he was told to buy his kinsman's land in Anathoth (Jer 32), since the word used in Daniel 9:25 technically is not "decree" but "word." Others favor the return under Zerubbabel in 536 B.C. or under Ezra in 457 B.C.

[7]The view that Daniel indicates the *exact* date of the Messiah's coming by assuming that the time units used in the account of Noah become normative for all the rest of Scripture and prophecy is a gratuitous assumption as far as we can tell, since nothing in Scripture warrants transferring the evidence from the Noah story to the rest of Scripture, much less to eschatological data!

"seventieth 'week.'" The fact that such a gap exists is explained by the data of Scripture that declares that during this time "the Anointed One will be cut off" and "the city and the sanctuary" will be destroyed by those who belong to that opposing ruler of the end times (i.e., the Antichrist). Since Christ's death took place sometime around A.D. 30 and the fall of Jerusalem around A.D. 70, it seems reasonable to conclude that the natural sequence in the weeks has been interrupted.

How long this gap in the 490 years can be extended is also a matter of debate, but since the people of Daniel and his city have not experienced anything like the greatness they had prior to the Babylonian captivity, nor have the promises mentioned in the six infinitives of verse 24 been fulfilled, it seems that the gap must still be in effect even to the present moment.

The "Anointed One" (v. 26) and "the ruler" (v. 25) we understand to be the same as the "son of man" in 7:14 and the one promised in the line of David in 2 Samuel 7. Over against this Anointed One stands the "little [horn]" (Da 7:8), the "prince" (9:26b–27 NASB) or "king" who "will do as he pleases"; he will "magnify himself above every god and will say unheard-of things against the God of gods" (11:36). But just as the kings of Babylon in Isaiah 14 and the king of Tyre in Ezekiel 28 function as surrogates for the coming evil one in their challenge against God and his people, so Daniel envisages the appearance of someone who turned out to be Antiochus (Epiphanes) IV, who fulfilled the same role in his dastardly deed of sacrilege in 165 B.C. These rulers are but foretastes of the Antichrist who is to come (Da 11:36–45; 2Th 2; Rev 13).

But that is not how history will end. Just as Antiochus IV set up his abomination in the Holy Place, so the Antichrist will do the same in the last days (Da 9:27). But the end will come swiftly, and the Messiah will be left the sole Ruler and God's uniquely "Anointed One."

◆ 9 ◆

The Messiah in the Postexilic Prophets

The decree of Cyrus, king of Medo-Persia, permitted the Jewish people to return to their own land and to rebuild the temple (Ezr 1:2–4). Under the leadership of Zerubbabel (from the house of David) and Joshua the high priest, the people at first enthusiastically began the task of erecting the temple of God that was destroyed in 587 B.C. However, the initial excitement and enthusiasm gave way to discouragement as many realized how small this temple would be in comparison to what they had before they were carried off into captivity. Therefore, from 536 until 516 B.C. the work of reconstructing the temple lay dormant. About that time, God sent two prophets to stir up the hearts and resolve of the people to return to rebuilding the destroyed temple: Haggai and Zechariah.

A. THE MESSIAH IN HAGGAI

Haggai gave four messages in a short period, all recorded in his compact book. The first came on August 29, 520 B.C. (to use our Julian calendar dates), urging the people to renew God's work by returning to the abandoned project of building the house of God (ch. 1). The second came on October 17, 520 B.C. (2:1), with its word that God calls us to reject a negative spirit. Haggai's last two recorded messages both came on December 18, 520 B.C. (2:10, 20).

Not much more is known about Haggai than what we have in this brief book and the references to him in Ezra 5:1; 6:14. He did, however, leave us with two predictions about the coming Messiah.

1. The Messiah As the Desire of the Nations (Haggai 2:6–9)

To Haggai, the future belongs totally to God. As history moves to its final countdown, God will reorder all things and establish his kingdom on earth as a preparation for his eternal kingdom.

As preparation for three immovable and irreplaceable innovations that God will bring in—an immovable kingdom (2:6), an immovable King (2:7), and an immovable glory (2:8–9)—God will first shake up this world as it has never been shaken before. True, once before God rocked the earth, ever so slightly, at the exodus from Egypt (Ps 114) and at Sinai (Ex 19:18; Jdg 5:4–5; Ps 68:6; Hab 3:6), but this time he will do so in an extraordinary way. In those previous shakings, God came to aid only his people in their time of deep need. But in the last day, in connection with his second coming, there will be a worldwide shake-up that will signal the final appearance of Christ as he comes to reign forever.

The writer to the Hebrews uses this section of Haggai as the basis of his message that God will shake everything that is movable in order that the things that cannot be shaken may remain, not being subject to any of the vicissitudes of life (Heb 12:26–28). And that unshakable thing, he affirms, is the kingdom of God, whom we ought to serve with reverence and godly fear (cf. 1Co 7:29, 31; 2Pe 3:10–11). His kingdom is an everlasting one.

At the heart of this text is the word that God will "shake all nations, and the *desire* [*treasure*] of all nations will come" (Hag 2:7, emphasis added). In modern times, this passage has fallen from being regarded as a messianic text, mainly because the Hebrew verb translated "come" is plural ("they will come"), whereas its subject, the noun "desire" (Heb. *ḥemdâ*), is singular. Thus, the 1901 ASV changed "desire" into "precious things," considering the noun as a singular collective. Others, like the NASB, keep the singular reading, but changed the rendering to, "They will come with the *wealth* of all nations." Likewise, the NEB reads: "The *treasure* of all nations shall come hither," and the NIV reads: "And the *desired* of all nations will come." The third-century B.C. Septuagint also rendered the noun as a plural, apparently by the changing the vowels of the Hebrew word *ḥemdâ*, but retaining its consonants.

The truth of the matter is that *ḥemdâ*, "desire," occurs twenty-five times in the OT. In the singular it depicts the land God will give Israel (Ps 106:24; Jer 3:19; 12:10; Zec 7:14), their houses (Eze 26:12), and their valuables (2Ch 32:27; 36:10; Isa 2:16; Jer 25:34; Da 11:8; Hos 13:15; Na 2:10). But it is also used of persons. Saul was the "desire of Israel" (1Sa 9:20). Three times the word is used of Daniel, though interestingly enough in the plural (Heb. *ḥamûdôt*, Da 9:23; 10:11, 19, rendered in the NIV as "highly esteemed").

Can Haggai be deliberately using a form of "desire" that has both a singular and plural connotation in order to bring out the idea that God is the head of all precious things *and* that he is also more precious than all the wealth of the world? There is, after all, much biblical evidence to suggest that the "wealth" of the nations will flow to God's people in that day: "The riches of the nations will come" (Isa 60:5, using a different word for "wealth," *ḥayîl*), and "the wealth of all the surrounding nations will be collected" (Zec 14:14; cf. Rev 21:26).

We conclude that the word "desire" in Haggai 2:7 refers to the Messiah,[1] who will come at the end of history to set up his kingdom. He is the "desired [One]" par excellence, the most precious of all prized possessions or persons. But, just as he is the epitome and center of all that is valuable, so in his train will flow all the wealth and treasures of the nations. The most sought-after Person of all persons is also the one to whom all "desirable items" and "wealth" will flow in that day, for everything that is valuable, prized, and precious belongs to him as Lord, creator, and owner of all things (Ps 24:1). That explains adequately the singular and plural connotation that most commentators and translators have failed to grasp.

Some, no doubt will ask, as James E. Smith anticipates and answers,

> How is the concept of the Desire of all Nations to be reconciled with Isaiah 53:2 which says that the Servant would have no beauty that one should desire him (*nechmedehu*) him? What is implied here is not that nations definitely desired him, but that he is the only one who could satisfy the yearnings which they all felt for a Savior. In Isaiah 53 it is the Jews as a nation who do not desire him because of his lowly origins, [but] here it is the Gentiles who are particularly in view.[2]

Along with the unshakable kingdom and unshakable King is the promise in verses 8–9 of an unshakable glory. God promises to fill the temple that the people will rebuild with a glory that is his when he shakes the heavens and the earth once more in the last day. The glory referred to here is nothing short of the real presence of the incarnate God, though it can also refer to the material splendor, since the silver and gold are

---

[1]Herbert Wolf, "The Desire of All Nations in Haggai 2:7," *JETS* 19 (1976): 97–102, points to other OT passages where the plural verb and noun clearly refer to an individual, thus allowing this to be the case here as well.

[2]James E. Smith, *What the Bible Teaches About the Promised Messiah* (Nashville: Thomas Nelson, 1993), 402.

his to spread lavishly on the temple that will be built in the day when he rules as King of kings and Lord of lords.

2. The Messiah As God's Signet Ring (Haggai 2:21–23)

As part of the inauguration of God's kingdom, Haggai now declares God's victory over all human governments in the most graphic terms possible (2:22). But since this takeover lies far in the future for Haggai, how can he describe such an event when he has not experienced what will happen, much less can the people, who likewise have no access to the events, persons, and implements of that coming day, grasp any part of his meaning?

The solution is the same as that used by other previous writers of Scripture: The future is described in terms of the past. (1) God will "overturn royal thrones," similar to his "overturning" or "overthrow" of Sodom and Gomorrah (Dt 29:23; Isa 13:19). That is how he will suddenly work the collapse of the kingdoms of this earth.

(2) In that future day God will vanquish all warring rivals that challenge his coming reign on earth the same way as he took care of Pharaoh and his armies when they were "hurled" or "went down" in the sea (Ex 15:1, 4). Both horse and rider were vanquished when Pharaoh's army tried to oppose God and his people.

(3) The nature of God's victory in that day comes from Gideon's victory in Judges 7:22. The Midianite soldiers "turn[ed] on each other with their swords." Similarly, so completely disarmed will God's enemies be in that coming day that in their confusion they will kill each other (Hag 2:22). The nations who oppose God will only succeed in destroying themselves.

In the same day that God introduces his kingdom, he will make his Messiah a "signet ring" (v. 23). This God-ordained emblem of the office and authority of the Davidic kingship—the family through whom Messiah comes—was taken from one of David's descendants, King Jehoiachin, and given to someone else in David's line (Jer 22:24). Rather than continuing the Davidic line through Solomon, God shifts it at this point to David's other son, Nathan (not to be confused with the prophet Nathan), whose descendant in Haggai's day is Zerubbabel. The signet ring on the king's hand stands for much the same that the seal of the presidency stands for in the United States: It conveys all the rights, privileges, and authority of the office to the office holder.

Three other messianic expressions are used along with "signet ring": "my servant," "[my] chosen," and "I will take you" (v. 23). (1) The Servant of the Lord, of course, is one of the most frequently used titles for the Messiah. Not only did it appear frequently in Isaiah 41–66, but it was the title Ezekiel used for the coming David, the Messiah (Eze 34:23; 37:24).

(2) The fact that Zerubbabel has been chosen, like God's Servant (Isa 42:1), should not surprise us, for God has singled out this anointed one for the task he now assigns him. The words used here are later applied to the long-expected Messiah on the day that John baptized Jesus. A voice came from heaven saying, "This is my Son, whom I love; with him I am well pleased" (Mt 3:17; cf. Mk 1:11; Lk 3:22; cf. also at Jesus' transfiguration, Lk 9:35). The Messiah is God's chosen, his Elect One.

(3) God also tells Haggai that he will take Zerubbabel and make him his signet ring. The words "I will take you" refers to God's special selection of Zerubbabel, just as God took others in the past. Historically, the words carried overtones of God's call for a special task (Ex 6:7; Jos 24:3; 2Sa 7:8). In the same way, the Messiah will be marked out by God for a special task by this distinctive designation.

God will give an unshakable kingdom to the Messiah with the emblem of his office, the signet ring. That ring, though stripped from the hand of Jehoiachin, will be transferred to the

Messiah, while still coming through the line of David, as God's promise-plan predicted.

B. THE MESSIAH IN ZECHARIAH

Zechariah began his prophetic ministry in November 520 B.C., two months after Haggai delivered his first message on August 29, 520 B.C. Zechariah's book is not only the longest of the twelve minor prophets, it is one of the most frequently quoted OT books in the NT (seventy-one quotations or allusions). One-third of these appear in the Gospels and thirty-one are found in Revelation. Zechariah is second only to Ezekiel in its influence on the book of Revelation.

Zechariah, whose name means "God remembers," was from the tribe of Levi and therefore served as both priest and prophet. His prophecies both advance the doctrine of the Messiah and summarize the previous promises made about the coming son of David.

1. The Messiah's Work As High Priest
(Zechariah 3:8–10)

Just as Isaiah and his sons were signs (Isa 8:18), so Joshua the high priest (whose name, incidentally, is the same as Jesus in the Greek) and his companions are signs or "men symbolic of things to come" (Zec 3:8). Therefore, Zechariah's vision is given to instruct the readers of that day and ours about the work of the final and greatest high priest who will come in the last day.

In Zechariah's vision in 3:1–7, Satan accuses Joshua, who appears in priestly robes that are severely dung-spattered (representing the filthiness of sin). But the "angel of the LORD," who is no doubt a preincarnate form of Christ, orders the foul clothes to be removed from Joshua. The Lord then recommissions Joshua and grants him direct access to God the Father.

In what way are Joshua and his associates "symbolic of things to come?" Two marvelous titles of the Messiah appear in the last part of verse 8: "my servant" and "the Branch." Both have been discussed in the chapter on Isaiah: the first in Isaiah 42–53, the second in 4:2. The "servant of the LORD" embraces a corporate solidarity in which all who believe are included with the key representative of the group—in this case, the coming Messiah. In the four presentations of "the Branch" discussed above (see. pp. 156–58, 187), it is the servant role that Zechariah 3:8 focuses on. And in this context, as in Isaiah 53, the chief work of serving is in the Messiah's high priestly work of "remov[ing] the sin of this land in a single day" (Zec 3:9d).

There is a third messianic term in this text: the title "stone" (v. 9a). This title has also been discussed in our comments on Isaiah 28:16. What is unique here, however, is that the Stone has seven eyes and an inscription engraved on it: "I will remove the iniquity of this land in a single day" (v. 9c-d). Clearly, this Stone must be the same Stone that Isaiah mentioned in Isaiah 28:16. It was announced in Psalm 118:22 as the Chief Cornerstone that the builders rejected and in Daniel 2:44–45 as the Stone that represented the kingdom of God that grew and filled the whole earth after smashing the great image. The number seven may indicate completeness, as it often does, or it may be a deliberate reference to the sevenfold fullness of the one Spirit of the Lord given to the Messiah (see Isa 11:2).

The cleansing that God predicts he will bring to the land in a single day is a type of the spiritual cleansing that the Messiah accomplished on Calvary in a single day, later called Good Friday. The "one day" promised is "that day" of Zechariah 9–14, that is, the day of Israel's national repentance when the people will look on the One whom they have pierced and mourn as one mourns for an only son (12:10). The one day of Zechariah is equivalent to the "once for all" of Christ's death emphasized in Hebrews 7:27; 9:12; and 10:10.

Zechariah's fourth vision concludes with a picture of tranquillity and rest, since each sin has been pardoned and removed (v. 10). This scene of domestic tranquillity, in which everyone sits under his own vine and fig tree, is the epitome of contentment and happiness in the future age when the Messiah reigns supreme without any rivals (1Ki 4:25; 2Ki 18:31; Mic 4:4).

2. The Messiah As the King-Priest: Ruler Over All Nations (Zechariah 6:9–15)

David Baron has remarked concerning this passage:

> This is one of the most remarkable and precious Messianic prophecies, and there is no plainer prophetic utterance in the whole OT as to the Person of the promised Redeemer, the offices He was to fill, and the mission He was to accomplish.[3]

This passage marks the climactic act to the eight night visions of Zechariah. It involves the symbolic crowning of Joshua the high priest.

Rather than portraying this message in a vision, God has the prophet placed in the midst of his people, where he receives, in the house of Josiah son of Zephaniah (v. 10c), a delegation of three men from Babylon who bear a special gift of "silver and gold" (v. 11). Zechariah must take this gift of silver and gold and fashion from it an elaborate crown that will eventually be set on the head of Joshua the high priest (v. 11). But the most surprising aspect of this action is that the Hebrew word for "crown" is actually plural, "crowns." Therefore, it may well point to the double-ringed priestly and royal tiara. If so, then it points to the Messiah, who will come as both priest and king (as the context will make clear later on).

---

[3]David Baron, *The Visions and Prophecies of Zechariah* (Grand Rapids: Kregel, 1972), 149.

This text introduces five messianic promises that are of great significance for the doctrine of the Anointed One. (1) The text begins with the presentation: "Here is the man whose name is the Branch" (v. 12b). This announces the promise that the Davidic king who will come in the new age of God will be from human stock, yet he will have the title of Branch (see our comments on "Branch" in Isa 4:2; Jer 23:3–5; 33:14–26; Zec 3:8).

(2) "He will branch out from his place" (v. 12c). Even though Messiah will come from what many regard as dry and parched ground (cf. Isa 53:2; he will be somewhat of a rural country bumpkin in the eyes of most uninformed observers), God will exalt, elevate, and prosper the Messiah in accordance with his own nature. That is why the Branch will branch out and be extremely successful (cf. 2Sa 23:1; Ps 89:19)!

(3) "[He will] build the temple of the LORD" (v. 12d). While Zerubbabel the governor, under the prompting of the prophets Haggai and Zechariah, built the so-called second temple in 516 B.C., the Messiah himself will build a new temple in that coming age (Isa 2:2–4; Eze 40–42; Mic 4:1–5; Hag 2:7–9). Not only will he be in charge of building this new temple, "he will [also] be clothed with majesty" (v. 13b). Thus, all the splendor that the glory and honor of his position afford will belong to Messiah in that day and will be observable by all (Ps 96:6).

(4) "[He] will sit and rule on his throne" (v. 13c). Long ago God promised to David that one of his sons would sit and rule on his throne over a worldwide and everlasting kingdom (2Sa 7:12–16). All power in heaven and earth will belong to Messiah, who will personally rule and reign from that point on forever and ever.

(5) "He will be a priest on his throne. And there will be harmony between the two" (v. 13d-e). This is the clearest statement in the OT that the coming Messiah will be both a king and a priest (cf. Heb 7). So amazing is this prediction that it has troubled many interpreters. How is it possible that a priest

should sit on a throne? The Greek Septuagint tried to soften this prediction by substituting "at his right hand" for "on his throne." But as is known from the royal psalms (e.g., Ps 110:4), the Messiah will exercise an everlasting priesthood in addition to his royal and prophetic offices. Accordingly, Zechariah daringly combines the priestly and kingly offices into one person, the Branch. Only when this has taken place can the Lord bring "harmony between the two," as he removes the sin of the earth in one day (Zec 3:8–9). Thus, the tensions between the offices of the religious and political leadership will be resolved.

The crown of verse 11 will be preserved as a "memorial in the temple" (v. 14), both as a reminder of the gift of the captives in Babylon and as a testimony to the coming union of the priest and king into one messianic office. There it will remain "until he comes to whom it rightfully belongs" (Eze 21:27; cf. Ge 49:10).

In the last day, even "those who are far away will come and help to build the temple of the LORD" (Zec 6:15a)—a reference to the temple of the final day that Isaiah (Isa 2:1–4), Micah (Mic 4:1–4), and Ezekiel (Eze 40–48) spoke about. The expression "those who are far away" is the same one used in the NT for the Gentiles (e.g., Ac 2:39; Eph 2:13), who will pitch in to help construct this edifice. Thus, the princely gifts that come from as far away as Babylon are but a harbinger and a precursor of the wealth of the nations that will pour into Jerusalem when the Messiah, the Branch, will be received as King of kings and Lord of lords.

3. The Messiah As the King (Zechariah 9:9–10)

These two verses stand at the heart of chapter 9, forming a pivot point between verses 1–8 and 11–17. In many ways, verses 9–10 enlarge on the messianic teaching of 3:8 and 6:9–15, as four announcements are made.

a. The arrival of the king (v. 9a-c)

Spontaneous outbursts of exuberant joy break out in an enormous celebration over the fact that the earth will finally receive her king. It is indeed, "Joy to the world, the Lord has come," as Isaac Watts paraphrased Psalm 98. The invitation to sing and rejoice is similar to that issued earlier in Zechariah 2:10, for in that coming day, the Lord will dwell in Jerusalem.

b. The character of the king (v. 9d-f)

The Messiah is described as "righteous" (i.e., "in the right"). His nature and character will set the norms for what is lawful, just, and correct. This characteristic also implies a quality of impartiality in judgment as he exercises his kingly office.

He is also described as "having salvation." The form of the word for "salvation" is either a passive one or reflexive one. If it is passive, then the Messiah will "be saved"—that is, he will be delivered from the power of death. If it is reflexive, as the ancient versions such as the Septuagint, the Vulgate, the Syriac, and the Targum took it, then the Messiah will show himself to be the Savior. Both ideas may be intended.

The Messiah will also come in a "gentle" (or "lowly") spirit. This may also be translated as one who has experienced humility, affliction, or the trial of being stricken. Certainly our Lord was brought low on the cross on behalf of all sinners (cf. Isa 53:7).

Finally, he will present himself to his people "riding on a donkey." In the ancient Near East, the donkey was not thought of as a beast of burden, as we think of it today; instead, the donkey was the preferred mount of princes (Jdg 5:10; 10:4; 12:14), kings (2Sa 16:1–2), and leaders who mingled with the people in a peaceful manner (Ge 49:11; 2Sa 19:26; 1Ki 1:33). Since horses were most often linked with chariots as instruments of war (Dt 17:16; Ps 33:16–17; Isa 33:1), it is significant that the Messiah will not enter Jerusalem mounted on a horse; that is, Jesus will not come the first time as a conqueror. Moreover, these verses allude to Jacob's blessing given to the line of Judah in Genesis 49:10–11, where the "one whose right it was" (cf. Eze 21:27) is described as "tether[ing] his donkey to a vine, his colt to the choicest branch." Accordingly, the Ruler promised in Genesis 49 will come mounted on a donkey, indeed, on the colt of an ass (i.e., a purebred, not born of a mule). Both Matthew 21:2–7 and John 12:12–15 refer to Zechariah 9:9–10 in their depiction of Jesus's triumphal entry into Jerusalem on Palm Sunday.

c. The disarmament of the world (v. 10a-c)

Three weapons will be abolished when the Messiah returns a second time: the "chariots," "the war-horses," and "the battle bow." These, or their modern equivalents, will be banished from his kingdom and realm. Thus, peace will come not only to the northern ("Ephraim") and southern ("Jerusalem") kingdoms of Israel, but also to the "nations" of the world (next section).

d. The kingdom of the Lord (v. 10d-f)

The Messiah "will proclaim peace to the nations." The strength and might of this king will not need to be measured, as other kings do, in terms of his military arms and hardware. His laws and decrees will settle disputes and introduce peace over all nations and territories.

The scope of Messiah's realm will be from "sea to sea and from the River to the ends of the earth." This terminology is similar to that of Psalm 72:8 as celebrated in Isaac Watt's paraphrase of that psalm:

> Jesus shall reign wher'er the sun
> > Does its successive journeys run.
> His kingdom spread from shore to shore.
> > Til' moons shall wax and wane no more.

Then will have happened what this earth has always longed for—a just and lasting peace.

4. The Messiah's Four Titles (Zechariah 10:4)

By using the metaphor of the shepherd as a leader, Zechariah contrasts the good and bad leaders who have shepherded (or will shepherd) God's people. The one who will restore the house of Judah and Joseph by returning them once again to their ancient homeland will be the true shepherd (v. 6)—and this restoration was promised in 518 B.C., well after the return from Babylon under Zerubbabel!

In the past, the bad shepherds looked in the wrong direction for guidance—to "idols" and "diviners" (v. 2). The result of such misguided leadership was devastating, for the people wandered around "like sheep oppressed for lack of a shepherd" (v. 2). Thus the anger of God is burning against these shepherds and leaders who have, in effect, abandoned their flock (v. 3). In contrast to these actions, God will take care of his bullied sheep and turn them into his "proud horse in battle" (v. 3e). Strengthened by God, the people will one day overthrow their oppressive shepherds.

At this point Zechariah suddenly interrupts this litany of judgment to announce God's surprising provision of a new, stable leadership that will be granted directly "from [the Lord]."[4] Even though several passages imply that the Messiah will come from God the Father, this is the only one that states it directly. This new brand of leadership, therefore, finds its model in the one whose four titles now appear in this brief messianic passage.[5]

---

[4]The Hebrew at the beginning of verse 4 reads, "From him." The NIV translates this, "From Judah will come" the fourfold titled person named here. But Judah is treated as a plural throughout this passage, as James E. Smith has pointed out (*What the Bible Teaches*, 430–43). Thus, the most "likely . . . antecedent of the singular pronominal suffix ['From him'] is Yahweh."

[5]See the excellent discussion by David Baron in "Four Precious Titles of the Messiah," in his *Rays of Messiah's Glory: Christ in the Old Testament* (1886; reprint, Grand Rapids: Zondervan, n.d.), 151–78.

(1) His first title is "corner" or "cornerstone" (v. 4a). The Messiah will be the *foundation* and the *unifier* of the people who belong to him by right of redemption. The term *cornerstone* was used in Isaiah 28:16 to refer to the Messiah as the Stone that human beings rejected, but which eventually became the cornerstone. The Messiah was also styled "the capstone" in Psalm 118:22 (cf. Mt 21:42). Surely this metaphor depicts steadfastness, reliability, and headship. In other passages in the OT, it is used figuratively to refer to a ruler (cf. Isa 19:13).

(2) A "tent peg" or "nail" is depicted either a hook in the center of a tent where frequently used items are kept (Isa 22:22–23; Eze 15:3) or as the peg in the ground that secures the tent and keeps it secure (Ex 27:19; 35:18; Jdg 4:21, 22). This imagery is the same as Isaiah used to refer to Eliakim, the son of Hilkiah, who also had a leadership position. God declared that he would "fasten [Eliakim] as a peg in a secure place" (NKJV), or that God would "drive him like a peg into a firm place" (NIV), for God had placed "on his shoulder the key to the house of David" so that "what he opens no one can shut, and what he shuts no one can open" (Isa 22:22–23; cf. Rev 3:7). Thus Eliakim, a son of David, is merged into another son of David, the Messiah, in whom all the promises made to David are centered and fulfilled. Accordingly, the Messiah will be the Nail in a sure place on whom his people can hang all their burdens, cares, and anxieties. For those who do not belong to Messiah, the Nail "will be cut down," along with the load hanging on it (Isa 22:25).

(3) "The battle-bow" is a symbol of strength for military conquests (2Ki 13:17). It describes the same character of the Messiah that was given in Psalm 110:5–6 and Isaiah 63 (cf. Rev 19). When the Messiah comes again, he will be like a sharp sword in the hand of the Almighty, for he will smite the nations who have by then filled up the cup of iniquity. He will rule them with a rod of iron and dash them in pieces like a potter's vessel (cf. Ps 2:9).

(4) This final title is difficult to translate since it involves a peculiar expression in the Hebrew. In the previous chapters, the Messiah has been called a "ruler" (*môšēl*) and a "king" (*melek*), but here in Zechariah 10:4 he is called a *nôgēš*. What is that? In a negative sense, the term is used in the OT of a "taskmaster" or an "exacter"; but the sense here must be a positive one. In Isaiah 3:12; 14:2; and 60:17 it is used in the sense of someone who rules. Accordingly, a *nôgēš* is an absolute Ruler, on whom all sovereignty rests.

These four titles demonstrate what the Messiah will be able to do in both the present and future vis-à-vis the bad shepherds whom the people had to put up with for so many years.

5. The Messiah As the Rejected Good Shepherd
(Zechariah 11:4–14)

In one of Zechariah's more difficult sections, the Lord requests a shepherd to look after a flock that has been destined for slaughter. The prophet, so it appears, is to act out a parable with a prophetic truth. Accordingly, he dresses in the garb of a shepherd and begins to act out a ministry to the people that assumes both religious and civic functions (v. 7a). The flock entrusted to this shepherd is Israel, a nation abused by other owners who have slaughtered the people without any feeling of guilt (v. 5a). Meanwhile, Israel's own shepherds have no pity and in effect have abandoned God's flock for motives of profiteering. What then will happen to this flock? God himself will abandon them in the future (v. 6) and hand the whole land over to Israel's neighbors and to foreign kings as the prize of conquest (v. 6b).

Where, then, does the prophet, now dressed as a shepherd, fit in? He becomes Israel's shepherd, despite the certain doom that awaits the nation (v. 7a). Using two staffs, one named "Favor" (or "beauty, grace") and the other named "Union" (or "bonds"), Zechariah symbolizes what he hopes to achieve through his ministry. He wants God's favor to rest on the people and for them to experience national unity again, in which the southern and northern kingdoms will be reunited as a single kingdom, just as they were in the days of David and Solomon.

What verse 8 means, however, is most problematic. The shepherd dismisses three shepherds in one month, but whether these three shepherds are Judah's last three kings (i.e., Jehoiakim, Jehoiachin, and Zedekiah, so that "one month" means a short period of time, cf. Hos 5:7) or something else is not certain. It is best to leave open the interpretation of this verse for the time being, for it may have relevance to an eschatological event as well.

Zechariah's patience begins to give out as the flock detests him (v. 8b). It is impossible for him to perform his duties as shepherd under these conditions. He therefore gives up, declaring that he will no longer shepherd the flock of God (v. 9b). Instead, the herd may just as well cannibalize each other (v. 9c), which is what happened in the awful sieges of Jerusalem in 587 B.C. and 70 A.D. (cf. Dt 28:54–57; La 4:10; Josephus, *Wars* 6.201–13). The people may be acting like cannibals in the way they verbally and emotionally attack each other, for one does not attack God's messenger without developing the bad habit of attacking each other. From there it is an easy step to move to the dire need for food during a siege, with only one's children and their afterbirth as an available source of sustenance.

The prophet, therefore, takes the staff called Favor and breaks it, thereby revoking the covenant that God made with the nations (v. 10). It is important to notice that God does not break the covenant he made with the patriarchs or with David (Ge 12:1–3; 2Sa 7:12–16), for God promises again, even to Zechariah, that he will never break that covenant (Zec 8:11–15; 10:6–12). Rather, it is the covenant made "with all the nations" (v. 10b) that he revokes. One need only to remember that God's people were protected from decimation from the nations by a covenant restraining those Gentile nations (Job

5:23; Eze 34:25; Hos 2:18). That covenant is now broken. God removes the protecting shadow of his hand from over Judah so that the nations can be his rod of punishment, just as the Assyrians were once used by God in the past (Isa 10:15–16).

As Zechariah continues to act out this parable of the Good Shepherd, he requests to be paid his wages for shepherding the people (v. 12). The authorities determine that "thirty pieces of silver" (v. 12c) is all he is worth—the going price for a slave under the Mosaic law (Ex 21:32) and the same sum Judas received for betraying Jesus (Mt 26:15; 27:9)![6] Thus the thirty pieces are weighed out.

After Zechariah receives such a "handsome price" (v. 13b; note the irony), he throws them, on God's command, "into the house of the LORD to the potter" (v. 13d). Since the Hebrew words for "potter" (yôṣēr) and "treasury" ('ôṣār) sound alike, and since both ideas are found in Matthew 27:6–9 (the money Judas threw into the treasury was used to buy a potter's field), many have adopted the Syriac emendation for verse 13, "throw it into the treasury." But that is unnecessary, since to "throw it to the potter" is simply a proverbial expression that has a note of contempt, meaning "throw it away."

Clearly, the money is cast into "the house of the LORD to the potter" (v. 13d). To make sense of this connection one need only recall that potters were connected with the temple in order to make the sacrificial vessels (Lev 6:28). Therefore, there must have been a guild of potters serving on a regular basis in the temple, to whom the money of the authorities' lavish generosity, now refused, is deposited (Jer 18:6; 19:1).

Once Zechariah has cast away the thirty pieces of silver paid to him, he breaks the other staff, Union (v. 14). The na-

---

[6]Matthew ascribes the quotation to Jeremiah rather than to Zechariah. This may be because Jeremiah, in the order of some of the Hebrew collections of the prophets, appears at the head of the whole corpus of the prophets, or it may be that Matthew combines Zechariah 11:12–13 with Jeremiah 18:1–4 and 32:6–9, thus referring to the entire quotation by the name of the more prominent prophet.

tional deed is complete. The people have rejected their Good Shepherd, the Messiah, which role the prophet has been depicting. As a result, the national unity they hope for will not be realized for some time to come. In fact, the prophet Ezekiel has predicted that the nation will remain divided until the One Good Shepherd (i.e., the Messiah) will come again to reunite the stick of Judah with the stick of Joseph in that final day (Eze 37:16–28).

6. The Messiah As the Pierced One (Zechariah 12:10)

The opening section of this chapter describes a vicious battle against Jerusalem unlike any others in the past. It will take place "on that day, when all the nations of the earth are gathered against [Jerusalem]" (v. 3). But on that future day, God will directly intervene with his personal presence to win a decisive victory. The only similar event to this one is the triumph God won over Pharaoh at the Red Sea.

The rest of the chapter (including 13:1) describes two mercies or gifts out of God's abundance that he will pour out "on that day" (vv. 4, 6): (1) a new spirit of grace and supplication (12:10–14), that is, a grace that will awaken guilty persons to cry out in supplication for pardon; and (2) a new cleansing for sin and uncleanness (13:1). The dominant feature of this grace or compassion from our Lord is a grace that forgives sin; in fact, it is a grace that can forgive even the piercing of the Messiah. "They will look on me, the one they have pierced, and they will mourn for him as one mourns for an only son" (12:10b).[7]

---

[7]This is not to add fuel to the fires of those who have castigated our Jewish neighbors by the stigma of being "Christ killers." That slur is as unfair as it is untrue! In fact, the Messiah was put to death by the Jews *and the Romans*. It is also true that he was put to death for the sins of all the world. So caution must be exercised in this area when describing the roles that were carried out by the first-century participants in the death of Christ.

Much controversy surrounds the translation of this text. The 1988 New Jewish Publication Society translation of the *Tanakh* (i.e., the OT) renders Zechariah 12:10 as: "But I will fill the House of David and the inhabitants of Jerusalem with a spirit of pity and compassion; and they shall lament to Me about those who are slain, wailing over them as over a favorite son and showing grief as over a first-born." The 1896 Jewish translation, in an appendix to the Revised Version, read: "And they [i.e., the house of David and the inhabitants of Jerusalem] shall look up to Me because of Him whom they [i.e., the nations which came up against Jerusalem] have pierced." An even more ancient Jewish interpretation understood this prophecy to refer to Messiah ben ["son of"] Joseph, a separate individual from Messiah ben David. But the creation of two Messiahs, one who suffers (ben Joseph) and the other who rules over all (ben David) is without textual support in the *Tanakh* itself and seems to have arisen as a response to the case Christians and first-century Jewish converts made for the Messiah's suffering prophesied in the OT.

But what of the differences between most translations and the Jewish versions listed above? The most difficult fact that these Jewish translations must face is that "me"[8] ("they will look on *me*") and "him" ("will grieve for *him*") both refer to the same person. Most Jewish interpreters prefer to have the Gentile nations look to God, whom these nations have been attacking indirectly by afflicting suffering on his people Israel. This cannot be correct, however. The subject of the verb "look" and the verb "pierce" is the same in Hebrew. Accord-

---

[8]The One who pours out the Spirit is the one upon whom they must look; thus the first person singular pronoun makes it clear that the object of looking is deity. While a few manuscripts do read "him" instead of "me," all the ancient versions, the greater majority of Hebrew manuscripts (including all the better texts) read "me." It appears that a marginal reading in some later Hebrew manuscripts crept into a few texts, but the witness of the better texts remains united in its reading of the first person singular pronoun.

ingly, those who pierced[9] the Messiah, the same One who will pour out a spirit of grace and supplication in that day, belong to the same national group that will "look" and "mourn" over the pierced One, as one mourns over the loss of a "firstborn son"—a phrase that also serves as a reminder of the Messiah according to the informing theology that began to develop in Exodus 4:22.

The first line of argument against this interpretation has been that it is impossible to pierce God, since he is not flesh and blood (Isa 31:3; cf. also Jn 4:24). But that is precisely the point: It is the Messiah's flesh that has been pierced—he who is one with God the Father in essence and being. Note that whenever the first person pronoun appears elsewhere in this chapter (vv. 2, 3, 4, 6, 9, 10), it refers to the Messiah.

Since Zechariah has just referred to the Good Shepherd being rejected by Israel in chapter 11, the context is most suitable to the interpretation suggested here. Only the character and person of the Messiah fits all the details given here. His piercing must come in a separate advent, for when he carries out the victory described in 12:1–9, he comes as a conquering hero who was already pierced at some previous point in time. The prediction of the Messiah's death on the cross and his being literally pierced is another startling fulfillment of prophecy.

The mourning in that day will be so intense that the only mourning that even begins to compare with it is the "weeping of Hadad Rimmon in the plain of Megiddo" (12:11b). If Hadad Rimmon is the name of a place in the plains that flow out from Megiddo, then the prophet is referring to the national mourning that took place at the tragic death of good King Josiah,

---

[9]While the Septuagint has rendered the Hebrew verb *dāqar* as to "grieve" or to "insult," the word is never so used in the OT. It always has the sense of a literal piercing (e.g., Zec 13:3). Surely King Josiah died from a literal piercing, not an insult or grieving!

killed at Megiddo while trying to stop Pharaoh Neco (2Ki 23:29; 2Ch 35:25). Few kings compiled a greater record for godliness and righteousness than Josiah, but he was shot by archers, and the nation went into bitter lamentation over his death. That period of national grief is but a foretaste of the national lament that will suddenly dawn on the nation of Israel as she realizes one day that the Pierced One who died on the cross on Golgotha was the Messiah and that he died for their sins as well as for the sins of the whole world (Isa 53:5).

7. The Messiah As the Smitten Companion of the Lord (Zechariah 13:7)

The Shepherd who is struck by the sword in Zechariah 13:7 is obviously the same as the one described as being pierced in 12:10 and as being rejected in chapter 11. There is, however, one major difference: this time Yahweh will wield the sword and smite the shepherd (13:7). The personal pronoun in *"my* shepherd" (v. 7), as well as the "I" of verses 7d, 9a-b, d-e, and the "my" of verse 9d-e, all refer to Yahweh.

Earlier the flock was destined for slaughter (11:4, 7). Then the sword was to strike the worthless shepherd (11:17). Next, the people wielded the sword against the one who was the source of grace and supplication, the Messiah himself (12:10). Now, once again, a sword is being called for. It will happen "on that day" (13:4) that Yahweh himself will use the sword, figuratively speaking, for it will "please the LORD to bruise him" (Isa 53:10a; NIV "it was the LORD's will to crush him").

But who is this shepherd? Certainly he is no ordinary herder of sheep and goats, for he is called "my shepherd" by the Lord (v. 7). Moreover, he is "the man who is close to me" (v. 7b) (Heb. *geber 'amîtî,* "the man with me," or "the man who is my companion"). Surely this is high praise, for the term "companion" or "associate" refers to a close neighbor or close companion in Leviticus 6:2; 7:21; 18:20; 19:15; 24:19. Thus, the shepherd is one who is side by side with Yahweh; that is, he is his equal. Once again, this messianic prophecy is speaking about a human being ("the man") who is also divine (he is "close to me," or is "my associate").

When the messianic Shepherd is smitten, the sheep "will be scattered" (v. 7e). In other words, following the death of the Messiah, the dispersion of the Jews around the world will take place. Every Jew, from the poorest to the richest, will be affected by this scattering. The tradition of resisting the divine implications of the hideous death of the Messiah, however, has been passed on from Jewish parents to their "little ones." And so the opposition to his person and work has continued to this day.

C. THE MESSIAH IN MALACHI

1. The Messiah As the Messenger of the Covenant (Malachi 3:1)

The revelation of the character and work of the Messiah in Malachi 3 comes as an answer to the grievances of the complainers in the prophet's day who have wearied God with the old saws: "All who do evil are good in the eyes of the LORD, and he is pleased with them." Their punch line is: "Where is the God of justice [anyway]?" (Mal 2:17). It is as if they are saying, "God must love wicked people because he made so many of them!"

But these crybabies will find out soon enough that God means business with evildoers, just as he means business with people who complain about them and in effect hide behind them to vindicate their own deeds of evil. God "will send [his] messenger, who will prepare the way before [him]" (Mal 3:1a). This messenger is a development of the preparer predicted in Isaiah 40:3–5. He is to be identified as John the Baptist, who came in the spirit and the power of Elijah (Mt 3:1–3; Mk 1:3;

Lk 1:17, 76; 3:4; Jn 1:19–23).[10] His job was to prepare the people morally and spiritually for the coming of the Messiah.

Where, then, is the God of justice? The answer is surprising: "Then suddenly the Lord you are seeking will come to his temple; [even] the messenger of the covenant, whom you desire, will come, says the LORD Almighty" (3:1c-e). There are a number of significant matters here. First, the word "Lord" (Heb. *hā'ādôn*) used in verse 1c is singular and is preceded by the definite article. Since *'ādôn* preceded by the definite article always refers to the divine Lord (e.g., Ex 23:17; 34:23; Isa 1:24; 3:1; 10:16, 33), he is certainly the one being referred to here. In fact, that was the Messiah's title in Psalm 110:1 ("The LORD says to my Lord").

This Lord is also "the messenger of the covenant." The covenant referred to here is the single plan of God contained in the succession of covenants that began with the word issued to Eve in Genesis 3:15, continued in the word given to Shem in 9:27, to Abraham in 12:2–3, to David in 2 Samuel 7:12–19, and renewed and enlarged in Jeremiah 31:31–34. This messenger of the covenant is the same person God sent ahead of Israel as they left Egypt (Ex 23:20–23), in whom Yahweh placed his own "name" (23:21). There can be no mistaking his identity, for to equate the name of God with his angel or messenger is to call him divine! Elsewhere this messenger is called "the Angel of the LORD," which is also understood to be a preincarnate appearance of Christ, or a Christophany (Ex 33:14–15; Jdg 6:12; Isa 63:9). The Messiah is the mediator of all the covenants of the Bible (Heb 8:8–13; 12:24); he is the communicator, executor, administrator, and consummator of that divine plan.

---

[10]For further development of this topic, see Walter C. Kaiser, Jr., "The Promise of the Arrival of Elijah in Malachi and the Gospels," *GTJ* 3 (1982): 221–33; reproduced as "Witnessing and Expecting the Arrival of Elijah," in idem., *The Uses of the Old Testament in the New* (Chicago: Moody Press, 1985), 77–88.

The Messiah, then, is the One these complainers of Malachi 2:17 are in fact seeking. He is the God of judgment; injustice will be rectified despite the skeptics' cynical remarks. He is also the legitimate owner of the temple. That is why the Messiah has the right to expect that it will be a house of prayer, not a place for exchanging money and for selling or trading of animals, as Jesus found it and had to clean it out at the beginning and at the end of his earthly ministry.

When the Messiah comes, he will "purify the Levites" (v. 3) and "come near ... for judgment ... against sorcerers, adulterers and perjurers, against those who defraud laborers of their wages, who oppress the widows and the fatherless, and deprive aliens of justice, but do not fear me" (v. 5). For those who are unprepared morally and spiritually, two questions come to mind: "Who can endure the day of his coming?" and "Who can stand when he appears?" (v. 2). Few, if any, especially among the malefactors, will survive those penetrating tests that Yahweh will impose. But a cleansed priesthood and a sentenced world of evildoers will be necessary to prepare for the coming rule and reign of the Messiah.

2. The Messiah As the Sun of Righteousness
(Malachi 4:2)

The title "sun of righteousness" is a messianic title, for it has roots in the previous revelations about the Messiah. It is connected with the star that will come out of Jacob (Nu 24:17), the great light that will arise in Zebulun and Naphtali (Isa 9:2), indeed, the light that will be for all the Gentiles to see (42:6; 49:6). Did not Jeremiah call the Messiah "the LORD Our Righteousness?" (Jer 23:5–6; 33:15–16)? Later on, a priest named Zechariah will blend together Malachi 4:2 with Isaiah 9:2 in Luke 1:76–79, because he will see the messianic connotation in the name Branch, which has the same root, "to sprout or to spring forth," as "the sun of righteousness *will rise*." Thus, like Malachi, Luke links the Messiah up with the "sunrise."

While there is little agreement among scholars as to the meaning of the phrase "sun of righteousness," those scholars are closer to the mark who regard the sun as pointing to the Messiah as the One characterized by righteousness and acting in righteous ways so as to produce righteousness.

The picture of the Messiah coming with healing in his wings is also a figure of speech that has not gained unanimity among interpreters. Whether the figure of the winged solar disc of Egypt, Assyria, Babylon, or Persia provides the prophet's imagery or just the observed rays of sunlight is difficult to say. Others appeal to Ezekiel 5:3, where the word translated "wings" here refers to "the folds of [one's] garment" in which possessions and gifts are stored. But the point remain the same: healing in all of its aspects belongs exclusively to the Messiah. This he will bring with him when he returns.

The rising of the Sun of Righteousness will signal the appearance of a whole new day for God's people. On that day they will break out into exuberant joy, like calves released for the first time in the spring of the year (4:2; cf. Mic 2:12–13). It will also signal a day when the Messiah's victory over all evildoers will be complete (Mal 4:3). The wicked will be trampled under foot as ashes on the soles of the Messiah's feet. His will be the kingdom and the glory and the power forever and ever. Amen.

Conclusion

Judging from the plethora of OT references to the Messiah in the promise-plan of God, it is impossible for us to conclude with Joachim Becker that "there was not even such a thing as messianic expectation until the last two centuries B.C."[1] But even Becker sensed something was wrong with that conclusion, for he went on in the same context to inquire:

> Does this eliminate the traditional picture of messianic expectation? Such a conclusion would contradict one of the most central concerns of the New Testament, which insists with unprecedented frequency, intensity, and unanimity that Christ was proclaimed in advance in the Old Testament. Historical-critical scholarship can never set aside this assertion of the New Testament.[2]

How, then, does Becker propose to account for these two irreconcilable facts? His way around the impasse that he himself created was to fall back on an exegetical method that was found in late Judaism, namely, the *pesher* method of exegesis seen in the Qumran community of the Dead Sea Scrolls. Therefore, while Becker held that the conclusions of historical criticism ruled out any supernatural predictions of the Messiah

---

[1]Joachim Becker, *Messianic Expectation in the Old Testament*, trans. David E. Green (Philadelphia: Fortress, 1980), 93.
[2]Ibid.

in the OT, it was neither deceptive nor unnatural that the NT projected a messianic overlay to the OT where none actually existed! In other words, it was not even the NT's alleged formal exegetical method that was distinctive and important in its use of the OT; instead, it was the fact that the uniqueness of Jesus Christ made it necessary that the church declare that in Christ everything was fulfilled. Thus, the facts of the OT remain the same in that they do not, according to Becker, point to the Messiah. But all of this can be relativized as long as the apologetic proof from prophecy is not used, as it has been done so naively (in Becker's view) in the past.

A. EXEGESIS, BIBLICAL THEOLOGY, AND JESUS

All of this sounds like a will to believe in spite of the facts. But what we have discovered, if the text is taken simply on its own terms without any Western assumptions laid on top of it as a preunderstanding and a precondition to accepting its message, is that there is an apologetic case to be made for the Messiah in the OT. The evidence is simply overwhelming.

Never does the OT hint that it must be understood as a *pesher* or a *midrashic* method of interpretation. A straightforward understanding and application of the text leads one straight to the Messiah and to Jesus of Nazareth, who has fulfilled everything these texts said about his first coming.

A similar complaint can be lodged against those who argue that the older discussions of the *unity* of the Bible and a search for a *center* for a biblical theology are without merit in these modern times. Gerhard Maier has given a powerful rebuke to the modern rejection of the case for the unity of and a center to the Bible. As he reviews the situation, that was not true from the beginning. So convinced were the Jewish interpreters of the first century A.D. that it was a point of emphasis for writers such as Josephus and Philo. In fact, Scripture's unity "was first seriously called into question with the advent of modern historical criticism."[3]

Maier outlines four bases for the *unity* of Scripture. (1) The unity of Scripture is based on the One who ultimately brought forth Scripture: God. (2) The unity of the Bible is grounded in the fact that all the books of the Bible summon all its readers to faith in the one and same God. (3) There is also a unity of history created through God's Word, for Christ gives history this unity. (4) Finally, where this unity of the Scriptures is lost, the church has also lost its means to fight against heresy.[4] This is what we have attempted to argue in our case for the Messiah in the OT. As Maier puts it elsewhere, "Because God gives history a purpose, each individual event and its respective form lie in a more or less direct connection to that purpose. The purpose of events is not exhausted in their isolated occurrence; it rather reaches beyond them."[5]

The same case can be made for biblical theology's *center*, providing, of course, that the rubric of a "center of Scripture" is not separated from the topic of the "unity of Scripture."[6] Our argument has been that the promise-plan of God comprises that center. It is a center that is personal in that it focuses on God's Son, the Messiah. But it is also dynamically historical in nature, for it involves a larger plan that took its distinctive shape in history and a plethora of provisions that embraced the whole of biblical revelation.

Recently, some have been so offended and disappointed with the meager results, not to mention the contradictory conclusions, offered by historical criticism that a total reaction

---

[3]H. Freiherr Campenhausen, *Die Entstehung der christlichen Bibel* (Tübingen, 1968), 335, as cited by Gerhard Maier, *Biblical Hermeneutics*, trans. Robert W. Yarbrough (Wheaton, Ill.: Crossway, 1994), 188. See Maier's note 12 on the same page for three other writers who came to the same conclusion.

[4]Maier, *Biblical Hermeneutics*, 191–93.

[5]Ibid., 198.

[6]Ibid., 202.

against the historical aspects of Scripture has set in. But the excesses of one method must not so polarize us that we swing to the opposite extreme. "God is the ultimate ground of history."[7] Therefore, he is the one who initiated and shaped history. Faith and history must not be made out to be opposites, for faith depends on real historical deeds and words. The fact that history can never lift the inquirer beyond the realm of probability must be accepted as true, but that is not to say that faith must stop at the point where history is obliged to halt.

However, one must not fall into the ditch on the other side of the road either and conclude that since faith takes us further along the road to belief in Christ, we may just as well abandon the historical aspects and dissolve the ties between faith and history. To opt for that solution is to reject the mainstream of biblical revelation. In fact, the heart of the Apostles' Creed directly hinges on the historical facts that Jesus suffered under Pontius Pilate, was crucified, died, was buried, and rose again on the third day. As Maier warns, "Where Protestant theology took up the retreat from history, even declaring that faith having a historical component is damaging, an idealistic spirit-religion with Platonic features streamed into the vacuum. . . . In this way Protestant theology became an advocate of historical skepticism."[8]

B. CONTINUITIES AND DISCONTINUITIES IN THE TESTAMENTS

As far as the case for the Messiah is concerned, the relationship between the OT and NT is one of strong continuity and progressive revelation. While the Bible does exhibit an enormous amount of complexity of revelation, this must not lead to despair in finding a stream of continuity and a pattern

---

[7]Ibid., 210.
[8]Ibid., 217.

of wholeness that is rooted in organic and seminal beginnings that eventually emerge in the full-grown organism of truth implicit in the seed ideas announced in each of its seminal states.

C. PREDICTION AND FULFILLED PROPHECY

As soon as the case for supernaturalism is accepted, the claim that God can announce beforehand what he intends to do in the future is, for all intents and purposes, secured. As we argued in the volume entitled *Back Toward the Future: Hints for Interpreting Biblical Prophecy*, "prediction is so natural to and so much a part of the divine activity that it can almost be ascribed as an attribute of God himself."[9] That was the very challenge that God himself made to the dead idols of the nations: If you are truly deities, then say something about the future and how events will turn out (Isa 41:22–23; 45:21b-c; 46:9b–10; Am 3:7). So important is prediction to the very nature of the Bible that it is estimated that it involves approximately 27 percent of the Bible. God certainly is the Lord of the future.

But no less significant is the fact that the fulfillment of prophecy is also a major part of biblical revelation. That fulfillment did not come about merely by the church's determination to say that it was so. There would be very little, if any, apologetic value in coming to that conclusion. No! The realities of what eventually happened had to fit perfectly what had been declared in word prior to its happening.

---

[9]Walter C. Kaiser, Jr., *Back Toward the Future: Hints for Interpreting Biblical Prophecy* (Grand Rapids: Baker, 1989), 17–18.

◆ Appendix I ◆

Chart Of New Testament Fulfillments Of Old Testament Predictions

Messiah's Birth From a Virgin

Isaiah 7:14	Matthew 1:33

Messiah's Birthplace

Micah 5:2	Matthew 2:1, 6

The Forerunner of Messiah

Isaiah 40:3–5	Matthew 3:3
	Mark 1:3
	Luke 3:4–6
	John 1:23
Malachi 3:1	Matthew 11:10
	Mark 1:2
	Luke 1:76; 7:27
Malachi 4:5	Matthew 11:14; 17:10–12
	Mark 9:11–13
	Luke 1:16–17

Messiah's Triumphal Entry into Jerusalem

Zechariah 9:9–10	Matthew 21:9
Psalm 118:25–26	Mark 11:9
	Luke 19:38
	John 12:13

The Betrayal of Messiah

Judas:
    Psalm 69:25   Acts 1:20
    Psalm 109:8

Thirty Pieces of Silver:
    Zechariah 11:12–13   Matthew 26:15; 27:9–10

The Suffering of Messiah

Mocked by his Enemies:
    Psalm 22:7; 109:25   Matthew 27:35
                             Mark 15:29
                             Luke 23:35
    Psalm 22:8   Matthew 27:43

Messiah's Thirst:
    Psalm 69:21   Matthew 27:34, 48
                             Mark 15:36
                             Luke 23:36
                             John 19:28

Messiah's Words on the Cross:
    Psalm 22:1   Matthew 27:46
                             Mark 14:34
    Psalm 22:31   John 19:30

Messiah's Side Is Pierced:
    Zechariah 12:10   John 19:37

Messiah's Gethsemane:
    Isaiah 50:4–9   Mark 14:65
                             John 18:22; 19:3

Messiah's Vicarious Suffering:
    Isaiah 53:6, 9   1 Peter 2:21–25
    Isaiah 53:7–8   Acts 8:32–35
                             Revelation 5:6, 12; 13:8

Isaiah 53:12   Romans 4:25
                                      Hebrews 9:28

The Resurrection of Messiah

Psalm 16:10   Acts 2:27; 13:35–37

The Offices of Messiah

Prophet:
Deuteronomy 18:15–19   Acts 3:22–23; 7:37

Faithful Priest:
1 Samuel 2:35   Acts 3:24

King:
Psalm 2:6   Revelation 19:16

Messiah's Second Coming

Daniel 7:13   Mark 13:26
                                     Luke 21:27
                                     Matthew 24:44
Zechariah 12:10   Matthew 24:30
                                     Revelation 1:7

Chart of the Progress of Sixty-Five Direct Predictions of the Messiah in the Promise Doctrine

Six Direct Messianic Predictions in the Pentateuch

Two in Genesis 1–11: Two in the Patriarchal Era: Two in the Mosaic:

Genesis 3:15	Genesis 12:1–3	Numbers 24:15–19
"Seed"	"all . . . be blessed"	"star"
Genesis 9:27	Genesis 49:8–12	Deut 15:15–18
"live in . . . Shem"	"Shiloh"	"prophet"

Four Messianic Texts in Job

Job 9:33;	Job 16:19–21;	Job 19:23–27;	Job 33:23–28
"Arbitrator"	"Witness"	"Redeemer"	"Mediator"

Five Messianic Texts Prior to and During the Davidic Era

1 Sam 2:1–10;	1 Sam 2:35–36;	2 Sam 7;	Psalm 89;	Psalm 132
"Anointed"	"faithful Priest"	David's "house, throne, kingdom"		

Eleven Psalms Celebrating the Person and Work of the Messiah

As Conqueror and Enthroned Ruler:
> Psalm 110
> Psalm 2

As a Rejected Stone:
Psalm 118

As Betrayed:
Psalm 69
Psalm 109

As Dying and Resurrected:
Psalm 22
Psalm 16

As Planner and Groom:
Psalm 40
Psalm 45

As Triumphant King:
Psalm 68
Psalm 72

Thirty-Nine Predictions of the Messiah in the Prophets of the Old Testament

Ninth Century: One Prediction

Joel 2:23	Messiah as "Teacher"

Eighth Century: Four Non-Isaianic Predictions

Hosea 3:4–5	Messiah as the Second David
Amos 9:11–15	Messiah as the Raised House of David
Micah 2:12–13	Messiah as the "Breaker"
Micah 5:1–4	Messiah as the Coming Ruler

Eighth Century: Isaiah: Fourteen Isaianic Predictions

Isaiah 4:2	Messiah the "Branch of the LORD"
Isaiah 7:14	Messiah Born of a Virgin
Isaiah 9:1–7	Messiah Whose Name is "Wonderful Counselor"
Isaiah 11:1–16	Messiah's Reign
Isaiah 24:21–25	Messiah's Universal Triumph
Isaiah 28:16	Messiah the "Foundation Stone"
Isaiah 30:19–26	Messiah as "Teacher"

Isaiah 42:1–7	Messiah the "Servant of the LORD"
Isaiah 49:1–6	Messiah's Mission to the World
Isaiah 50:4–9	Messiah's Gethsemane
Isaiah 52:13–53:12	The Atonement By Messiah
Isaiah 55:3–5	Messiah and the Unfailing Grace Promised to David
Isaiah 61:1–3	Messiah as Proclaimer of the Good News
Isaiah 63:1–6	Messiah as the Conqueror

Seventh Century: Three Predictions

Jeremiah 23:5–6	Messiah as "the LORD our Righteousness"
Jeremiah 30:9, 21	Messiah as the Priestly King
Jeremiah 33:14–26	Messiah's Inviolable Promise

Sixth Century: Six Predictions

Ezekiel 17:22–24	Messiah as the Tender Sprig
Ezekiel 21:25–27	Messiah as the Rightful King
Ezekiel 34:23–31	Messiah as the Good Shepherd
Ezekiel 37:15–28	Messiah as the Unifier of the Nation
Daniel 7:13–14	Messiah as the Son of Man
Daniel 9:24–27	Messiah as the Coming Anointed Ruler

Fifth Century: Eleven Predictions

Haggai 2:6–9	Messiah as the "Desire of the Nations"
Haggai 2:21–23	Messiah as God's "Signet Ring"
Zechariah 3:8–10	Messiah's Work as High Priest
Zechariah 6:9–15	Messiah as King-Priest Over the Nations
Zechariah 9:9–10	Messiah as the Entering King
Zechariah 10:4	Messiah's Four Titles
Zechariah 11:4–14	Messiah as the Rejected Good Shepherd
Zechariah 12:10	Messiah as the Pierced One
Zechariah 13:7	Messiah as the Smitten Companion
Malachi 3:1	Messiah as the "Messenger of the Covenant"
Malachi 4:2	Messiah as the "Sun of Righteousness"

Author Index

◆ Subject Index ◆

◆ Scripture Index ◆

◆ Hebrew Words ◆